D0091329

BERMUDA

18th Edition

By David LaHuta

FrommerMedia LLC

FROMMER'S STAR RATINGS SYSTEM

Every hotel, restaurant, and attraction listed in this guide has been ranked for quality and value. Here's what the stars mean:

★   Recommended
★★   Highly Recommended
★★★   A must! Don't miss!

AN IMPORTANT NOTE

The world is a dynamic place. Hotels change ownership, restaurants hike their prices, museums alter their opening hours, and buses and trains change their routings. And all of this can occur in the several months after our authors have visited, inspected, and written about, these hotels, restaurants, museums, and transportation services. Though we have made valiant efforts to keep all our information fresh and up-to-date, some few changes can inevitably occur in the periods before a revised edition of this guidebook is published. So please bear with us if a tiny number of the details in this book have changed. Please also note that we have no responsibility or liability for any inaccuracy or errors or omissions, or for inconvenience, loss, damage, or expenses suffered by anyone as a result of assertions in this guide.

Known locally as the Unfinished Church, this Gothic Revival ruin never had a roof, thanks to financial squabbles among the congregation. The site's crumbling beauty has made it one of the top proposal spots in Bermuda. See p. 110.

CONTENTS

The rosy peach sands of Horseshoe Bay (p. 67).

A LOOK AT BERMUDA

The Bermuda Triangle: a mysterious force that causes ships to disappear in the Atlantic Ocean? Or a triumvirate of elements that makes Bermuda irresistible to travelers? Let's go with the latter, citing (a) the island chain's stunning good looks, from the cerulean blue of the Sargasso Sea lapping pink sand beaches to the pastel homes on land; (b) a surfeit of exciting outdoor adventures; and (c) Bermuda's surprisingly varied and cosmopolitan culture. The pages that follow highlight those lures as well the many other aspects of this dreamy archipelago's magnetic pull. Enjoy!

—Pauline Frommer

Pauline Frommer

Editorial Director

An aerial shot of Bermuda.

Inside the Unfinished Church.

The view from the terrace of the White Horse Pub (p. 149).

Flatts Village was one of the first British settlements in Bermuda. Today, it's best known for its rainbow assortment of pastel homes.

Rebuilt five times over the centuries, Fort St. Catherine now houses an evocative museum (p. 110).

Lemurs aren't native to Bermuda, but they are among the biggest draws at the Bermuda Aquarium, Museum & Zoo (p. 105).

Protected from the open sea by dramatic limestone columns, Tobacco Bay is an ideal spot for rock climbing and snorkeling. See p. 69.

A vacationer climbs the rock formations in Tobacco Bay (p. 69).

ABOVE: Attend a cricket match to get into the spirit of a sport Bermudians are passionate about. See p. 86. BELOW: When Mark Twain visited the Crystal Caves (p. 61), he called them "the most beautiful . . . in the world," with "a brilliant lake of clear water under our feet and all the roof overhead splendid with shining stalactites, thousands and thousands of them as white as sugar, and thousands and thousands brown and pink and other tints."

HAMILTON & CENTRAL BERMUDA

Horseshoe Bay, a pristine arc of pink sand backed by cliffs, is Bermuda's most popular beach and the site of the annual Beachfest (p. 67).

Traditional Gombey dancers perform. See p. 182.

Sessions House, home to Bermuda's Supreme Court and Parliament (p. 102).

Cathedral of the Most Holy Trinity (p. 101).

A small fleet of jet skiers.

Stained-glass window from the cathedral.

Front Street in Hamilton.

Treacherous reefs encircle Bermuda. Of the many shipwrecks along the coast, this is one that can easily be explored by snorkelers as well as scuba divers.

ABOVE: Romantic "Moongates" serve as entry points across Bermuda. To read about their history, see p. 12. BELOW: A view of Hamilton from the city's bustling harbor.

Dine right on the sand at Mickey's Beach Bistro (p. 126).

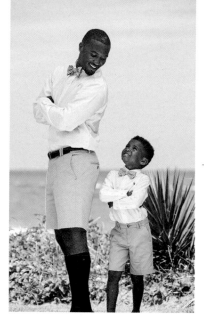

Bermuda shorts are worn for formal and informal occasions (p. 161).

Island-made jewelry from Alexandra Mosher (p. 165).

A flowering poinciana tree.

Plush canvas cabanas can make a day at the beach a luxe experience for guests of the Hamilton Princess Hotel (p. 197).

ABOVE: The Bermuda Underwater Exploration Institute (p. 101) offers a compelling look at the region's sea life. BELOW: A bevy of columns at historic Fort Hamilton (p. 101).

The pool overlooks the iconic strand for which the Elbow Beach Hotel (p. 194) is named.

ABOVE: Because of its position in the center of a number of migration routes, this island is a birder's paradise. Pictured is the Bermuda longtail. BELOW: The old-fashioned red phone booths in front of Fort Hamilton are just for photo ops these days.

DOCKYARD & WEST END

An aerial view of the Royal Naval Dockyard shows the vast scope of the area (p. 94).

ABOVE: A closer view of the no-longer-in-use commissioner's house and keep at the Dockyard.
BELOW: Colorful overwater cabanas.

The majestic clock tower of the Dockyard.

A scuba diver explores the *Hermes* shipwreck (p. 72).

"Muralized" history of Bermuda at the National Museum of Bermuda (p. 93).

The fabulous Fun Golf course (p. 82).

A Celebrity cruise ship docks at St. George's.

ABOVE: Jobson's Cove (p. 65) is one of the island's best hidden beaches. BELOW: Golfers practice their swings on the Port Royal driving range (p. 80). The island boasts a number of world-class golf courses.

THE BEST OF BERMUDA

Adrift in its own dreamy archipelago in the balmy Gulf Stream, this rich little oasis of pink sand beaches and sparkling blue waters is simultaneously slightly British, slightly American, and very Bermudian. Whether you've come to unwind on Elbow Beach, shop among the pretty pastels and whites of historic Hamilton, or discover 400 years of history at Fort St. Catherine, you'll discover a pleasant mix of formal British culture dressed in a pair of Bermuda shorts.

THE most unforgettable
BERMUDA EXPERIENCES

o **Beachcombing:** Nothing says Bermuda more than its famous pink sand beaches. With their rosy hue, and dramatic off-shore rock formations, they're among the most beautiful on the planet. See below for our best beach picks.

o **Exploring the Colonial Heritage:** Originally founded in 1612, the Town of St. George's and its related fortifications were recognized as a UNESCO World Heritage Site in 2000 alongside world treasures like The Great Wall of China and Stonehenge. Stroll its labyrinthine cobblestone alleys and streets to the oldest Anglican church in continuous use in the Western Hemisphere, among other historic treasures (see chapter 3 for a walking tour).

o **Harbour Night in City of Hamilton:** On Wednesday nights from May through September, Front Street transforms itself into a pedestrian-only, and quite boisterous, street party. Buy locally made arts and crafts; eat quintessential Bermudian foods; and watch live performances including the island's own Gombey dancers—a colorful troupe that jumps, whirls and twirls to the music of snare drums and whistles.

o **Sailing Away:** Despite popular belief Bermuda is not one island, but an archipelago of more than 180 islands, islets and cays. To explore them for yourself, rent a boat and explore like a local. Islanders spend entire weekends on private vessels anchored in places like Mangrove Bay or in Paradise Lakes near Hamilton (see chapter 4).

- **Going Underground:** Bermuda has the highest concentration of limestone caves in the world, many with echo patterns and sedimentary deposits that some spelunkers consider mystical. Collectively, these caves form one of the island's major natural wonderlands. Their surreal formations took millions of years to come into being, and the great stalactites and stalagmites have a gothic grandeur. **Crystal Caves** (p. 61), at Bailey's Bay, are among the best, and among the few whose tunnels and chambers can be navigated by laypersons as part of a guided tour.

- **Friday Night Happy Hour:** By far the biggest night of the week on the Bermudian social calendar is Friday, when the island's well-dressed workforce punches out at the stroke of 5pm, then heads to bars, restaurants and hotels to mingle and mix. Among the best of the happy hour bunch? Marina Nights at the Hamilton Princess, where the partying is dockside next to swank yachts.

- **Cup Match:** No one sporting event is as universally beloved as Bermuda's annual Cup Match Cricket Tournament, a 2-day match between rival clubs St. George's and Somerset. Held the first Thursday and Friday in August, it's akin to a feisty Yankees/Red Sox game, albeit one with crowded tents filled with Bermudians rolling dice and betting cash at the Crown & Anchor tables, since it's the only 2 days of the year where open betting is legal. Can't get here in August? Then watch the Bermuda National Team play in matches throughout the year at the Bermuda National Sports Centre in Devonshire (for more, see "Cricket" in chapter 4).

- **Afternoon Tea:** Bermuda is Britain's oldest remaining colony, and the island nation still adheres to many traditions of its founding fathers. One is afternoon tea, a ritual meal held in private homes and hotels alike (p. 32).

BERMUDA'S best BEACHES

Your first priority on your Bermuda vacation probably will be to kick back at the beach. But which beach? Hotels often have private stretches of sand; if so, we describe the beach in each hotel's review (see chapter 9). There are many fine public beaches, as well. Here are our top choices, arranged clockwise around the island, beginning with the south-shore beaches closest to the City of Hamilton. For more details, see chapter 4.

- **Elbow Beach** (Paget Parish): The pale pink sand stretches for almost 1.6km (1 mile) at Elbow Beach, one of the most popular beaches in Bermuda. Because protective coral reefs surround it, Elbow Beach is one of the safest places on the island for swimming. See p. 64.

- **Warwick Long Bay** (Warwick Parish): This popular beach, on the south side of South Shore Park, features a 1km (⅔-mile) stretch of sand against a backdrop of scrubland and low grasses. Despite frequent winds, an offshore reef keeps the waves surprisingly small. Less than 60m (200 ft.) offshore, a jagged coral island appears to be floating above the water. There is excellent snorkeling here. See p. 57.

- **Jobson's Cove** (Warwick Parish): No more than 50 feet across, this secluded swimming hole is surrounded by tall limestone cliffs that protect it from ocean swells and strong breezes. Wade into calm, chest deep waters or climb the natural rock steps at its southern edge for an unparalleled view of the coastline. Schools of parrotfish are easy to spot so bring snorkeling gear.

- **Horseshoe Bay** (Southampton Parish): The Grand Dame of Bermuda beaches, this quarter-mile crescent is consistently rated as one of the world's finest. It's one of the few beaches in Bermuda with lifeguards in addition to an on-site bar and restaurant, changing facilities and beach rental concessions. *Family tip:* Baby Beach, just west of the main entrance, has a large shallow pool perfect for young swimmers. See p. 67.

- **Shelly Bay** (Hamilton Parish): On the north shore, you'll discover calm waters and soft, pink sand—and you'll want for nothing else. This beach is well known among beach buffs, but it's rarely overcrowded and there's always a spot in the sun just waiting for you. See p. 69.

- **Church Bay** (Southampton Parish): This small southwestern beach is one of the island's best for snorkeling, thanks to a thriving coral reef that starts at the water's edge and continues about 100 yards offshore. See p. 68.

- **Tobacco Bay** (St. George's Parish): A popular stretch of pale pink sand, this is the most frequented beach on St. George's Island. It offers lots of facilities, including equipment rentals and a snack bar. See p. 69.

- **Clearwater Beach** (St. George's Parish): Aptly named for its gin-clear waters where sea turtles can be spotted, this long sandy strip on the eastern tip of St. David's Island is often dotted with local families who come for its shallow approach, adjacent playground and casual restaurant.

BERMUDA'S best of OUTDOORS

- **Golf:** Once the home of the PGA Grand Slam of Golf, Bermuda attracts the world's leading golfers. Over the years, movie stars, former U.S. presidents, and the Duke of Windsor, have hit the island's links. Rolling, hummocky fairways characterize the courses, some of which were designed by luminaries like Robert Trent Jones and Richard Rulewich (see p. 79).

- **Boating & Sailing:** Many people forget that Bermuda isn't one island, but an archipelago, with all kinds of nooks and crannies waiting to be discovered. With the fresh wind of the Atlantic blowing in your hair, you can embark on your own voyage of discovery. See "Boating & Sailing," in chapter 4.

- **Hiking the Railway Trail:** Once home to a working rail line that ran across the island from 1931 to 1948, the Railway Trail is now a scenic pedestrian and bicycle path. Today, 18 of the railway's original 21 miles are open to the public and much of it is adjacent to Bermuda's stunning coastline or through lush, shaded forests. The trail is split into nine individual sections and the terrain varies throughout. Its highlight: Bailey's Bay footbridge, a 740-feet walkway that connects Coney Island to Crawl Hill in Hamilton Parish.

o **Snorkeling & Diving:** If you're happiest under the sea, Bermuda has what you're looking for. That includes the wrecks of countless ships, underwater caves, rich reefs, and, during most of the year, warm, gin-clear waters. All around the island you'll find a kaleidoscope of coral and marine life that's the most varied in this part of the world. Many scuba experts consider Bermuda one of the safest and best places to learn the sport. Seasoned divers will not be disappointed, either. Depths begin at 7.5m (25 ft.) or less but can exceed 24m (79 ft.). Some wrecks are in about 9m (30 ft.) of water, which puts them within the range of snorkelers. See "Bermuda's Best Dive Sites," below, and "Scuba Diving," in chapter 4.

BERMUDA'S best MUSEUMS

o **Masterworks Museum of Bermuda Art** (Pembroke Parish): Island-inspired artwork from such 19th-century masters as Georgia O'Keefe, Winslow Homer and E. Ambrose Webster make up the permanent collection at this impressive purpose-built gallery in the heart of the Botanical Gardens. Also featured: changing exhibits from local artists. See p. 96.

o **Bermuda Underwater Exploration Institute** (City of Hamilton, Pembroke Parish): This 21,000-square-feet science center features three floors of exhibits dedicated to Bermuda's discovered and undiscovered underwater world. View artifacts recovered from shipwrecks, tour a collection of over 1,200 shells or take a ride on a virtual submersible to see what life is like at 12,000 feet. See p. 101.

o **Bermuda Aquarium, Museum & Zoo** (Flatts Village): At this trio of family-friendly attractions you can watch local reef fish swim in a 140,000-gallon tank, learn how Bermuda was formed from a volcanic eruption, and view animals found around the globe (think lemurs from Madagascar or kangaroos from Australia). See p. 105.

o **National Museum of Bermuda** (Royal Naval Dockyard, Sandys Parish): This impressive collection of maritime history and art exhibits is housed in former munitions warehouses within the stone walls of Bermuda's largest fort. See p. 93.

BERMUDA'S best FAMILY EXPERIENCES

o **Find a Slice of Sand:** All kids love the seashore, but not all beaches are created equal. If you've got little ones in tow, head to Jobson's Cove in Warwick Parish, Baby Beach at Horseshoe Bay or Shelly Bay in Smith's Parish, all of which boast protected bays or shallow pools perfect for active, but safe, splashing.

- **Have Fun in Flatts:** Families can easily spend a full day in Flatts Village (p. 61), home to the Bermuda Aquarium, Museum & Zoo and its menagerie of fish, birds and mammals.
- **Do Dockyard:** The Royal Naval Dockyard is ground zero for families: Play miniature golf at Fun Golf, swim with dolphins at Dolphin Quest, eat burgers at the Frog & Onion, grab ice cream at the Clocktower Mall and frolic in the saltwater fountains located next to the playground shaped like a pirate ship.
- **Snorkel & Sail:** Budding marine biologists will love a daytrip spent sailing and snorkeling aboard one of Bermuda's many charter boats, which run half- and full-day excursions. See p. 71 for companies.
- **Spend a Day in Bailey's Bay:** Head to Bermuda's east end for a tour of the Crystal and Fantasy Caves followed by lunch at the Swizzle Inn (scribbling on the walls is encouraged here). Then head to Bailey's Bay Ice Cream Parlour for the best homemade ice cream on island.

BERMUDA'S best DIVE SITES

- **The *Constellation:*** This 60m (197-ft.), four-masted schooner, which wrecked en route to Venezuela with a cargo of glassware, drugs, and whiskey in 1943, lies in 9m (30 ft.) of water off the northwest side of the island, about 13km (8 miles) northwest of the Royal Naval Dockyard. The true story of this ship inspired Peter Benchley to write *The Deep.*
- **The *Cristóbal Colón:*** The largest known shipwreck in Bermuda's waters is this 144m (472-ft.) Spanish luxury liner; it ran aground in 1936 on a northern reef between North Rock and North Breaker. It lies in 9 to 17m (30–56 ft.) of water.
- **The *Hermes:*** This 50m (164-ft.) steamer ship rests in some 24m (79 ft.) of water about 1.5km (1 mile) off Warwick Long Bay on the south shore. It foundered in 1985. The *Hermes*, the *Rita Zovetta*, and the *Tauton* (see below) are Bermuda favorites because of the incredible multicolored variety of fish that populate the waters around the ships. You'll have a chance to see grouper, brittle starfish, spiny lobster, crabs, banded coral shrimp, queen angels, tube sponges, and more.
- **L'Herminie:** A first-class, 60-gun French frigate, *L'Herminie* was 17 days out of its Cuban port, en route to France, when it sank in 1838. The ship lies in 6 to 9m (20–30 ft.) of water off the west side of the island, with 25 cannons still visible.
- **The *Mary Celeste:*** This paddle-wheeler sank in 1864. Its 4.5m-diameter (15-ft.) paddle wheel, off the southern portion of the island, is overgrown with coral standing about 17m (56 ft.) off the ocean floor.
- **The *North Carolina:*** One of Bermuda's most colorful and well-preserved wrecks, this English sailing barkentine foundered in 1879 and now lies in about 12m (39 ft.) of water off the western portion of the island. The bow, stern, masts, and rigging are all preserved, and all sorts of vibrant marine life call the wreck home.

o **The *Rita Zovetta:*** A 120m (394-ft.) Italian cargo ship, lying in 6 to 21m (20–69 ft.) of water off the south side of the island, the *Rita Zovetta* ran aground off St. David's Island in 1924. It's a favorite with underwater photographers because of the kaleidoscope of fish that inhabit the area.

o **South West Breaker:** This coral-reef dive off the south shore, about 2.5km (1½ miles) off Church Bay, has hard and soft coral decorating sheer walls at depths of 6 to 9m (20–30 ft.).

o **The *Tauton:*** This popular dive site is a Norwegian coastal steamer that sank in 1920. It lies in 3 to 12m (10–39 ft.) of water off the north end of the island and is home to numerous varieties of colorful marine life.

o **Tarpon Hole:** Featuring a series of caves and tunnels that divers can swim through, this honeycombed reef near Elbow Beach is known for its plentiful varieties of coral, including yellow pencil, elkhorn, star and fire.

BERMUDA'S best GOLF

o **Belmont Hills Golf Club** (Warwick Parish): When California-based designer Algie M. Pulley, Jr. reconfigured this par-70, 6,017-yd. course in 2003, he created a heavily contoured 18 holes—a radical new design that forced the club to add the word "Hills" to the end of its name when it reopened that year. Expect tricky pin placements, challenging greens and water hazards galore. See p. 79.

o **Turtle Hill Golf Club** (Southampton Parish): On the doorstep of the Fairmont Southampton where ocean views abound, this par-54, 2,684-yd. stunner is a true test of your short game with elevated tees, strategically placed bunkers and undulating fairways—chiefly the reason why it annually hosts the Grey Goose World Par Three Championship. See p. 81.

o **Port Royal Golf Course** (Southampton Parish): Former home of the PGA Grand Slam of Golf and originally designed by Robert Trent Jones, this 6,842-yd course is Bermuda's longest. Its cliff-hugging par three 16th, with nothing but the Atlantic between the tee and the pin, is one of golf's greatest holes. See p. 80.

o **Tucker's Point Golf Club** (Hamilton Parish): This 6,361-yd Robert Rulewich-designed course features scenic views of Castle Harbour and challenging TifEagle greens (a fine blade of grass that allows for smoother, more consistent putting). See p. 81.

o **Mid Ocean Club** (Hamilton Parish): Originally designed by Charles Blair McDonald in 1921 then rearchitected by Robert Trent Jones in 1953, this ocean-hugging, 6,548-yd course is commonly ranked among the top 100 courses outside the U.S. The elite private course is for club members only on weekends, but nonmembers can play midweek. See p. 80.

BERMUDA'S best DAY HIKES

o **From the Royal Naval Dockyard to Somerset** (Sandys Parish): A 6.5km (4-mile) walk leads from the dockyard, the former headquarters of the

British navy on Bermuda, to Somerset Island. Along the way you'll cross a beautiful nature reserve; explore an old cemetery; view the Royal Naval Hospital, where thousands of yellow-fever victims died in the 19th century; and be rewarded with a sweeping panoramic view of Great Sound. Sandy beaches along the route are perfect for pausing from your hike to stretch out on the sand or take a dip in the ocean.

o **Spittal Pond Nature Reserve** (Smith's Parish): This 59-acre sanctuary is the island's largest nature reserve, home to both resident and migratory waterfowl; some 25 species of birds can be spotted here from November to May. Scenic trails and footpaths cut through the property, so short and long walks can easily be achieved. See p. 104.

o **Horseshoe Bay to Stonehole Bay** (Southampton Parish): A long walk on Horseshoe Bay Beach is always a good idea, but when the tide is low this nearly one-mile-long hike along the shoreline is certifiably blissful. Start your walk at the western entrance of Horseshoe Bay and simply head east. At low tide you can pass through craggy rock formations and dip in natural pools. And if the tide is high, walk along the dunes for incomparable views of the south shore.

o **The Railway Trail:** We've got to give another plug to this superb trail. For full details, see p. 43.

BERMUDA'S best VIEWS

o **Warwick Long Bay:** This stretch of pristine pink sand is a dream beach of the picture-postcard variety. It backs up to towering cliffs and hills studded with Spanish bayonet and oleander. A 6m-high (20-ft.) coral outcrop, rising some 60m (200 ft.) offshore, and resembling a sculpted boulder, adds variety to the stunning beachscape. See p. 65.

o **Achilles Bay:** For the greatest sunset view in all of Bermuda, head to this east end cove adjacent to Fort St. Catherine, about a 5-minute taxi from the Town of St. George's. Better yet, reserve a table for dinner at Blackbeard's (p. 148), which overlooks the bay.

o **Gibbs Hill Lighthouse:** One up Queen Elizabeth II! She visited but did not climb this lighthouse in 1953. Built in 1846, it's the oldest cast-iron lighthouse in the world. From the top, you can relish what locals consider the single finest view in all of Bermuda—a 360-degree panorama of the island and its shorelines. See p. 95.

BERMUDA'S best HISTORIC SITES

o **National Museum of Bermuda (The Keep Fort)** (Sandys Parish): Built in the 1880s to protect the Royal Naval Dockyard against enemy attacks, this 6-acre fortress is a proud symbol of British naval might with ramparts, bastions and gunnery from every period of armament (like 32-lb. Napoleonic era cannons, 18-ton rifled muzzle loaders from the 1870s, and 6-in. steel breech loaders from the 1950s). See p. 93.

o **St. Peter's Church** (St. George's Parish): This is the oldest Anglican house of worship in the Western Hemisphere. At one time, virtually everyone who died on Bermuda was buried here and to the west of the church lies a graveyard of slaves. The present church sits on the site of the original, which colonists built in 1612. A hurricane destroyed the first structure in 1712, but some parts of the interior survived, like the original wooden alter, which was kept when the church was rebuilt on the same site in 1713. See p. 109.

o **Fort St. Catherine** (St. George's Parish): This massive stone fort—with its tunnels, cannons and ramparts—towers over the beach where the shipwrecked crew of the *Sea Venture* first came ashore in 1609, thus becoming Bermuda's first settlers. The fort was completed in 1614 and extensive rebuilding and remodeling continued until the 19th century. Visitors view antique weapons, learn about military living quarters and pop into dark blockades where prisoners were held. See p. 110.

BERMUDA'S best RESTAURANTS

o **Best of the Best: Marcus'** (p. 131): You may have seen chef Marcus Samuelsson crushing the competition on TV's Top Chef Masters. He's done the same here on Bermuda, opening the island's friendliest, tastiest, chicest eatery. Really: This is a place that gets everything right, and it's a singular pleasure to dine here (and to see how Bermuda's other restaurateurs are upping their own games in response).

o **Most Romantic: Mickey's Beach Bistro** (p. 126): The stars will be twinkling above, and the surf crashing just 20 feet from your table when you dine at this alfresco favorite, located right on iconic Elbow Beach. It's a charming spot, with excellent food, and discreet waitstaff.

o **Best Bang for Your Buck: D'angelini's** (p. 141): Sometimes you just need simple, tasty sandwiches and baked goods to be happy. You'll get them, along with excellent coffee, at this little cafe adjacent to the public ferry dock and a stone's throw from the Visitor Services Center, in the City of Hamilton.

o **Best Splurge: Waterlot Inn** (p. 121): Its setting is a handsome and historic 1830s-era Bermuda cottage, and its schtick is steak. This is the island's classic "big night out" choice, serving hearty cuts of meat, succulent seafood and famous (and dramatic) flaming bananas foster. A three-course meal for two will cost around $400 with wine, but it's worth every penny.

o **Best Sushi: Pearl** (p. 138): Thanks to all the fresh-caught seafood Bermuda gets, sushi is served at many island restaurants—even pubs. But here it's taken to another level, with creative preparations like rockfish *usuzukuri*, thinly sliced grouper with rice wine vinegar and chili oil.

- **Best Pub: Frog & Onion Pub** (p. 119): Of the many pubs on Bermuda, this is most fun to visit, thanks to its historic setting (an 18th-c. cooperage built by the British Navy), the quality of food (traditional fish and chips, Cornish Pasties, meat pies, and burgers of all kinds) and the suds on tap, which include locally brewed ale from the Dockyard Brewing Company. It doesn't hurt that there's live music throughout the week.

- **Best Ice Cream: Bailey's Bay Ice Cream Parlour** (p. 147): All-natural, homemade ice cream is served here, and it comes in very Bermudian flavors like Dark n' Stormy, Bermuda banana, and rum raisin.

- **Best Asian: L'Oriental** (p. 137): This is the only restaurant in Bermuda with a traditional Japanese *teppanyaki* table, where a chef theatrically prepares Asian-style beef, chicken, shrimp, and scallops on a hot tabletop. Also on offer: well-executed Szechuan, Hunan, and Cantonese dishes.

- **Best Bermuda Seafood: Wahoo's Bistro & Patio** (p. 148): Try wahoo tacos, wahoo nuggets, wahoo burgers, smoked wahoo pate, wahoo chowder, and of course, simply grilled wahoo. And if you *must*, other types of seafood are served—they're darn good, too.

- **Best View: Blackbeard's** (p. 148): Adjacent to Fort St. Catherine on Bermuda's far eastern tip, this open-air restaurant has an unending view of the horizon and stunning Achilles Bay. Come at sunset.

BERMUDA IN CONTEXT

Mark Twain once famously wrote: "You can go to heaven if you want. I'd rather stay here in Bermuda." The acclaimed American writer visited the island a handful of times from 1867 to 1910—a prolific period, during which Bermuda's natural beauty inspired some of his finest travel writing. Considering much of the island's natural landscape has gone unchanged, this twenty-one-square mile archipelago continues to lure travelers by air and sea, all who have come to explore this jewel of the Atlantic.

Often lumped in with the islands of the Caribbean, Bermuda is actually tucked away in the middle of the Atlantic. *Fun fact:* Bermuda lies closer to Nova Scotia than any nation in the Caribbean. That placement carries with it some important perks. It is one of the few islands near to the United Stated where the Zika virus has never been recorded. It's also, in general, safer than many Caribbean isles, with a relatively hassle-free environment (no aggressive vendors selling their wares—or worse, drugs). If you're into sunning and swimming, it doesn't get much better than Bermuda between May and September. Pink sand and turquoise seas—it sounds like a corny travel poster, but it's for real. As Mark Twain also wrote, "Sometimes a dose of Bermuda is just what the doctor ordered."

This is also a nation with uniquely British roots. It's not uncommon to spot judges and barristers wearing white wigs as they walk through the City of Hamilton (pity them in the hotter summer months!); right-hand drive vehicles operate on the left side of the road; and pictures of Her Majesty the Queen can be found hanging in most public buildings (and until recently on bank notes, which are now adorned with tropical flora and fauna). Tea is still taken by many, come afternoon, and people mind their manners. If you don't say "please" and "thank you" with most every interaction, you'll get dirty looks. Some visitors find all the British decorum rather silly on a remote island that's closer to Atlanta than to London. But many others find the stalwart commitment to British tradition colorful and quaint, enhancing the unique charm of the lovely place that is Bermuda.

This chapter covers how Bermuda forged its character, as well as the elements of that personality, and advice on when to go. Please read on!

BERMUDA TODAY

If there's a sore point among Bermudians today, it's their extreme desire to separate themselves from the islands of the Caribbean, particularly from the Bahamas, in the eyes of the world. They've been known to send angry letters to publishers of maps, reference sources, and travel guides, insisting that Bermuda is not in the Caribbean. As one irate Bermudian put it, "You don't claim that Washington, D.C., is part of Dallas, Texas. They're the same distance apart that Bermuda is from the Caribbean."

Bermuda prides itself on its lack of economic, socioeconomic, and racial problems. Because of this, you won't see many homeless people on its streets and there are few living below the poverty line, despite the fact that Bermuda is far costlier than its sister isles in the Caribbean.

Instead, what the island would like to be known for is its performance in banking and multinational business. During the first decade of the millennium, international business positioned itself to overtake tourism as Bermuda's primary source of revenue. The trend began in the 1970s, when some Hong Kong businesspeople formed low-profile shipping, trading, and investment companies in Bermuda—companies that became, in essence, corporate cash cows.

When Britain surrendered Hong Kong to China in 1997, Bermuda became the largest British colony. A local businessman watched the televised ceremonies in which Britain handed over control, and gleefully remarked, "All we can say is: Thank you very much, Hong Kong, because here come the insurance companies and pension funds." By the end of the 20th century, nearly half of the companies listed on the Hong Kong Stock Exchange—and even some of the Chinese government's own holding companies—had established a legal presence in Bermuda, because the island provides such hefty tax breaks. Amazingly, tiny Bermuda emerged as the biggest and most prosperous of all of Britain's colonies, the bulk of which are now in the Caribbean.

Bermuda by the Numbers

Believe it or not, many visitors are surprised to learn that Bermuda is not anywhere near the Caribbean, even though its waters are turquoise in color. Located **665 nautical miles** due east of Cape Hatteras, N.C., Bermuda is situated well within the mid-Atlantic Ocean, at a **latitude and longitude of 34°N/64°W** (common numbers that you'll see on Lili Bermuda colognes and on novelty T-shirts). Another popular belief is that Bermuda is a singular island. Not so. An archipelago of more than **180 islands,** **islets, and cays,** Bermuda is a nation connected by bridges and causeways and one that's encircled by a thriving coral reef. Indeed, the reason why its waters are home to **more than 400 shipwrecks.** The most famous of them all is the *Sea Venture,* a three-masted schooner that **crashed upon Bermuda's shores in 1609,** the year that English settler's first arrived on the island and a number you'll spot nearly everywhere (like the Hamilton Princess restaurant simply named 1609 and the tiny jewelry shop 1609 Design).

In the 21st century, Bermuda is attracting a growing number of American companies that are incorporating in Bermuda to lower their taxes without giving up the benefits of doing business in the United States. Insurance companies have led the way, but now other kinds of companies are following, including tech firms and investment banks. It's been trumpeted in the press as "profits over patriotism," since becoming a Bermudian company is a paper transaction that can save millions annually.

And as aggressively as Bermuda is pursuing business, it's also more aware than ever of its fragile environment. Bermuda's population density is the third highest in the world, after Hong Kong's and Monaco's. Because the number of annual visitors is 10 times higher than the population, Bermuda has had to take strong initiatives to protect its natural resources. Environmental protection takes the form of stiff antilitter laws, annual garbage cleanup campaigns, automobile restrictions, cedar replanting (a blight in the '40s and '50s wiped out the native trees), and strict fishing policies, among others.

Along the shaky road to self-government, Bermuda had some ugly racial conflicts. Riots in 1968 built up to the assassination of the British governor in 1973. But that was a long time ago; today, Bermuda has the most harmonious race relations in this part of the world, far better than those in the United States, or the Caribbean. There's still a long way to go, but Bermudians of African descent have assumed political, administrative, and managerial posts in every aspect of the local economy. Bermuda hasn't quite reached the point where the color of your skin is unimportant, but it has made more significant advancement toward that goal than its neighbors to the south.

In 2016 (the last year for which there are records), Bermuda's average household income was $131,074—a stark contrast with some of the less fortunate islands in the Caribbean, many of which don't even have the budgets to compile such statistics. Compared with residents of densely populated Caribbean islands like Puerto Rico or Jamaica, no one is really poor in Bermuda. On the downside, home prices in Bermuda are at least three times the median cost of a house in the United States or Canada.

Say Cheese!

If you're searching for a spot to snap a memorable photograph, look no further than Bermuda's limestone moongates. Said to give newlyweds enduring happiness if they pass through the stone archway hand-in-hand, these semi-circle openings first began popping up in Bermuda around 1860, following a local sea captain's trip to a Chinese garden. By the 1920s, handcrafted moongates had spread throughout the island and had widely been ingrained into Bermuda's architectural culture. These days, they can be found most everywhere including hotels, restaurants and public parks, and are a perfect natural frame for any photo (look for the one on back patio of the Hamilton Princess Hotel, which lights up at night). Even if you're not a newlywed, step underneath and steal a kiss from your loved one: Local lore says that moongates will bring you good luck whether or not you just said, "I do."

As a tourist destination, Bermuda was a resort long before Florida, Hawaii, Mexico, and many other places. Over the years, it has exploited its position in the northwest Atlantic between North America and Europe. The United States remains its largest market—about 80% of visitors are Americans—but in recent years more and more travelers from Europe, Asia and Canada have been recorded visiting the island.

Life in the Onion Patch
GETTING TO KNOW THE "ONIONS"

Even though Bermuda isn't in the onion business the way it used to be, a born and bred islander is still called an "Onion." The term dates from the early 20th century, when the export of Bermuda onions and Easter lilies to the U.S. mainland were the island's major sources of income.

The "Onions"—a term that still carries a badge of pride—have their own lifestyle and even their own vocabulary. For example, an "Ace boy/girl" is your best friend"; if you're "hot" you're drunk; if you're "full hot" you're *really* drunk; "chingas" is an expression of amazement, used as a synonym for "wow"; "dahn de country" means to head eastward towards St. George's; "up de country" means to head westward towards Somerset; "greeze" is a large, filling meal; and "stop ya noize" is exclaimed when something is simply unbelievable.

Residents of more troubled islands to the south often look with envy upon the "Onions," who have a much higher standard of living than Caribbean islanders do; they also pay no personal income tax and suffer from only a 7% unemployment rate. The literacy rate is high: An estimated 99% of females age 15 and older can read and write, as can 98% of Bermudian males.

Today's native residents are mostly of African, British, and Portuguese descent however one-third of Bermuda's 65,000 permanent residents are foreign nationals who've been granted temporary work permits. Bermuda's population density, one of the highest in the world, is about 3,210 per 2.5 sq. km (1 sq. mile). The population is about 54% black, 31% white. Many ethnic minority groups are represented, the largest and most established being the Portuguese; most inhabitants, however, are islanders from the Caribbean or the Bahamas. Some Bermudians can even trace their ancestry back to the island's first settlers, and others to freed slaves.

Britain's influence in Bermuda is obvious in the predominantly English accents and spelling, police who wear helmets like those of London bobbies, and cars that drive on the left. Schools are run along the lines of the British system and provide a high standard of preparatory education. Children 5 to 16 years of age must attend school and higher education is provided at The Bermuda College, a trade school that offers academic and technical studies.

WHO'S MINDING THE STORE?

In essence, Bermuda is a self-governing dependency of Britain, which protects its security and stability. The governor, appointed by the queen, represents Her Majesty in the areas of external affairs, defense, and internal security.

An Island of Religious Tolerance

About a third of Bermuda's population adheres to the Church of England, which has been historically dominant in the colony. Indeed, the division of Bermuda into nine parishes dates from 1618, when each parish was required by law to have its own Anglican church, to the exclusion of any other. That division still exists today, but more for administrative purposes than for religious ones.

Religious tolerance is now guaranteed by law. There are some 20,000 Catholics, many of them from the Portuguese Azores. There are also many members of Protestant sects whose roots lie within what were originally slave churches, among them the African Methodist Episcopal Church. Established in 1816 by African Americans, the sect was transported to Bermuda from Canada around 1870. Today, the church has about 7,000 members.

Also found in Bermuda are Seventh-day Adventists, Presbyterians, Baptists, Lutherans, and Mormons. There are also a handful of Jews, Muslims, Rastafarians, and Jehovah's Witnesses.

Bermuda today boasts more than 110 churches, an average of five per 2.5 sq. km (1 sq. mile). They range from the moss-encrusted parish churches established in the earliest days of the colony to modest structures with only a handful of members.

By choosing to remain a British dependency, Bermuda rejected the trail that many former colonies in the Caribbean blazed by declaring their independence. Although they remain under the protection of the British, Bermudians manage their own day-to-day affairs. And ever since the people of Bermuda were granted the right to govern themselves in 1968, they have done so admirably well.

Bermuda has a 12-member cabinet headed by a premier. The elected legislature, referred to as the Legislative Council, consists of a 40-member House of Assembly and an 11-member Senate. Bermuda's oldest political party is the Progressive Labour Party (PLP), formed in 1963. In 1964, the United Bermuda Party was established; it stayed in power until it was toppled by the Progressive Labour Party in 1998. In 2011, the One Bermuda Alliance (OBA) was formed by merging the members of the existing two non-Labour parties, the United Bermuda Party (UBP) and the Bermuda Democratic Alliance (BDA). Currently Bermuda operates a two-party system with the PLP and OBA being its main players.

Bermuda's legal system is founded on common law. Judicial responsibility falls to the Supreme Court, headed by a chief justice in a powdered wig and a robe. English law is the fundamental guide, and in court, English customs prevail.

TOURIST DOLLARS & NO INCOME TAX

Bermuda's political stability has proved beneficial to the economy, which relies heavily on tourism and foreign investment.

For much of the island's early history, the major industry was shipbuilding, made possible by the abundant cedar forests. In the second half of the 19th century, when wooden ships gave way to steel ones, the island turned to tourism. Today, tourism is the country's second leading industry, next to insurance and international business. In 2018, Bermuda had more than 770,600 visitors—a record number in a single year, higher even than 2017 when the America's Cup brought scores of fans to the island. Those 2018 travelers spent more than $500 million, up from $320 million in 2017.

Because Bermuda has enacted favorable economic measures, more than 16,000 international companies are registered here. The companies engage mostly in investment holding, insurance, commercial trading, consulting services, and shipping—but fewer than 5,000 companies are actually on the island. The reason for this curious situation? Bermuda has no corporate or income tax, so companies register on Bermuda but conduct business in their home countries, thereby avoiding taxes that their home countries would otherwise deduct.

The island's leading exports are rum and other beverages while leading imports include foodstuffs, alcoholic beverages, clothing, furniture, fuel, electrical appliances and motor vehicles. Bermuda's major trading partners are the United States, Great Britain, Canada and the Caribbean states.

THE MAKING OF BERMUDA

The Early Years

The discovery of Bermuda is attributed to the Spanish—probably the navigator Juan Bermúdez—sometime before 1511, because in that year a map published in the *Legatio Babylonica* included "La Bermuda" among the Atlantic islands. A little over a century later, the English staked a claim to Bermuda and began colonization.

In 1609, the flagship of Admiral Sir George Somers, the *Sea Venture,* was wrecked on Bermuda's reefs while en route to the colony at Jamestown, Virginia. The dauntless crew built two small sailing ships called the *Deliverance* and the *Patience* and headed on to the American colony, but three sailors hid out and remained on the island. They were Bermuda's first European settlers. Just 3 years later, the Bermuda islands were included in the charter of the Virginia Company and 60 colonists were sent there from England. The Town of St. George's was founded soon after in 1612.

Bermuda's status as a colony dates from 1620, when the first parliament convened. Bermuda's is the oldest parliament in continuous existence in the British Commonwealth. In 1684, Bermuda became a British Crown Colony under King Charles II and Sir Robert Robinson was appointed the colony's first governor.

Slavery became a part of life in Bermuda shortly after the official settlement. Although most slaves came from Africa, a few were Native Americans. Later, Scots imprisoned for fighting against Cromwell were sent to the islands, followed in 1651 by Irish slaves. This servitude, however, was not as lengthy as that of plantation slaves in America and the West Indies. The British Emancipation Act of 1834 freed all slaves.

Bermuda History

1. **1609** *The Sea Venture*, captained by Sir George Somers, shipwrecked at Achilles Bay.
2. **1809** Royal Engineers began construction on the Royal Naval Dockyard.
3. **1815** Hamilton became the new capital of Bermuda, superseding St. George's.
4. **1937** The first scheduled air service to Bermuda from New York landed.
5. **1946** The first private cars appeared on Bermuda's roads.
6. **1973** Governor Richard Sharples was assassinated at Government House.
7. **2017** Foiling catamarans raced on the Great Sound during the 35th America's Cup.

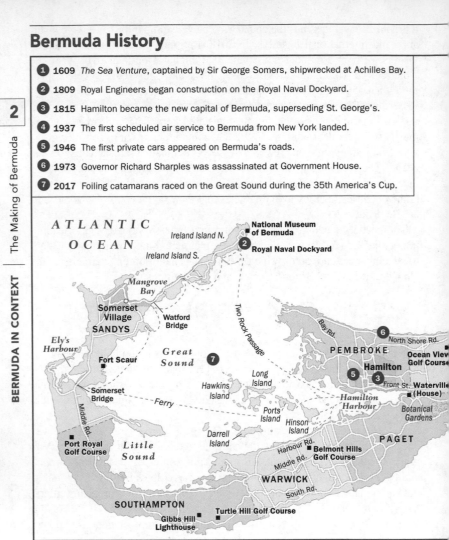

Relations with America

Early on, Bermuda established close links with the American colonies. The islanders set up a thriving mercantile trade on the Eastern Seaboard, especially with southern ports. The major commodity sold by Bermuda's merchant ships was salt from Turks Island.

During the American Revolution, the rebellious colonies cut off trade with Loyalist Bermuda, despite the network of family connections and close friendships that bound them. The cutoff in trade proved a great hardship for the islanders, who, having chosen seafaring over farming, depended heavily on America for their food. Many of them, now deprived of profitable trade

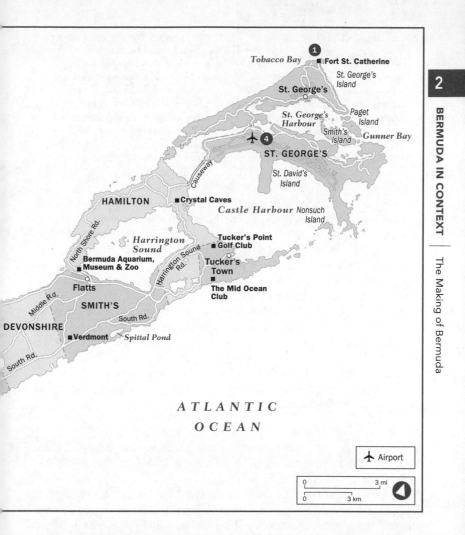

routes, turned to privateering, piracy, and "wrecking" (salvaging goods from wrecked or foundered ships).

Britain's loss of its important American colonial ports led to a naval buildup in Bermuda. Ships and troops sailed from Bermuda in 1814 to burn Washington, D.C., and the White House during the War of 1812.

Bermuda got a new lease on economic life during the American Civil War. The island was sympathetic to the Confederacy. With the approval of the British government, Bermuda ran the blockade that the Union had placed on exports, especially of cotton, by the southern states. St. George's Harbour was a principal Atlantic base for the lucrative business of smuggling manufactured goods into Confederate ports and bringing out cargoes of cotton and turpentine.

Puritan Justice

Many tales are told about the fate of persons condemned for witchcraft during the 1600s. Anyone suspected of collusion with the devil was thrown into St. George's Harbour; whoever did not sink was judged guilty. Many women floated because of their skirts and petticoats. The first woman to be found floating after her trial was Jeanne Gardiner, in 1651. Since her failure to plunge to the depths "proved" that she was a witch, the court ordered her removed from the water; she was then burned at the stake. Not only women were tried for witchcraft; in 1652, a man was condemned to death for having cast a spell over his neighbor's turkeys. Justice in those Puritan times was stern, in Bermuda no less than in the American colonies.

When the Confederacy fell, so did Bermuda's economy. Seeing no immediate source of income from trading with the eastern states, the islanders turned their attention to agriculture and found that the colony's fertile soil and salubrious climate produced excellent vegetables. Portuguese immigrants arrived to farm the land, and soon celery, potatoes, tomatoes, and especially onions were being shipped to the New York market. So brisk was the onion trade that the City of Hamilton became known as "Onion Town."

During Prohibition, Bermudians again profited from the situation in the United States—they engaged in the lucrative business of rum running (smuggling alcohol to the U.S.). The distance from the island to the East Coast was too great for quick crossings in small booze-laden boats, which worked well from the Bahamas and Cuba. Nevertheless, Bermuda accounted for a good part of the alcoholic beverages transported illegally to the United States before the repeal of Prohibition in 1933.

A Hotbed of Espionage

Bermuda played a key role in World War II counterespionage for the Allies. The story of the "secret war" with Nazi Germany is told dramatically in William Stevenson's *A Man Called Intrepid*.

Inside the Hamilton Princess Hotel, a carefully trained staff worked to decode radio signals to and from German submarines and other vessels operating in the Atlantic, close to the United States and the islands offshore. Unknown to the Germans, the British, early in the war had broken the Nazi code using a captured German coding machine called "Enigma." The British also intercepted and examined mail between Europe and the United States.

Bermuda served as a refueling stop for airplanes flying between the two continents. While pilots were being entertained at the Yacht Club, the mail would be taken off the carriers and examined by experts. An innocent-looking series of letters from Lisbon, for example, contained messages written in invisible ink. The letters were part of a vast German spy network. The British became skilled at opening sealed envelopes, examining their written contents, and carefully resealing them.

The surreptitious letter readers were called "trappers." Many of them were young women without any previous experience in counterespionage work, yet a number of them performed very well. As Stevenson wrote, it was soon discovered that "by some quirk in the law of averages, the girls who shone in this work had well-turned ankles." A medical officer involved with the project reported it as "fairly certain that a girl with unshapely legs would make a bad trapper." So, amazingly, the word went out that women seeking recruitment as trappers would have to display their gams.

During their work, the trappers discovered one of the methods by which the Germans were transmitting secret messages: They would shrink a whole page of regularly typed text to the size of a tiny dot, then conceal the dot under an innocuous-looking punctuation mark. The staff likened these messages, with their secret-bearing dots, to the English dessert plum duff, for these "punctuation dots [were] scattered through a letter like raisins in the suet puddings." The term "duff method" came to be applied to the technique that the Germans used to send military and other messages through the mail.

When the United States entered the war, FBI agents joined the British in their intelligence operations in Bermuda.

Bermuda Comes into Its Own

In 1953, British Prime Minister Winston Churchill chose Bermuda, which he had visited during the war, as the site for a conference with U.S. President Dwight D. Eisenhower and the French premier. Several such high-level gatherings have followed in the decades since. Former British Prime Minister John Major and former U.S. President George H. W. Bush met on the island in 1991 and the most recent was a visit by Her Majesty the Queen in 2009, when she and the Duke of Edinburgh came to commemorate the 400th anniversary of the settlement of Bermuda.

Bermuda's increasing prominence led to changes in its relations with Great Britain and the United States, as well as significant developments on the island itself. In 1957, after nearly 2 centuries of occupation, Britain withdrew its military forces, and decided to grant self-government to its oldest colony.

Impressions
"The short-pant is a terrible fashion choice. Unless it is from Bermuda."   —Winston Churchill

As Bermudians assumed greater control over their own affairs, they began to adopt significant social changes, but at a pace that did not satisfy some critics. Although racial segregation in hotels and restaurants ceased in 1959, schools were not integrated until 1971. Women received the right to vote in 1944, but the law still restricted suffrage to property holders. That restriction was rescinded in 1963, when voter registration was opened to all citizens.

On the rocky road to self-government, Bermuda was not without its share of problems. Serious rioting broke out in 1968, and British troops were called back to restore order. Then, in 1973, Sir Richard Sharples, the governor, was assassinated (he's buried in the churchyard of St. Peter's Church in St. George's).

These events, which occurred when several of the islands in the region and in the Caribbean were experiencing domestic difficulties, proved to be the exception rather than the rule. In the years since, the social and political climate in Bermuda has been markedly calm—all the better for the island's economic well-being, because it encourages the industries on which Bermuda depends, including tourism.

During the 1990s, the political status of the island again became a hot topic among Bermudians. Some people felt it would be advantageous to achieve complete independence from Britain, whereas others believed it was in Bermuda's best interest to maintain its ties to the Crown. In 1995, most voters in an independent referendum rejected a proposal to sever ties with Great Britain.

In 1997, the governing party of Bermuda, the United Bermuda Party, chose the daughter of a well-known civil rights leader as its prime minister. Pamela Gordon, former environment minister, was named to the post at the age of 41, the youngest leader in the island nation's 400-year history and the first woman to be prime minister. David Saul, the reigning prime minister, resigned in favor of this younger and more popular leader. In her first months in office, Gordon, a relative political newcomer, pledged to bridge differences between Bermuda's majority black population and its white business elite.

In that stated goal, at least based on subsequent election returns, she failed. In November 1998, the Progressive Labour Party, supported by many of Bermuda's blacks, ended 30 years of conservative rule by sweeping its first victory in general elections. Although Gordon is black, as was most of her cabinet, many locals saw her party as part of the "white establishment."

The Labour Party's leader, Jennifer Smith, became the new prime minister, claiming Bermuda's residents had met their "date with destiny." The Labour Party has moved more from the left to the center in recent years, and Smith sought to reassure the island's white-led business community that it would be "business as usual" with her party in power. The Labour Party made the economy an issue in the campaign, promising higher wages and better benefits to workers, even though Bermuda residents enjoy one of the highest standards of living in the world. In 2003, W. Alexander Scott replaced Smith as the prime minister and head of the party.

Also in 2003, tragedy struck the island in the roaring fury called Hurricane Fabian, Bermuda's worst hurricane in 40 years. For some 12 hours, Fabian pummeled the island with 190 to 225kmph (120–140 mph) winds. This caused small tornadoes to spawn and unleashed a towering surge of ocean that drenched almost all of Bermuda in saltwater, uprooting trees.

In October 2006, Dr. Ewart Brown, also of the PLP, took over the helm as premier. Four years later, in 2010, he was replaced by Paula Cox who served 2 years as head of the party until a new party was formed and took power in 2012. Called the One Bermuda Alliance (OBA), the party campaigned on "Putting Bermuda First," which included polices like balancing the budget, cutting ministers' pay and allocating government contracts to small business.

THE BAFFLING bermuda triangle

The area known as the Bermuda Triangle encompasses 2,414,016 sq. km (932,057 sq. miles) of open sea between Bermuda, Puerto Rico, and the tip of Miami. This bit of the Atlantic is the source of the most famous, and certainly the most baffling, legend associated with Bermuda. Tales of the mysterious Bermuda Triangle persist, despite attempts by skeptics to dismiss them as fanciful. Below are three of the most popular.

- In 1881, a British-registered ship, the *Ellen Austin*, encountered an unnamed vessel in good condition sailing aimlessly without a crew. The captain ordered a handful of his best seamen to board the vessel and sail it to Newfoundland. A few days later, the ships encountered each other again on the high seas. But to everyone's alarm, the crewmen who had transferred from the *Ellen Austin* were nowhere to be found—the ship was completely unmanned.

- Another tale concerns the disappearance of a merchant ship, the *Marine Sulphur Queen*, in February 1963. It vanished suddenly without warning, and no one could say why. The weather was calm when the ship set sail from Bermuda, and everything onboard was fine—the crew never sent a distress signal. In looking for explanations, some have theorized that the ship's weakened hull gave way, causing the vessel to descend quickly to the ocean floor. Others attribute the loss to more mysterious forces.

- The most famous of all the legends concerns an incident in 1945. On December 5, five U.S. Navy bombers departed from Fort Lauderdale, Florida, on a routine mission. The weather was fine; no storm of any kind threatened. A short time into the flight, the leader of the squadron radioed that they were lost, and then the radio went silent. All efforts to establish further communication proved fruitless. A rescue plane was dispatched to search for the squadron, but it, too, disappeared. The navy ordered a search that lasted 5 days, but there was no evidence of any wreckage. To this day, the disappearance of the squadron and the rescue plane remains a mystery as deep as the waters of the region.

So how can we explain these strange phenomena? While conspiracy theorists like to blame aliens or biblical prophecies, it's best to listen to scientists who surmise that rogue waves or huge bubbles of methane gas might be the culprit. No matter what your views are, you're bound to provoke an excited response by asking locals what they think since everyone has an opinion about Bermuda's most fascinating legend.

Following the resignation of Premier Craig Cannonier, who left office amidst abuse of power allegations, Michael Dunkley was appointed premier in 2014 and his administration is largely credited for bringing the 35th America's Cup to Bermuda, which in turn stoked local and foreign investment on the island. After 3 years in power, the OBA was defeated by the PLP, which rode a wave of nationalism into the premier's office when 38-year-old David Burt was elected premier—indeed the youngest in Bermuda's history—in 2017.

BERMUDA ART & ARCHITECTURE

Art

Bermuda has long been a favorite among international artists and sculptors. Much of this island-inspired artwork can be viewed at the **Masterworks Museum of Bermuda Art,** where a permanent collection of works from 19th-century painters including Winslow Homer, Georgia O'Keefe and E. Ambrose Webster have hung since its opening in 2009.

But to get a full understanding of Bermuda's artistic past, its roots must be traced to colonial days, when most works were portraits painted by itinerant artists for the local gentry. Most of these were by the English-born Joseph Blackburn, whose brief visit to Bermuda in the mid-1700s led to requests by local landowners to have their images recreated on canvas. Many of these portraits can be found today in the **Tucker House** in St. George's (p. 109). A handful of portraits from the same period were done by the American-born artist John Green. Also prized are a series of paintings from the mid–19th century depicting sailing ships; they're signed "Edward James," but the artist's real identity remains unknown.

During the 19th century, the traditions of the English landscape painters, particularly the Romantics, came into vogue in Bermuda. Constable, with his lush and evocative landscapes, became the model for many. Other than a few amateur artists however, whose works showed great vitality but little sense of perspective, most of Bermuda's landscape paintings were executed by British military officers and their wives. Their body of work includes a blend of true-to-life landscapes with an occasional stylized rendering of the picturesque or Romantic tradition then in vogue in England. Among the most famous of the uniformed artists was Lt. E. G. Hallewell, a member of the Royal Engineers, whose illustrations of the island's topography were used for planning certain naval installations.

Another celebrated landscapist was Thomas Driver, who arrived as a member of the Royal Engineers in 1814 and remained on the island until 1836. Trained to reproduce detailed landscape observations as a means of assisting military and naval strategists, he later modified his style to become more elegant and evocative. He soon abandoned the military and became a full-time painter of Bermuda scenes. Because of Driver's attention to detail, his works are frequently reproduced by scholars and art historians who hope to recapture the aesthetic and architectural elements of the island's earliest buildings.

Later in the 19th century, other artists depicted the flora of Bermuda. Lady Lefroy, whose husband was governor of the island between 1871 and 1877, painted the trees, shrubs, fish, flowers, and animals of the island in much detail. Later, at scattered intervals during their careers, such internationally known artists as Winslow Homer, Andrew Wyeth, George Ault, and French-born Impressionist and cubist Albert Gleizes all painted Bermudian scenes.

Among prominent Bermuda-born artists was Alfred Birdsey, who died in 1996. His watercolors represented some of the most elegiac visual odes to Bermuda ever produced. Birdsey's paintings, as well as those of other artists mentioned above, are on display in galleries around the island.

Today, Bermuda has more artists painting and creating than at any point in its history. Local favorites include Eric Amos, whose illustrations of Bermuda's wild birds are sought by collectors all over the world; Captain Stephen J. Card, who has developed an international reputation by specializing in marine art; Vivienne Gardner, known not just for her paintings but also for her sculpture, stained glass, and mosaics; Christine Phillips-Watlington, who has achieved an international reputation for her botanical paintings; and Graham Foster, a prolific modernist best known for his 1,000-square-foot mural *The Hall of History,* depicting 500 years of Bermuda's past (the work took him 3 years to complete and was officially opened at the Commissioner's House in the Royal Naval Dockyard by Her Majesty the Queen in 2009). In addition to its painters, Bermuda also boasts several noted sculptors, including Chelsey Trott, who produces cedar-wood carvings, and Desmond Hale Fountain, who creates works in bronze found in hotels and private homes alike. Fountain's life-size statues often show children in the act of reading or snoozing in the shade.

Architecture

Today, Bermuda's unique style is best represented by its architecture: primarily, those little pink cottages that grace postcards. The architecture of the island—a mélange of idiosyncratic building techniques dictated by climate and the types of building materials available—is the island's only truly indigenous art form.

Bermuda's early settlers quickly recognized the virtues of the island's most visible building material, coral stone. A conglomerate of primeval sand packed with crushed bits of coral and shells, this stone has been quarried for generations on Bermuda. Cut into oblong building blocks, it is strong yet porous. However, it would be unusable in any area where the climate has cycles of freezing and thawing, because it would crack. Mortared together with imported cement, the blocks provide solid and durable foundations and walls.

Bermuda's colonial architects ingeniously found a way to deal with a serious problem on the island: the lack of an abundant supply of fresh water. During the construction of a house or any other sort of building, workers excavated a water tank, or **cistern,** first. The cistern was created either as a separate underground cavity away from the house or as a foundation for the building. These cisterns served to collect rainwater funneled from rooftops via specially designed channels and gutters. The design of these roof-to-cellar water conduits led to the development of what is Bermuda's most distinct architectural feature: the gleaming **rooftops** of its houses. Gently sloping, and invariably painted a dazzling white, they are constructed of quarried limestone slabs sawed into "slates" about an inch thick and between 77 and 116 sq. cm (12–18 sq. in.). Roofs are installed over a framework of cedar-wood beams (or, more recently, pitch pine or pressure-treated wood beams), which are interconnected with a series of cedar laths. The slates are joined with cement-based mortar in overlapping rows, then covered with a cement wash and one or several coats of whitewash or synthetic paint. This process corrects the porosity of the coral limestone slates, rendering them watertight. The result is a layered effect, since each panel of limestone appears in high relief atop its neighbor. The angular, step-shaped geometry of Bermudian roofs has inspired watercolorists and painters to emphasize the rhythmically graceful shadows that trace the path of the sun across the rooflines.

Unlike those in the Caribbean, Bermudian houses are designed without amply proportioned hanging eaves. Large eaves may be desirable because of the shade they afford, but smaller ones have proved to be more structurally sound during tropical storms. The interiors of Bermudian houses are usually graced with large windows and doors and in older buildings, floors and moldings crafted from copper-colored planks of the almost-extinct Bermuda cedar. Also common is a feature found in colonial buildings in the Caribbean and other western Atlantic islands as well: **tray ceilings,** so named because of their resemblance to an inverted serving tray. This shape allows ceilings to follow the lines of the inside roof construction to create what would otherwise be unused space. The effect of these ceilings, whether sheathed in plaster or planking, gives Bermudian interiors unusual height and airiness.

Despite the distinctively individualistic nature of Bermuda's architecture, decor remains faithfully British, and somewhat more formal than you might expect. Interior designs seem to be a felicitous cross between what you'd find in a New England seaside cottage and how a nautically minded society hostess would accent her drawing room in London. Bermuda homes usually have lots of Chippendale or Queen Anne furniture (sometimes authentic, sometimes reproduction). Whenever possible, decorators love to include any piece of antique furniture crafted from Bermuda cedar. Combine these features with the open windows, gentle climate, and carefully tended gardens of the fertile, mid-Atlantic setting, and the result is some very charming and soothing interiors.

Did You Know?

o **Unlike most Caribbean islands, Bermuda is Zika free,** making it one of the most popular tropical destinations in North America for babymoons.

o **Bermuda inspired William Shakespeare's 1610 play *The Tempest*.**

o **Somerset Bridge is the world's smallest drawbridge.** At only 32 inches wide, the opening is just large enough for a ship's mast to pass through.

o **Sir Brownlow Gray, the island's former chief justice, played the first** game of tennis in the Western Hemisphere on Bermuda in 1873.

o **Bermuda has no source of fresh water,** which is why most of the water its residents use to wash dishes, bathe and flush down the toilet is rain water collected on stepped white roofs that funnel the flow to underground cisterns.

o **Bermuda has no billboards.** There is a ban on outdoor advertising and neon signs.

No discussion of Bermudian architecture should neglect to mention a garden feature that many visitors consider unique to Bermuda: the **moongate**. A rounded span of coral blocks arranged in a circular arch, the moongate was first introduced to Bermuda around 1860, following a local sea captain's trip to China. The structures didn't become prevalent until the 1920s, when the landscape architect of English aristocrat the Duke of Westminster incorporated one into the now defunct Bermudiana Hotel after finding similar inspiration from such gates in China and Japan.

BERMUDA IN POP CULTURE
The Literary Scene

Bermuda has long been a haven for writers, and has figured in many works of literature, beginning with Shakespeare's *The Tempest*. Shakespeare never visited the island himself but was inspired to set his play here by accounts he had read or heard of the island.

The Irish poet Thomas Moore (1779–1852), who visited Bermuda for several months in 1804, was moved by its beauty to write:

> *Oh! could you view the scenery dear*
> *That now beneath my window lies.*

Moore left more memories—literary and romantic—than any other writer who came to Bermuda. He once stayed at Hill Crest Guest House in St. George's (now called **Aunt Nea's Inn** [p. 202]) and soon became enamored of Nea Tucker, the adolescent bride of one of the most prominent men in town. "Sweet Nea! Let us roam no more," he once wrote of his beloved. It's said that the lovesick poet would gaze for hours upon Nea's veranda, hoping that she'd appear. One day a jealous Mr. Tucker could tolerate this no more and banished the poet from his property. Moore was chased down a street that now bears the name Nea's Alley to commemorate his unrequited romance.

Today, one of the oldest restaurants in Bermuda is **Tom Moore's Tavern** (p. 146). The building was once the home of Samuel Trott, who constructed it in the 17th century. Unlike Tucker, the descendants of Samuel Trott befriended Moore, who often visited the house. Moore immortalized the calabash tree on the Trott estate in his writing; he liked to sit under it and write his verse there.

Following in Moore's footsteps, many famous writers visited Bermuda in later years. None, however, have left their mark on the island like Tom Moore.

For Americans, it was Mark Twain who helped make Bermuda a popular tourist destination. He published his impressions in the *Atlantic Monthly* in 1877 through 1878, and in his first book, *The Innocents Abroad.* He became so enchanted by the island that, as he wrote many years later to a correspondent, he would happily choose it over heaven.

After Twain, Eugene O'Neill came to Bermuda in 1924, and returned several more times, at least through 1927. While here, he worked on *The Great God Brown, Lazarus Laughed,* and *Strange Interlude.* O'Neill was convinced that cold weather adversely affected his ability to write. He thought that

Bermuda would "cure" him of alcoholism. At first, O'Neill and his family rented cottages on what is now Coral Beach Club property. Later, O'Neill bought the house "Spithead," in Warwick. In 1927, however, his marriage ended, and O'Neill left his family—and Bermuda.

During the 1930s, several eminent writers made their way to Bermuda, in hopes of finding idyllic surroundings and perhaps a little inspiration: Sinclair Lewis, who spent all his time cycling around "this gorgeous island"; Hervey Allen, who wrote *Anthony Adverse,* his best-selling novel, at Felicity Hall in Somerset; and James Ramsey Ullman, who wrote *The White Tower* on the island. James Thurber also made several visits to Bermuda during this time.

In 1956, Noël Coward came with his longtime companion, Graham Payn, to escape "the monstrously unjust tax situation in England." He was not, he said, "really mad about the place," yet he purchased "Spithead" in Warwick (O'Neill's former home) and stayed some 2 years, working on *London Mornings,* his only ballet, and the musical *Sail Away.* "Spithead" is now privately owned.

Other well-known authors who visited Bermuda over the years include Rudyard Kipling, C. S. Forester, Hugh Walpole, Edna Ferber, Anita Loos, John O'Hara, E. B. White, and Philip Wylie.

Bermuda's own writers include William S. Zuill—a former director of the Bermuda National Trust who wrote *The Story of Bermuda and Her People,* an excellent historical account—and Nellie Musson, Frank Manning, Eva Hodgson, and Dale Butler, who have written about the lives of African Bermudians.

RECOMMENDED READING

Most of the books listed below have been printed in Bermuda. So while they're readily available on the island, they may be hard to find in the United States and beyond. Check with your favorite online bookseller or used bookstore.

The Bermuda Triangle

Many writers have attempted to explain the Bermuda Triangle. None has sufficiently done so yet, but all these books make good reads for those of us intrigued by this tantalizing mystery.

The best of the lot is *The Bermuda Triangle Mystery Solved* by Larry Kusche. It's a good read even though it doesn't actually "solve" the mystery. A mass-market paperback, *Atlantis: Bermuda Triangle,* by Greg Donegan, also digs into the puzzle; as does another paperback, *The Mystery of the Bermuda Triangle* by Chris Oxlade.

Art & Architecture

For Bermuda style, both inside the house and outside, two books lead the pack: *Bermuda Antique Furniture and Silver,* published by Bermuda National Trust; and *Architecture Bermuda Style,* by David R. Raine, issued by Pompano Publications.

Divers, Hikers & Shipwrecks

Daniel Berg has written the finest book on the shipwrecks of Bermuda—a great choice for a diver to read before actually going under the water. It's called *Bermuda Shipwrecks: A Vacationing Diver's Guide to Bermuda's Shipwrecks.* Divers might also like to pick up a copy of *Marine Fauna and Flora of Bermuda,* edited by Wolfgang Sterrer. Another good book for divers is *Diving Bermuda,* part of the Aqua Quest Diving Series, this one authored by Jesse Concelmo and Michael Strohofer. Its second edition is the most up-to-date of all the sports guides to Bermuda.

History

In Bermuda's bookstores, you can find several books devoted to the colorful history of the island. Making for the best reads are the following titles: *The Rich Papers—Letters from Bermuda* by Vernon A. Ives; *Biography of a Colonial Town* by Jean de Chantal Kennedy; *A Life on Old St. David's* by Ernest A. McCallan; *Chained on the Rock: Slavery in Bermuda* by Cyril O. Packwood; and *Bermuda's Story* by Terry Tucker.

Flora & Fauna

If you're a devotee of Mother Nature, seek out *Bermuda Houses and Gardens* by Ann B. Brown and Jean Outerbridge; *Bermuda: Her Plants and Gardens 1609–1850* by Jill Collett; and *A Guide to the Reef, Shore, and Game Fish of Bermuda* by Louis S. Mowbray.

Fiction

One of the most sensitive portraits, capturing Bermuda of long ago, is *The Back Yard* by Ann Z. Williams, an account of growing up in Bermuda in the 1930s and '40s.

Non-Fiction

If you'd like to know what life is like as a Canadian expat relocating to a quirky island in the middle of the Atlantic, then pick up *Tea with Tracey: The Woman's Survival Guide to Bermuda* by Tracey Caswell. This first-person account of settling into island life is full of laughs, including the trials and tribulations of adjusting to nightly tree frog serenades and invading ants among other island annoyances. For a decidedly more poetic take on island life, pick up *Mark Twain in Paradise: His Voyages to Bermuda* by Donald Hoffman, a comprehensive study of Samuel Clemens' love affair with the island.

Children's

Written and illustrated by Elizabeth A. Mulderig, *Tiny the Treefrog Tours Bermuda,* is a beloved picture book about a small green treefrog who visits popular sites across the island (think the Crystal Caves or pink sand beaches).

Film & Television

Film buffs may be surprised to discover that Bermuda has an indirect link to the movie *The Wizard of Oz*—Denslow's Island. The privately owned island is named after W. W. Denslow, who created the original illustrations for the book on which the movie is based, *The Wonderful Wizard of Oz* (1900) by L. Frank Baum, and thus with his pen gave form to many of the characters depicted on the screen. Denslow lived in Bermuda at the turn of the 20th century. The island, however, despite its famous association, is off limits to visitors.

Several films were shot in and around Bermuda. The most famous is *The Deep* (1977), starring Jacqueline Bisset, Nick Nolte, Robert Shaw, and Louis Gossett, Jr., a visually arresting movie about a lost treasure and drugs and, of course, scuba diving off the island's coast.

A movie that was filmed partly in Bermuda is *Chapter Two* (1979), with James Caan and Marsha Mason. Based on the successful Broadway play by Neil Simon, it is the story of a playwright's bumpy romance soon after the death of his wife. The Bermuda scenes were shot at Marley Beach Cottages.

Several television shows have been filmed on the island in recent years. Most watched was the ABC reality show *The Bachelorette* in 2012 and two live episodes of NBC's *Kathie Lee & Hoda* filmed in 2017. Bermuda was also featured in a 12-part documentary-style PBS series called *Ocean Vet,* which followed the late veterinarian Dr. Neil Burnie as he explored the island's marine creatures in 2014.

Music

Modern Bermudian music, which you can hear occasionally in hotel lounges, is a blend of traditional folk tunes with sounds from Jamaica, Trinidad, and Puerto Rico, as well as the United States and Britain. However, these aren't the sounds you'll predominantly hear: As elsewhere, American and British rock, modified by local rhythms, has proved the strongest and most lasting influence.

GOMBEY DANCING

Despite new pop forms, Bermuda is proud of its original musical idioms. Gombey dancing is the island's premier folk art. Gombey (commonly pronounced *goom*-bee or *gom*-bay) combines West Africa's tribal heritage with the Native American and British colonial influences of the New World. African Caribbeans brought to Bermuda as slaves or convicts introduced the tradition, and its rhythms are similar to Brazilian street samba. Gombey dancers are almost always male; in accordance with tradition, men pass on the rhythms and dance techniques from generation to generation in their family. Dancers outfit themselves in masquerade costumes, whose outlandish lines and glittering colors evoke the brilliant plumage of tropical birds.

Gombey (spelled "goombay" in some other places, such as the Bahamas) signifies a specific type of African drum, as well as the Bantu word for "rhythm." These rhythms escalate into an ever faster and more hypnotic beat as the movements of the dancers become increasingly uninhibited, and the response of the spectators grows ever more fervent. The most strenuous dances are usually performed during the Christmas season.

Although Gombey dancing, with its local rituals and ceremonies, can be seen as one of Bermuda's major cultural contributions, it's not unique to the island. Variations are found elsewhere in the western Atlantic, as well as in the Caribbean. Indeed, during its development, Bermuda's Gombey dancing was significantly influenced by some of these other versions. In colonial times, for example, when African Caribbeans were brought to Bermuda as slaves or convicts to help build the British military installations on the island, they carried with them their own Gombey traditions, which eventually combined with those that had already taken root in Bermuda. What's unique about the Bermudian version of Gombey, however, is its use of the British snare drum, played with wooden sticks, as an accompaniment to the dancing.

A handful of Gombey recordings are available, enabling you to hear this African-based music, with its rhythmic chanting and rapid drumbeat. Among the recordings, the album *Strictly Gombey Music,* performed by four members of the Pickles Spencer Gombey Group, offers a good selection of Gombey dances.

Aficionados of this art form, however, will argue that Gombey's allure lies not so much in the music as in the feverish—almost trancelike—dancing that accompanies it, as well as in the colorful costumes of the dancers. For that reason, they say, audio recordings can't convey the full mesmerizing power of a Gombey dance the way a visual recording can. So, while you're in Bermuda, consider filming a Gombey dance to show when you get back home.

THE BALLADEER TRADITION

Bermuda also has a strong balladeer tradition. Although its exponents are fewer than they used to be, local balladeers continue to enjoy considerable popularity among islanders and visitors alike. A wry, self-deprecating humor has always distinguished their compositions, and balladeers can strum a song for any occasion on their guitars. Today, many of their songs have to do with Bermuda's changing way of life.

By virtually everyone's estimate, the musical patriarch of Bermuda was **Hubert Smith,** who was the island's official greeter in song. A balladeer of formidable talent and originality, Smith composed and performed songs for the visits of nearly all the foreign heads of state who graced Bermuda's shores in recent memory. His performances for members of the British royal family included one of the most famous songs ever written about the island: *Bermuda Is Another World.* The song is now the island's unofficial national anthem; it's included in the best-selling album *Bermuda Is Another World.*

RECORDINGS

In the 1970s and 1980s, calypso was king in Bermuda, which is why you can still find CDs featuring beloved local artists like **The Bermuda Strollers, Jay**

Fox, Stan Seymour, and **The Talbot Brothers** for sale in the Music Box on Reid Street (58 Reid St.; ✆ **441/295-4839**). These days, its best to tune into music streaming services like Spotify if you'd rather listen to some of the island's most well-known artists. The biggest of the bunch is dance hall reggae singer Collie Buddz, whose top hits *Come Around* and *Blind to You* have been streamed nearly 60 million times combined. Mishka is another acclaimed reggae singer from Bermuda. His style is decidedly more mellow and his following smaller, but *Above the Bones* and *Give Them Love* are still well worth a listen. His sister, a singer-songwriter named Heather Nova, is another Bermudian artist whose music can be heard on Spotify.

EATING & DRINKING

For years, Bermuda wasn't known for its cuisine; the food was too often bland and lacking in flavor. However, the culinary scene has notably changed. Chefs are better trained, and many top-notch (albeit expensive) restaurants dot the archipelago. They represent most every major cooking tradition (Chinese food, pub grub, French bistros, etc.) except for the traditional foods of the island itself. You'll find few places serving the staples the islanders lived on for centuries, which included shark hash, mussel pie and Hoppin' John, a traditional side dish of black-eyed peas and rice.

The best choice at most restaurants is the catch of the day. Indeed, Bermuda's waters have long been the inspiration of many a chef, since the surrounding Atlantic is rich with fresh tuna, wahoo, mahi, rockfish and when in season, spiny Caribbean lobster. Of course, every good meal deserves an equally good drink and in Bermuda, most of those contain rum. Specifically, Gosling's Black Seal Rum, which has been integrated into the fabric of the island since it was first created in 1806.

What's Cooking?

SEAFOOD Any local fisherman will be happy to tell you that more species of shore and ocean fish—including wahoo, tuna, mahi, snapper, and the ubiquitous rockfish—are found off Bermuda's coastline than any other place.

Rockfish, which is similar to Bahamian grouper, appears on nearly every menu. From the ocean, it weighs anywhere from 15 to 135 pounds (or even

---

Dress Up for Your Evening Out

In years past, many of Bermuda's fanciest restaurants—including the Waterlot Inn and Fourways Inn—required that men wear jackets to dinner. These days, dress codes have relaxed significantly, but that doesn't mean you can show up in flip-flops. The dress code at most island restaurants is smart casual, meaning men should wear a collared shirt, shorts or slacks, and closed-toe shoes. Pretty much anything goes for ladies, but don't even think about showing up for lunch in a bikini, since coverups are expected to be worn everywhere except public beaches.

more). Steamed, broiled, baked, fried, or grilled, rockfish delicious any which way that it's prepared.

The most ubiquitous dish on the island is **Bermuda fish chowder,** a spicy seafood and vegetable stew traditionally served with a dash of Gosling's Black Seal Rum and Outerbridge's Sherry Peppers sauce.

Shark isn't as popular on Bermuda as it used to be, but many traditional dishes, including hash, are made from shark. Some people use shark-liver oil to forecast the weather; it's said to be more reliable than the nightly TV report. The oil is left in the sun in a small bottle. If it lies still, fair weather is ahead; if droplets form on the sides of the bottle, expect foul weather.

The great game fish in Bermuda is **wahoo,** a sweet fish that tastes like albacore. If it's on the menu, go for a wahoo steak. Properly prepared, it's superb.

The **spiny Caribbean lobster** has been called a first cousin of the Maine lobster. It's in season from September to March. Its high price tag has led to overfishing, forcing the government to issue periodic bans on its harvesting. In those instances, lobster is imported.

Mussels are cherished in Bermuda; one of the most popular traditional dishes is Bermuda-style mussel pie, with a filling of papaya, onions, potatoes, bacon, curry powder, lemon juice, thyme, and, of course, steamed mussels.

FRUITS & VEGETABLES In restaurants and homes, **Portuguese red-bean soup**—the culinary contribution of the Portuguese farmers who were brought to the island to till the land—precedes many a meal.

The **Bermuda onion** figures in many recipes, including onion pie. Bermuda-onion soup, an island favorite, is usually flavored with Outerbridge's Original Sherry Peppers.

Bermudians grow more **potatoes** than any other vegetable; the principal varieties are Pontiac red and Kennebec white. The traditional Sunday breakfast of codfish and bananas cooked with potatoes is still served in some homes.

"Peas and plenty" is a Bermudian tradition. Black-eyed peas are cooked with onions, salt pork, and sometimes rice. Dumplings or boiled sweet potatoes may also be added to the mix at the last minute. Another peas-and-rice dish, **Hoppin' John,** is eaten as a main dish or as a side dish with meat or poultry.

Both Bermudians and Bahamians share the tradition of **Johnny Bread,** or **Johnnycake,** a simple pan-cooked cornmeal bread. Fishermen would make it at sea over a fire in a box filled with sand to keep the flames from spreading to the boat.

The starchy **cassava** root, once an important food on Bermuda, is now used chiefly as an ingredient in the traditional Christmas cassava pie. Another dish with a festive holiday connection is **sweet-potato pudding,** traditionally eaten on Guy Fawkes Day (Nov 5).

Bermuda grows many **fresh fruits,** including strawberries, Surinam cherries, guavas, avocados, and bananas. Guavas are made into jelly, which in turn often goes into making the famous Bermuda syllabub, a sweet frothy drink traditionally accompanied by Johnnycake.

Teatime!

One of Bermuda's most delightful traditions is the English ritual of partaking in **afternoon tea,** which many hotels and small inns typically serve from 3pm to 5pm. For one of the Bermuda's best, head to the Crown & Anchor at the Hamilton Princess Hotel on Saturday and Sunday. There you'll be served a selection of dainty finger sandwiches like smoked salmon with cream cheese and roast beef with mustard plus a selection of scones, doughnuts, and sweet petit fours. Since Crown & Anchor's tea service is in collaboration with Lili Bermuda perfumes, your choice of tea is paired with a bottle of perfume that has similar floral notes, which you can take home as a gift. (Hamilton Princess Hotel & Beach Club, 76 Pitts Bay Rd.; www.thehamiltonprincess.com; ℂ 441/295-3000; $55, with champagne $75).

What to Wash It All Down With

For some 300 years, **rum** has been the drink of Bermuda and the Grand Dame of them all is none other than Gosling's Black Seal, a rich, dark rum that's been distilled on the island since the early 19th century. It's the key ingredient in Bermuda's two national drinks: the **Dark n' Stormy,** made with Gosling's Black Seal Rum and spicy ginger beer, and the **Bermuda Rum Swizzle,** a potent mix of Gosling's Black Seal Rum, Gosling's Gold Seal Rum, orange and pineapple juices, a dash of Angustora bitters, and a local sweetener called Falernum (to try the original, head to the Swizzle Inn in Bailey's Bay or Warwick Parish).

An intriguing drink is **loquat liqueur,** made with locally grown loquats (a small plumlike local fruit), sugar and gin—or more elaborately, with brandy instead of gin and the addition of such spices as cinnamon, nutmeg, cloves, and allspice.

You'll find all the usual name-brand alcoholic beverages in Bermuda, but prices on mixed drinks can run high, depending on the brand (expect to pay up to $11 for a beer).

WHEN TO GO

The Weather

A semitropical island, Bermuda enjoys a mild climate; the term "Bermuda high" has come to mean sunny days and clear skies. The Gulf Stream, which flows between the island and North America, keeps the climate temperate. There's no rainy season, and no typical month of excess rain. Showers may be heavy at times, but the skies clear quickly.

Being farther north in the Atlantic than the Bahamas, Bermuda is much cooler in winter. Springlike temperatures prevail from mid-December to late March, with the average temperature ranging from 60° to 70°F (16°–21°C). Unless it rains, winter is fine for golf and tennis but not for swimming; it can be cool, and you may even need a sweater or a jacket. Water temperatures in winter are somewhat like the air temperature, ranging from about 66°F (19°C) in January to 75°F (24°C) through March. Scuba divers and snorkelers will find Bermuda's waters appreciably cooler than Caribbean waters in winter. From mid-November to mid-December and from late March to April, be prepared for unseasonable spurts of spring or fall weather.

In summer, the temperature rarely rises above 85°F (29°C) and there's nearly always a cool breeze in the evening. Local water temperatures can be as high as 86°F (30°C) during the summer—warmer than many inshore and offshore Caribbean waters.

As a result, Bermuda's off season is the exact opposite of that in the Caribbean. It begins in December and lasts until about March 1. In general, hotels offer off-season rates, with discounts ranging from 20% to 60%. This is the time to go if you're traveling on a tight budget. During autumn and winter, many hotels also offer discounted package deals. Some smaller inns close for a couple of weeks or months at this period.

A look at the official chart of temperature and rainfall will give you a general idea of what to expect during your visit.

Bermuda's Average Daytime Temperatures & Rainfall

	JAN	FEB	MAR	APR	MAY	JUNE	JULY	AUG	SEPT	OCT	NOV	DEC
TEMP (°F)	65	64	64	65	70	75	79	80	79	75	69	65
TEMP (°C)	19	18	18	19	21	24	26	27	26	24	21	19
RAINFALL (IN.)	4	5	4.6	3	3.9	5.2	4	5.3	5.3	6	4.5	3

The Hurricane Season

This curse of the Caribbean, the Bahamas, and Bermuda lasts officially from June to November, but fewer tropical storms pound Bermuda than the U.S. mainland. Bermuda is also less frequently hit than islands in the Caribbean. Satellite forecasts are generally able to give adequate warning of any really dangerous weather. If you're concerned, check reports from the National Hurricane Center by visiting **www.nhc.noaa.gov** and to find the current weather conditions in Bermuda visit the Bermuda Weather Service at **www.weather.bm**.

Holidays

Bermuda observes the following public holidays: New Year's Day (Jan 1), Good Friday, Easter, Bermuda Day (celebrated on the last Fri in May), the Queen's Birthday (first or second Mon in June), Cup Match Days (cricket; Thurs and Fri preceding first Mon in Aug), Labour Day (first Mon in Sept), Christmas Day (Dec 25), and Boxing Day (Dec 26). Public holidays that fall on a Saturday or Sunday are usually celebrated the following Monday.

Bermuda Calendar of Events

JANUARY & FEBRUARY

Bermuda Festival of Performing Arts. Held in the City of Hamilton and a handful of venues in neighboring parishes, this 7-week performing arts festival features drama, dance, jazz, classical, and popular music, as well as other entertainment by a rotating lineup of international artists from January through March. For details about this year's festival, visit www. bermudafestival.org; © **441/295-1291.**

Bermuda Restaurant Weeks. Enjoy island-inspired cuisine at discount prices during these weeks in January, when restaurants in the City of Hamilton and across the island offer affordable prix fixe menus.

Bermuda Marathon Weekend. Not just one race, but a trio of competitive races that culminates with a challenging 26.2-mile run, this 3-day, weekend event is popular with local and international runners alike. For more information and entry forms visit www.bermudaraceweekend.com; ℂ **441/737-8835.**

MARCH

Bermuda International Film Festival. This independent film festival screens works from international and local filmmakers. In addition, the festival holds workshops and Q&A sessions with industry leaders. For more information, visit www.biff.bm or call ℂ **441/293-3456.**

Good Friday. On this day in March, Bermudians flock to Horseshoe Bay Beach to fly kites, many of which are handmade with brightly colored tissue paper, sticks and glue. The annual tradition—known as the Bermuda Kite Festival—is meant to replicate the ascension of Christ, who according to Christian tradition, rose from the dead on Easter Sunday.

APRIL

Peppercorn Ceremony. Meant to recreate the moment when the island's capital was transferred from St. George's to Hamilton in 1816, this annual ceremony full of pomp and circumstance follows his Excellency the Governor, as he collects the annual rent of one peppercorn for use of the Old State House in St. George's. Mid- to late April.

Bermuda Agricultural Exhibition. Held over 3 days in late April at the Botanical Gardens in Paget, this family-friendly event is a celebration of Bermuda's agrarian and horticultural bounty. In addition to prize-winning produce, the exhibition (locally known as the "ag show") features an equestrian competition and best-in-show awards for top pig, chicken, and other farm animals. For more information, visit www.theagshowbda.com.

International Race Week. Every year, during late April and early May, this yachting event pits equivalent vessels from seven classes of sailing craft against one another. Yachting enthusiasts around the world follow the knock-out elimination-style event with avid interest. The **Marion-to-Bermuda Race** and **Newport-Bermuda Race** (see below) take place in June. Unfortunately for spectators, the finish lines for the island's sailing races usually lie several miles offshore. Afterward, boats are often moored in Hamilton Harbour; any vantage point on the harbor is good for watching the boats come in. Even better: Head for any of the City of Hamilton's harborfront pubs, where racing crowds celebrate their wins (or justify their losses) over pints of ale.

For information on all sailing events held off the coast of Bermuda, contact the Royal Bermuda Yacht Club (www.rbyc.bm; ℂ **441/295-2214**).

MAY

Harbour Night. On Wednesday nights in the City of Hamilton from May through August, join a festive street party on a blocked off section of Front Street, where local vendors sell crafts, artwork and food. Expect family-friendly kid zones, cultural expositions and live musical performances, like Bermuda's very own Gombey dancers.

Bermuda Day. Celebrated every year on the last Friday of May, Bermuda Day is a public holiday that's Bermuda's equivalent of Independence Day. Bermuda Day is punctuated with parades through downtown Hamilton, dinghy and cycling races, and the Bermuda Half Marathon Derby, a 13-mile road race that's popular with locals. It's also the official start of summer, when you'll see Bermudians don their swimsuits and jump into the Atlantic for the first time of the year.

JUNE

Bermuda Heroes Weekend. One of the island's biggest summer celebrations, this Carnival-style event features a parade of bands, feverish Soca concerts, steel pan musicians and the J'Ouvert Celebration, a boisterous all-night fete where people party until the sun comes up.

Marion-to-Bermuda Race. This 1,038km (645-mile) sailboat race from Marion, Massachusetts, to Bermuda is held in mid-June. See the entry for "International Race Week," under April, above, for details on international sailing events. For more information, visit www.marionbermuda.com, or call the Royal Bermuda Yacht Club ℂ **441/295-2214.**

Newport-Bermuda Race. Also known as "The Thrash to the Onion Patch," this biannual, 635-nautical mile regatta starts in Newport, Rhode Island and ends in Bermuda. In 2016, the 100-foot high-performance racing yacht *Comanche* set a new course record by completing the race in less than 35 hours, smashing the old record by almost 5 hours. That record hasn't been broken since. For more information visit www.bermudarace.com.

JULY & AUGUST

Bermuda Triple Crown Billfish Championship. A trio of deep-sea fishing tournaments, this series of high-octane angling events is comprised of the Bermuda Billfish Blast, the Bermuda Big Game Classic and the Seahorse Anglers Club Billfish Tournament, all of which feature hefty cash purses. For more information visit www.bermudatriplecrown.com.

Cup Match. Held on Thursday and Friday before the first Monday in August, this 2-day cricket match is the most beloved sporting event of the year, when cricketers from the East End (St. George's Cricket Club) square off against those from the West End (Somerset Cricket Club). Come to watch the hotly contested match or join the throngs of well-dressed locals who crowd the neighboring tents to drink rum swizzle and win cash at the Crown & Anchor tables, a popular dice game where betting is permitted.

SEPTEMBER

Sand Sculpture Competition. This annual competition held on Horseshoe Bay Beach is perfect for kids of all ages, since prizes are awarded in categories including companies, tourists, adults, families and children 12 and under.

OCTOBER

The City Food Festival. Featuring wine tastings, walking tours, bartending competitions and live cooking demonstrations from some of the island's top chefs, this 3-day festival in the City of Hamilton celebrates everything food. For more information visit www.cityofhamilton.bm.

NOVEMBER

The Opening of Parliament. Typically held the first week of November, this traditional ceremony, with a military guard of honor, celebrates the opening of Parliament by His Excellency the governor, as the Queen's personal representative. In anticipation of the entry of the members of Parliament (MPs) at 11am, crowds begin gathering outside the Cabinet Building around 9:30 or 10am. Spectators traditionally include lots of schoolchildren being trained in civic protocol, as well as nostalgia buffs out for a whiff of British-style pomp.

Remembrance Day. Bermudian police, British and U.S. military units, Bermudians, and veterans' organizations participate in a small parade in remembrance of all who have given their lives in battle. November 11.

World Rugby Classic. Former international rugby players, who have recently retired from the international stage, compete with Bermudians at the Bermuda National Sports Club at this beloved annual event. Watch from the grandstands or splurge on a ticket to the Member's Tent, a VIP area located behind the goal post where all food and wine is included (www.worldrugby.bm; ℂ **441/295-6574**). Mid-November.

DECEMBER

National Trust Christmas Walkabout. Watch the Town of St. George's come to life in splendid holiday wonder during this beloved annual event when 17th-century homes are open to the public, carolers stroll the streets and live performances by choirs and dance troupes are held in festively decorated King's Square. For more information, visit www.bnt.bm.

Christmas Boat Parade. Typically held every other year in Hamilton Harbour, this festive parade features dozens of circling boats, all lit up in festive colored lights for the holidays. For a great view, grab a table at 1609, a harborside restaurant at the Hamilton Princess Hotel.

Bermuda Goodwill Tournament. The longest running Pro-Am in golf, this tournament features international pro-amateur foursomes who come to play 72 holes on three of

Bermuda's top courses (Port Royal, Tucker's Point, and the Mid Ocean Club). Anyone who wants to compete must pass the sponsors' stringent requirements and may appear only by invitation. Spectators are welcome to watch from the sidelines for free. For more information visit www.bermudagoodwill.org.

2 BERMUDA'S NATURAL WORLD

Lying 1,070km (665 miles) east-southeast of Cape Hatteras, North Carolina, Bermuda is actually a group of some 180 islands, islets and cays clustered in a fishhook-shaped chain about 35km (22 miles) long and 3km (2 miles) wide at its broadest point. The archipelago, formally known as "The Bermudas," forms a landmass of about 54 sq. km (21 sq. miles).

Only 20 or so of the islands are inhabited. The largest one, called the "mainland," is Great Bermuda; about 23km (14 miles) long, it's linked to nearby major islands by a series of bridges and causeways. Bermuda's capital, the City of Hamilton, is on Great Bermuda.

The other main inhabited islands include Somerset, Watford, Boaz, and Ireland in the west, and St. George's and St. David's in the east. This chain of major islands encloses the archipelago's major bodies of water, which include Castle Harbour, St. George's Harbour, Harrington Sound, and Great Sound. Most of the other smaller islands, or islets, lie within these bodies of water.

Bermuda is far north of the Tropic of Cancer, which cuts through the Bahamian archipelago. Bermuda's archipelago is based on the upper parts of an extinct volcano, which may date from 100 million years ago. Through the millennia, wind and water brought limestone deposits and formed these islands far from any continental landmass. Today, the closest continental landmass is the coast of the Carolinas. Bermuda is about 1,250km (775 miles) southeast of New York City, some 1,660km (1,030 miles) northeast of Miami, and nearly 5,555km (3,445 miles) from London. It has a balmy climate year-round, with sunshine prevailing almost every day. The chief source of Bermuda's mild weather is the Gulf Stream, a broad belt of warm water formed by equatorial currents. The stream's northern reaches separate the Bermuda islands from North America and, with the prevailing northeast winds, temper the wintry blasts that sweep across the Atlantic from west and north. The islands of Bermuda are divided, for administrative purposes, into parishes (see chapter 3).

More Than Onions: The Island's Flora

Bermuda's temperate climate, abundant sunshine, fertile soil, and adequate moisture account for the exceptionally verdant gardens that you'll find on the archipelago. Some of the best gardens, such as the Botanical Gardens in Paget Parish, are open to the public. Bermudian gardeners pride themselves on their mixtures of temperate-zone and subtropical plants, both of which thrive on the island, despite the salty air.

Bermuda is blessed with copious and varied flora. Examples include the indigenous **sea grape,** which flourishes along the island's sandy coasts (it prefers sand and saltwater to more arable soil), and the **cassava plant,** whose roots resemble the tubers of sweet potatoes. When ground into flour and soaked to remove a mild poison, the cassava root is the main ingredient for Bermuda's traditional Christmas pies. Also growing wild and abundant are **prickly pears, aromatic fennel, yucca,** and the **Spanish bayonet,** a spiked-leaf plant that bears a single white flower in season.

Bermuda's only native palm, the **palmetto,** proved particularly useful to the early settlers. Its leaves were used to thatch roofs, and when crushed and fermented, the palm fronds produced a strong alcoholic drink called bibby, whose effects the early Puritans condemned. Palmetto leaves were also fashioned into women's hats during a brief period in the 1600s, when they represented the height of fashion in London.

The **banana,** one of Bermuda's most dependable sources of fresh fruit, was introduced to the island in the early 1600s. It is believed that Bermudian bananas were the first to be brought back to London from the New World. They created an immediate sensation, leading to the cultivation of bananas in many other British colonies.

The plant that contributed most to Bermuda's renown was the **Bermuda onion** *(Allium cepa)*. Imported from England in 1616, it was grown from seeds brought from the Spanish and Portuguese islands of Tenerife and Madeira. The Bermuda onion became so famous along the East Coast of the United States that Bermudians themselves became known as "Onions." During the 1930s, Bermuda's flourishing export trade in onions declined due to high tariffs, increased competition from similar species grown in Texas and elsewhere, and the limited arable land on the island.

Today, you'll see oleander, hibiscus, royal poinciana, poinsettia, bougainvillea, and dozens of other flowering shrubs and vines decorating Bermuda's gently rolling land. Of the island's dozen or so species of morning glory, three are indigenous; they tend to grow rampant and overwhelm everything else in a garden.

Close Encounters with the Local Fauna
AMPHIBIANS

Because of the almost total lack of natural freshwater ponds and lakes, Bermuda's amphibians have adapted to seawater or slightly brackish water. Amphibians include **tree frogs** *(Eleutherodactylus johnstonei* and *Eleutherodactylus gossei),* whose nighttime chirping newcomers sometimes mistake for the song of birds. Small and camouflaged by the leafy matter of the forest floor, the frogs appear between April and November.

More visible are Bermuda's **giant toads,** or road toads *(Bufo marinus),* which sometimes reach the size of an adult human's palm. Imported from Guyana in the 1870s in hopes of controlling the island's cockroach population, giant toads search out the nighttime warmth of the asphalt roads—and are often crushed by cars in the process. They are especially prevalent after a soaking rain. The road toads are not venomous and, contrary to legend, do not cause warts.

Island reptiles include colonies of harmless **lizards,** often seen sunning themselves on rocks until approaching humans or predators scare them away. The best-known species is the Bermuda rock lizard *(Eumeces longirostris),* also known as a skink. It's said to have been the only nonmarine, nonflying vertebrate on Bermuda before the arrival of European colonists. Imported reptiles include the Somerset lizard *(Anolis roquet),* whose black eye patches give it the look of a bashful bandit, and the Jamaican anole *(Anolis grahami),* a kind of chameleon.

BIRD LIFE

Partly because of its ample food sources, Bermuda has a large bird population; many species nest on the island during their annual migrations. Most of the birds arrive during the cooler winter months, usually between Christmas and Easter. Birders have recorded almost 40 different species of eastern warblers, which peacefully coexist with martins, doves, egrets, South American terns, herons, fork-tailed flycatchers, and some species from as far away as the Arctic Circle.

Two of the most visible imported species are the **cardinal,** introduced during the 1700s, and the **kiskadee.** Imported from Trinidad in 1957 to control lizards and flies, the kiskadee has instead wreaked havoc on the island's commercial fruit crops.

The once-prevalent **eastern bluebird** has been greatly reduced in number since its preferred habitat, cedar trees, was depleted by blight. Another bird native to Bermuda is the gray-and-white **petrel,** known locally as a cahow, which burrows for most of the year in the sands of the isolated eastern islands. During the rest of the year, the cahow feeds at sea, floating for hours in the warm waters of the Gulf Stream. One of the most elusive birds in the world—it was once thought to be extinct—the petrel is now protected by the Bermudian government.

Also native to Bermuda is the **white-tailed tropic bird,** which you can identify by the elongated plumage of its long white tail. The bird resembles a swallow and is the island's harbinger of spring, appearing annually in March.

Although the gardens and golf courses of many of the island's hotels attract dozens of birds, some of the finest bird-watching sites are maintained by the Bermuda Audubon Society (www.audubon.bm) or the National Trust. Isolated sites known for sheltering thousands of native and migrating birds include Paget Marsh, just south of the City of Hamilton; the Idwal Hughes Nature Reserve in Hamilton Parish; and Spittal Pond in Smith's Parish.

SEA LIFE

In the deep waters off the shores of Bermuda are some of the finest game fish in the world: **blackfin tuna, marlin, swordfish, wahoo, dolphin, sailfish, and barracuda.** Also prevalent are **bonefish** and **pompano,** both of which prefer sun-flooded shallow waters closer to shore. Any beachcomber is likely to come across hundreds of oval-shaped **chitons** *(Chiton tuberculatus),* a mollusk that adheres tenaciously to rocks in tidal flats; locally, it is known as "suck-rock."

Beware of the **Portuguese man-of-war** *(Physalia physalis)*, a floating colony of jellyfish whose stinging tentacles sometimes reach 15m (50 ft.) in length. Give this venomous marine creature a wide berth: Severe stings may require hospitalization. Avoid the creature when it washes up on Bermuda beaches, usually between March and July—the man-of-war can sting even when it appears to be dead.

The most prevalent marine animal in Bermuda is responsible for the formation of the island's greatest tourist attraction—its miles of pale pink sand. Much of the sand consists of broken shells, pieces of coral, and the calcium carbonate remains of other marine invertebrates. The pinkest pieces are shards of crushed shell from a single-celled animal called foraminifera. Its vivid pink skeleton is pierced with holes, through which the animal extends its rootlike feet *(pseudopodia)*, which cling to the underside of the island's reefs during the animal's brief life, before its skeleton is washed ashore.

GREEN TRAVEL

The ecotourist will find Bermuda a rich stomping ground with its bird-watching and nature trails. See for yourself, by mapping out your own green tour. Some of these chief attractions include the following:

o **The Arboretum,** Middle Road in Devonshire Parish, is 7.7 pristine hectares (19 acres) close to the City of Hamilton, with a large expanse of open space and a small woodland.

o **Bermuda Railway Trail.** Totaling 34km (21 miles), this trail provides a scenic route from East to West. It is used by walkers and birders alike.

o **Blue Hole Park,** Hamilton Parish. An abundance of wildlife exists in nearly 5 hectares (12 acres), with a natural small pond and caves close by.

o **Hog Bay Park,** Sandys Parish. On 15 hectares (38 acres), this park has well-maintained trails, vegetable gardens, and wooded hillsides with native and endemic vegetation.

o **Spittal Pond Nature Reserve,** Smith's Parish. At South Road, 14 hectares (36 acres) of nature form the largest and most accessible nature reserve on the island. There are excellent trails plus bird-watching at several observation points, where you can see a large variety of wildlife.

SUGGESTED ITINERARIES

For visitors on the run (or on cruises), who are forced by their schedules to see Bermuda in anywhere from 1 to 3 days, we've devised a trio of 1-day itineraries. With these ready-made plans, you can have an unforgettable trip, even if time is short.

If your time on island is longer—lucky you! You can *still* use these itineraries, but you'll be able to break up your sightseeing trips with long stretches on the beach, boating, or engaging in some of the island's other outdoor activities, such as golf or scuba diving.

We're supplementing these short itineraries with special plans for families and those who might one day start families (but are romantic twosomes for now). Our itinerary section will be followed by a discussion of the parishes of Bermuda, so you can find your way around when crafting your *own* itineraries.

ICONIC BERMUDA IN 1 DAY

If you have only 1 day for sightseeing, spend most of it in and around the parish of Southampton, where Bermuda's iconic pink sand beaches seem to go on forever. Pack everything you'll need for a day at the beach—sunblock, hat, water and snorkel gear. Southampton, and most of Bermuda's south shore beaches for that matter, are easily accessible via the No. 7 bus from the City of Hamilton, but if you're hopping on elsewhere, just make sure you're headed in the right direction (bus stops are marked with blue poles for westward routes and pink poles for eastward routes; and all buses accept coins if you don't already have tickets, which can be purchased at the main bus terminal on Church St., at the ferry terminal on Front St., or at any post office).

We begin the tour at:

1 **Horseshoe Bay Beach**
The Grand Dame of Bermuda beaches, this quarter-mile slice of pink sand is consistently ranked among the world's finest— and it'll be easy to see why when you arrive at its entrance on South Road. Thanks to a recently constructed wooden boardwalk that gently slopes downwards as it nears the beach, you'll have an unsurpassed view of this mighty crescent, that tourists

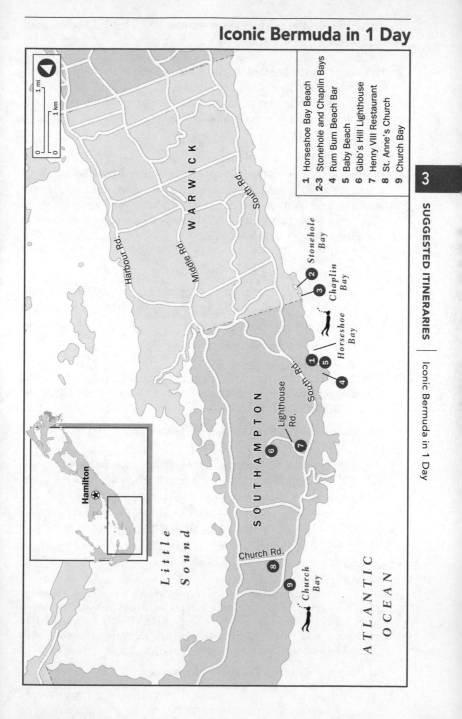

Iconic Bermuda in 1 Day

1 Horseshoe Bay Beach
2-3 Stonehole and Chaplin Bays
4 Rum Bum Beach Bar
5 Baby Beach
6 Gibb's Hill Lighthouse
7 Henry VIII Restaurant
8 St. Anne's Church
9 Church Bay

WARWICK

Harbour Rd.

Middle Rd.

South Rd.

SOUTHAMPTON

Lighthouse Rd.

Church Rd.

Stonehole Bay

Chaplin Bay

Horseshoe Bay

Church Bay

Little Sound

ATLANTIC OCEAN

Hamilton

1 mi
1 km

and locals alike flock to in summer months. If you needed a beach chair and umbrella, you'd continue past the bathrooms to where rentals are available. But you don't have the time to linger here all day, so head to the wooded pathway to the left, which exits closest to the lifeguard stand on the beachside. Once at the end of the path, you'll be in the middle of the beach and further from the cruise ship crowds that fill the western end. Pull up a piece of a sand and take a dip.

Next, hike to:

2 Stonehole & Chaplin Bays

This beach walk is particularly good at low tide, when the retreating Atlantic unveils dozens of natural tidal pools and volcanic rock formations. There are no signs demarking this hike, but if you hug the shoreline it'll be impossible to get lost. You'll know you've reached your destination when you can't walk any further.

Now grab a drink at:

3 Rum Bum Beach Bar

Make your way back to the entrance of open-air Horseshoe Beach. It may be before noon, but as the Alan Jackson/Jimmy Buffet song goes, it's five o'clock somewhere.

When you're done, walk 5 minutes west to:

4 Baby Beach

Completely encircled by a protected cove of volcanic rock, this massive natural pool is blissfully wave-free, which makes it the perfect place for a safe soak after a stiff drink.

Walk to the taxi stand just past the public bathrooms and hail a cab to:

5 Gibb's Hill Lighthouse

Originally powered by kerosene, the lighthouse now features a 1,000-watt, 2.75-ton electric bulb that can be seen by ships 40 miles out to sea and by airplanes at 10,000 feet and 120 miles away. Opened in 1846, this is one of the oldest cast-iron lighthouses in the world. Climb the 185 steps to the very top for a stunning, 360-degree panorama of the island. There's a modest $2.50 fee to enter (closed Feb).

Next walk to:

6 Henry VIII Restaurant ☕

Grab a late lunch at this traditional English pub, which is a 10-minute, 500-meter walk down Lighthouse Road. On the way there you'll pass Queen's View, where Queen Elizabeth II famously took in the view of Riddell's Bay, the Great Sound and beyond shortly after her coronation in 1953 (look for the bronze plaque mounted on a cement pedestal).

If you've got the energy for a 20-minute, 1.3-kilometer walk, cross the street and head west on South Rd, where you'll be treated to a jaw-dropping oceanview amble.

RATTLE & SHAKE: the bermuda railway trail

One of the island's most unusual sight-seeing adventures is following the Bermuda Railway Trail—an 18-mile pedestrian and cycle path, which was home to a working railway from 1931 to 1948. Affectionately known as the "Old Rattle & Shake," the train eventually gave way to the automobile after cars arrived the island in 1946. But signs of its demise had hovered over the railway for years since its construction originally cost investors a whopping $1 million (said to be the most expensive railway ever constructed) and locating spare parts for routine repairs was nearly impossible given Bermuda's isolated mid-Atlantic location.

The railway was eventually sold to British Guiana (Guyana), but thanks to an infusion of government capital in the 1980s, its railbed has been transformed into a popular recreational path for all to enjoy.

The trail is divided into nine separate sections, but two particularly picturesque routes are in Sandys Parish on the west end, from Morgan's Point to Somerset Bridge; and in Hamilton Parish on the east end, where you'll cross a newly constructed, 740-foot-long footbridge that connects Coney Island to Crawl Hill. The terrain varies throughout but expect to stroll through lush forests and past oceanview coastlines.

Otherwise, look for the blue pole on the roadside for routes west and take the No. 7 bus two stops to:

7 St. Anne's Church

The stone structure you see before you is the second church to stand on this site. The first, founded in 1616 and built of palmetto leaves and Bermuda cedar, was destroyed by the hurricanes of 1712 and 1716 (as were most of the wooden churches on the island). The current church, erected in 1719, is not only a hardier structure, it's a very fine example of Bermudian ecclesiastic architecture. Step inside to smell pews made with fragrant Bermuda cedar and view colorful stained-glass windows, some of which depict the island's maritime history. Stroll the old graveyard with its oddly angled headstones, some of which date back to 1668 (purportedly the oldest decipherable date on any Bermuda graveyard). *Important:* Make sure you don a coverup before entering the church.

Exit the church, cross South Road and head west. It's less than a 5-minute walk to the entrance of:

8 Church Bay

You've brought your snorkel gear, right? This small southwestern cove has a series of shallow reefs close to the shoreline. Descend the wooden stairway, enter the beach and walk to its western edge. There you'll find the beginnings of a coral trail that leads 100 yards offshore, to a pair of large outcroppings teaming with marine life. Almost immediately you'll see large reef fish like colorful parrotfish, sergeant majors and angelfish plus healthy clumps of elkhorn and brain coral.

ICONIC BERMUDA IN 2 DAYS

Spend **Day 1** as indicated above. Devote **Day 2** to exploring the historic colonial capital of **St. George's,** the second English town established in the New World after Jamestown, Virginia. In this maze of narrow streets, you can spend an entire day exploring British-style pubs, seafood restaurants, shops, old forts, museums, and churches.

---

1 King's Square

Also known as Market Square and King's Parade, the square is the very center of St. George. Only about 200 years old, it's not as historic as St. George itself. This was formerly a marshy part of the harbor—at least when the shipwrecked passengers and crew of the *Sea Venture* first saw it. At the water's edge stands a branch of the Visitor Services Centre, and on the square is a replica of a pillory and stocks. These devices were used to punish criminals—and, in many cases, the innocent. You could be severely punished here for such "crimes" as casting a spell over your neighbor's turkeys.

From the square, head south across the small bridge to:

2 Ordnance Island

The British army once stored gunpowder and cannons on this island, which extends into St. George's Harbour. Today, the island houses the *Deliverance,* a replica of the vessel that carried the shipwrecked *Sea Venture* passengers on to Virginia. Alongside the vessel is a ducking stool, a contraption used in 17th-century witch trials. Across the street is a bronze statue of Sir George Somers, captain of the *Sea Venture*—many of the island's parks and schools are named for him.

Retrace your steps across the bridge to King's Square. On its eastern border lies:

3 Town Hall

Located near the Visitor Services Centre and dating back to 1782, this is the meeting place of the corporation governing St. George's. On display here are antique cedar furnishings, a collection of photographs of previous lord mayors and letters written by Queen Elizabeth II.

From King's Square, head east along King Street, cutting north (left) on Bridge Street. You'll come to the:

4 Bridge House

Constructed in the 1690s, this white-washed home is one of the oldest residential buildings in Bermuda and an excellent example of British colonial architecture. Once the home of Governor Benjamin Bennet in the early 1700s, this stone structure is now a private residence.

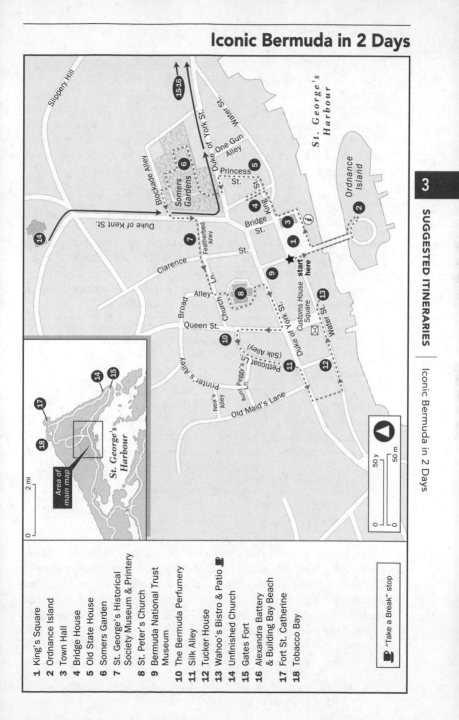

1 King's Square
2 Ordnance Island
3 Town Hall
4 Bridge House
5 Old State House
6 Somers Garden
7 St. George's Historical
  Society Museum & Printery
8 St. Peter's Church
9 Bermuda National Trust
  Museum
10 The Bermuda Perfumery
11 Silk Alley
12 Tucker House
13 Wahoo's Bistro & Patio 📖
14 Unfinished Church
15 Gates Fort
16 Alexandra Battery
  & Building Bay Beach
17 Fort St. Catherine
18 Tobacco Bay

📖 "Take a Break" stop

Return to King Street and continue east to the:

5 Old State House

Once the home of the Bermuda Parliament, this handsome hilltop building is one of the oldest on the island, dating back to 1620 when mortars like turtle oil and lime were used to bind its limestone bricks. Today it's the site of the Peppercorn Ceremony, an annual celebration commemorating when the capital of Bermuda was transferred from St. George's to the City of Hamilton in 1816. When parliament left the building that year, the Old State House was rented to the Freemasons for one peppercorn—a symbolic gesture that continues to this day (see p. 108).

Continue your stroll down King Street until you come to York Street and the entrance to:

6 Somers Garden

When *Sea Venture* Captain Sir George Somers died in 1610, he instructed his nephew to bury his heart in Bermuda. Lore has it that his heart was buried here while his remains were shipped and buried near his birthplace of Lyme Regis in West Dorset, England. Opened in 1920 by the Prince of Wales, the gardens are among St. George's few green spaces, complete with tall palm trees and tropical plants of all kinds.

Walk through Somers Gardens and up the steps to the North Gate onto Blockade Alley. Turn left, then left again onto Government Hill Road where at the next corner you'll find:

7 St. George's Historical Society Museum & Printery

With its traditional "welcoming arms" staircase, antique cedar furnishings and period artifacts throughout, this living history museum is fashioned to resemble a working Bermudian home in the early 1700s. Take a gander at the centuries-old tools used to cook in the stone kitchen, sniff around the fragrant herb gardens, and don't miss the working replica of the printing press invented by Johannes Gutenberg in Germany in the 1450s.

Go up Featherbed Alley and straight onto Church Street. Go through the church's backyard, opposite Broad Alley, to reach:

8 St. Peter's Church

We're taking you through the graveyard of the oldest Anglican place of worship in the Western Hemisphere so that you can read the headstones, some of which are 300 years old. There's a separate graveyard to the west of the church for slaves and free blacks—a solemn reminder of Bermuda's divided past. Once inside the church, view its handsome red-cedar altar carved in 1615 and a baptismal font brought by early settlers that's believed to be over 900 years old.

Exit through the main entrance. Across the street is the:

9 Bermuda National Trust Museum

This building has quite the history. Built in 1700 as the Governor's mansion, it eventually became the Globe Hotel—and a center of international intrigue. During the American Civil War, Maj. Norman Walker of the Confederate Army moved in, and not-so-quietly started smuggling guns, ammunition, and other supplies from England back to his troops. The history of the blockade running that followed is described in great detail in the permanent exhibit: "Rogues and Runners: Bermuda and the American Civil War."

Go west along York Street, then turn right on Queen Street. Head to Stewart Hall to find:

10 The Bermuda Perfumery

A Bermuda institution since 1928, this adorable boutique is set in a historic building (Stewart Hall) and still makes its own island-inspired perfumes and colognes from local botanicals such as cedar, freesias and lilies. If you have the time, watch the short video about perfume making, and then head back into the garden to see the shed where the scents are mixed.

Exit the Perfumery, make a right onto Queen Street, then turn right again onto:

11 Silk Alley

Also known as Petticoat Lane, this alley got its name during the 1834 emancipation, when two former slave women who'd always wanted silk petticoats like their former mistresses, finally purchased some, and then paraded down the lane to show off their new finery. The alley ends at York Street and then connects to Barber's Alley, which honors Joseph Hayne Rainey. A former slave from South Carolina, Rainey fled to Bermuda with his French wife at the outbreak of the Civil War. He became a barber in St. George's and eventually returned to South Carolina, where, in 1870, he was elected to the U.S. House of Representatives—the first African American to serve in Congress.

Continue west until you reach:

12 Tucker House

Opening onto Water Street, this was the former home of a prominent Bermudian family, whose members included an island governor, a treasurer of the United States and a captain in the Confederate Navy. The building houses an excellent collection of antiques, including silver, portraits, cedar furniture and an entire room devoted to memorabilia of the aforementioned Joseph Hayne Rainey (it's thought that his barber shop operated in this building).

Walk east down Water Street to get lunch at:

13 Wahoo's Bistro & Patio ☕

Casual but accomplished, this eatery serves wahoo (white, flaky, tasty fish) every which way. Request a table on its harborfront patio.

From here you'll want to hop on a scooter or negotiate a multi-stop ride with a taxi driver since the next few sights are beyond the city limits. Make a right out of the restaurant and follow Water Street to King's Square where you'll make a left. Turn right onto York Street and go straight. At the fork, bear left onto Government Hill Road. Walk straight to:

14 Unfinished Church

Intended to replace St. Peter's Church after it was damaged by a hurricane, this elegant edifice was beset by financial difficulties and a schism in the Anglican congregation after its construction began in 1874. Consequently, all that was constructed is this evocative, roofless cathedral.

Head back down Government Hill Road and make a left onto York Street, which turns into Mullet Bay Road. Stay right around the bend; it will turn into Cut Road. Follow Cut Road through a residential neighborhood until you reach:

15 Gates Fort

Named after Thomas Gates—the Governor-elect of Jamestown, Virginia, who, along with the other passengers aboard the *Sea Venture,* wrecked on a nearby reef in 1609—this small fort was built around 1612. For a picture-perfect view of Town Cut (the channel leading to the open sea), walk to the top of the watchtower.

Stay right on Cut Road, which immediately turns into Barry Road. In less than a quarter-of-a-mile you'll reach:

16 Alexandra Battery & Building Bay Beach

Like nearby Gates Fort, Alexandra Battery was built to protect eastern waterways in the 1860s. However, its adjacent beach is where you'll find most visitors since it's a popular spot to collect sea glass. At low tide you'll find treasures of all colors, but the most common are green, milky white and brown. Called Building Bay, this beach is also where *Sea Venture* shipwreck survivors built the *Deliverance,* a similar sailing vessel that eventually went on to save the famished colonists of Jamestown in 1610.

Stay right on Barry Road. Continue straight for several minutes, keeping the coastline on your right side. After about 1 mile you'll eventually reach:

17 Fort St. Catherine

Of Bermuda's historic stone fortresses, this mighty military structure is the most impressive. The original fort was built around 1614, but work continued steadily through the 19th century, making this one of Bermuda's largest. Tour its extensive gunnery collection (including 18-ton rifled muzzle-loaders); duck into dark tunnels, which lead into the fort's bowels; and enjoy some of Bermuda's finest water views over its ramparts.

Exit the fort and make a right onto Barry Road. In a quarter-of-a-mile you'll reach:

18 Tobacco Bay

You've earned some time on the beach after a full day exploring, so rent a chaise lounge on this idyllic slice of sand, grab a cool drink at the beachfront bar and relax in the Bermuda sun.

ICONIC BERMUDA IN 3 DAYS

Spend **Days 1 & 2** as indicated above. Devote **Day 3** to sightseeing and shopping in the City of Hamilton. If you're staying in Paget or Warwick, a ferry from either parish will take you right into the city. Or simply hop on any bus, since all public routes operate between the City of Hamilton and outer destinations. For many visitors, the City of Hamilton's shops are its most compelling attraction. Try to time your visit to avoid the arrival of cruise ships; on those days, the stores and restaurants in the city can get really crowded. You can obtain a schedule of cruise-ship arrivals and departures from the tourist office.

Begin your tour along the harbor front at the:

1 Visitor Services Centre

Start your self-guided city tour at this gleaming, purpose-built structure (it's across the street from D'angelini's, an Italian cafe where you can fuel up with espresso and freshly baked goods). From the VSC, you'll emerge onto Front Street, the City of Hamilton's main thoroughfare and principal shopping area. Before 1946, there were no cars here. This is where you'll eventually return if you're planning on taking a ferry to the outer parishes.

Walk south from the Ferry Terminal toward the water, taking a short side street between the D'angelini's and the six-story HSBC building. You'll come to:

2 Albouy's Point

This is a small, grassy park, which opens onto a panoramic vista of the boat- and ship-filled harbor. Nearby is the Royal Bermuda Yacht Club, which has been an elite rendezvous for the Bermudian and American yachting set since the 1930s. The private club is the official sponsor of the Newport-Bermuda Race—a 635-mile biennial sailing regatta that begins in Rhode Island and ends in Bermuda. Peek inside and you'll see trophies and ship hull models from past winners of this race, affectionately known as the "Thrash to the Onion Patch."

After taking in the view, walk directly north, toward Front Street. Look for a light pink awning across the street that reads:

3 Alexandra Mosher Studio Jewellery

Even if you're not in the market for a bangle, the artistry of the goods at this store make for good browsing. The artist/owner's sterling silver necklaces, rings, bracelets, earrings and cufflinks are made with brilliant grains of Bermuda pink sand.

Exit the store and make a left onto Front Street. You'll pass Coral Coast Clothing, where you can buy locally made men's shirts and Astwood Dickenson, which sells high-end watches and fine jewelry. At the corner of Front and Queen Streets you'll see:

4 The Birdcage

Originally designed to keep Bermuda shorts clad "bobbies" safe while directing traffic in the 1950s, this Hamilton landmark is now a popular spot for photographs; climb inside the white-and-blue metal shelter to snap a memorable moment. Although the birdcage closely resembles a home befitting of a parrot, it was in fact named after its designer, engineer Geoffrey "Dickie" Bird.

Continue north along Queen Street until you reach:

5 The Island Shop

Another fun place to explore this pretty shop sells ceramics, linens and glassware with hand-painted designs of local flora, fauna and architecture from Bermudian artist Barbara Finsness.

Continue north along Queen Street and make a left into:

6 Par-la-Ville Park

Although this green space was officially renamed Queen Elizabeth Park in 2012, following her Diamond Jubilee, this lovely woodland will forever be known to Bermudians as Par-la-Ville. Once the private gardens of Bermuda's first postmaster William B. Perot (for whom the adjacent post office is named), the winding paths, koi ponds, shaded pergolas, flowering plants, and sculpture garden make this a prime selfie spot.

Exit the park at its main entrance, then turn left into the:

7 Perot Post Office

Bermuda's first postmaster, William B. Perot ran this post office from 1818 to 1862. It's said that he'd collect the mail from the clipper ships, then put it under his top hat in order to maintain his dignity. As he proceeded through town, he'd greet his friends and acquaintances by tipping his hat . . . and delivering their mail at the same time. In 1848 he started printing his own stamps and of the thousands that he produced, only 11 are known to exist, making them extremely valuable. Queen Elizabeth II owns several and the last time a Perot stamp came on the market, in 2011, it fetched $205,000.

Adjacent to the Perot Post Office, set back behind a massive Indian Rubber Tree is the:

8 Bermuda Historical Society Museum

This small museum, set in a Georgian home, is filled with curiosities, including 18th-century cedar furniture, collections of antique silver flatware, a model replica of the *Sea Venture,* Boer War artifacts, Hogge money (the original monetary unit minted in Bermuda), and a 1775 letter from George Washington asking Bermuda to steal gunpowder from the British for America's revolutionary forces. Take half an hour here.

Continue to the top of Queen Street, then turn right onto Church Street to reach:

9 City Hall & Arts Centre

Designed in 1960 by Bermudian architect Wilfred Onions, this whitewashed building is home to the Bermuda National Gallery, an eclectic collection of international artwork (p. 100), and the Bermuda Society of Arts, which features revolving exhibits from local students and artists

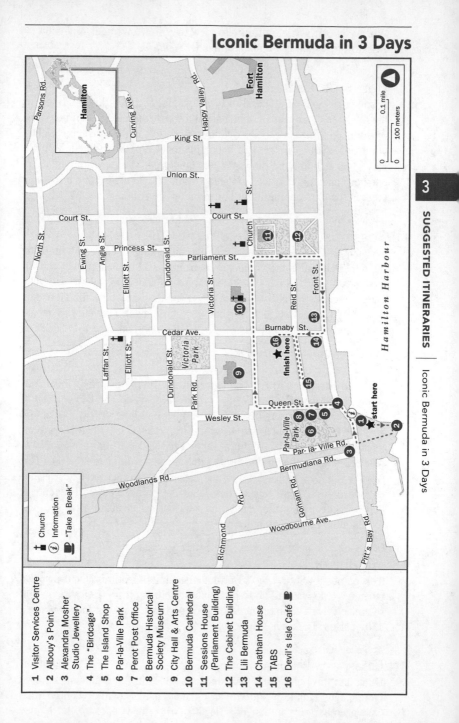

Iconic Bermuda in 3 Days

Hamilton

Parsons Rd.

Curving Ave.

Happy Valley Rd.

Fort Hamilton

King St.

Union St.

Court St.

Court St.

St.

Church St.

North St.

Ewing St.

Angle St.

Princess St.

Dundonald St.

Parliament St.

Reid St.

Front St.

Elliott St.

Victoria St.

Burnaby St.

Laffan St.

Cedar Ave.

Elliott St.

Dundonald St.

Victoria Park

Park Rd.

Wesley St.

Queen St.

Par-la-Ville Park

Par-la-Ville Rd.

Bermudiana Rd.

Woodlands Rd.

Rd.

Gorham Rd.

Woodbourne Ave.

Richmond

Pitt's Bay Rd.

Hamilton Harbour

finish here

start here

0.1 mile
100 meters

Church
Information
"Take a Break"

1 Visitor Services Centre
2 Albouy's Point
3 Alexandra Mosher Studio Jewellery
4 The "Birdcage"
5 The Island Shop
6 Par-la-Ville Park
7 Perot Post Office
8 Bermuda Historical Society Museum
9 City Hall & Arts Centre
10 Bermuda Cathedral
11 Sessions House (Parliament Building)
12 The Cabinet Building
13 Lili Bermuda
14 Chatham House
15 TABS
16 Devil's Isle Café

When you exit, look to the sky to view the bronze weather vane atop its clocktower, which is a replica of the *Sea Venture*.

Exit through its main entrance and make a left onto Church Street. One block east is the:

10 Bermuda Cathedral

Also known as the Cathedral of the Most Holy Trinity, this is the seat of the Anglican Church of Bermuda and it towers over the city skyline. Made of Bermuda limestone, this neo-Gothic beaut features ornate stained-glass windows, soaring arches and a pulpit modeled after architect William Hay's home church in Edinburgh, Scotland. Visit Monday through Friday and you can walk 155 steps to the top of the church tower for a bird's-eye view of the City of Hamilton. For more on the building, see p. 101.

Leave the cathedral and continue east along Church Street to the:

11 Sessions House (Parliament Building)

Located on Parliament Street, this Italian-style terra cotta building was built in 1819 after the capital of Bermuda was moved there from St. George's 4 years earlier (the clocktower was added in 1893 to celebrate Queen Victoria's Golden Jubilee). The building is where the House of Assembly (known as the lower house of parliament) convenes to debate policy and where the Supreme Court hears important cases of the day.

Continue south along Parliament Street to Front Street where you'll see:

12 The Cabinet Building

Originally designed in 1837 and home to the Premier's office, this handsome two-story building is also where the Senate (or Upper House) meets every Wednesday between November and June. In November, the building hosts the much ballyhooed "Throne Speech," when His Excellency the Governor arrives in a plumed hat and full military regalia to deliver a state of the union from a cedar throne dating back to 1642. Out front is the Cenotaph—a limestone monument to memorialize Bermuda's dead from both World Wars—and the bronze statue of legendary heroine Sally Bassett, a slave who was burned to death after she was found guilty of poisoning her master and his wife.

Head west on Front Street to do some shopping. Your first stop should be:

13 Lili Bermuda

This outpost of St. George's Bermuda Perfumery features island-inspired perfume, cologne, and body products (try citrusy Mary Celestia, a scent re-created from an unopened bottle of perfume that was found inside a 150-year-old Bermuda shipwreck).

Across the street on the corner of Front Street and Burnaby Street is:

14 Chatham House

Duck into this hole-in-the-wall smoke shop for its excellent collection of Dominican, Jamaican and Cuban cigars. Thanks to the recently lifted Cuban embargo, you can now legally bring them back to the United States.

Spend **Days 1 through 3** as outlined above. Use **Day 4** to explore the Royal Naval Dockyard, especially fun with little ones in tow. Within the walls of this 16-acre west end hub—one that was once a working shipyard for the British royal navy and is now Bermuda's main cruise port—is a large selection of shops, restaurants and attractions. The latter includes **Bermuda Fun Golf** with 18 miniature-sized replicas of the world's most iconic holes; **Dolphin Quest** (p. 77); the **Bermuda Crafts Market** and the **Bermuda Arts Centre;** and the **National Museum of Bermuda,** with maritime and history exhibits that are housed in one of the island's largest stone fortresses. Looking for an adrenaline fix? Then don't miss **KS Watersports,** where you can rent jet skis for a glimpse of sunken shipwrecks, soar high over the turquoise ocean during a paragliding excursion or join a Wildcat Tour, where you'll zip past Bermuda's coastline aboard a 50-feet-long high-speed catamaran powered by twin 1,000hp turbo-charged engines.

Exit the store, make a left and walk straight up Burnaby Hill. Make your first left onto Reid Street, then walk straight until you reach:

15 TABS

An acronym for The Authentic Bermuda Shorts, this boutique sells knee length shorts for men, women and children in all colors of the rainbow, lovingly designed by Bermudian Rebecca Singleton. The cotton-twill and cotton-linen shorts are all color-blocked to match existing island hues (like oleander pink and sea fan purple) and feature whimsical island-inspired lining.

Retrace your steps on Reid Street, then turn left on Burnaby Street for lunch at:

16 Devil's Isle Café ☕

This sidewalk bistro specializes in wholesome fare made with mostly locally sourced veggies and proteins (like the Nourish Bowl with red cabbage, kale, swiss chard, and coconut oil–roasted beets). Finish with some java: Devil's Isle roasts and brews its own beans.

A WEEKEND FOR ROMANCE

FRIDAY: Happy Hour, a Photo Op & a Soulful Dinner

After touching down at L. F. Wade International Airport, check into your hotel and then get ready to party. Friday is Bermuda's busiest night and that's true especially in the City of Hamilton where bars and restaurants host boisterous happy hours at the stroke of 5pm. The best of the bunch is at the **Hamilton Princess Hotel and Beach Club** (p. 197), which is held dockside at the hotel's luxury marina—you'll sip cocktails overlooking gleaming super yachts. When you've got a "rum swizzle-glow" going, walk towards the hotel's main courtyard to its **illuminated moongate,** said to give eternal love and happiness to those who walk through

Romantic Bermuda & Bermuda for Families

Bermuda for Families

Day 1 **A** Bermuda Underwater Institute
B Bermuda Botanical Gardens
C Homer's Cafe
D Elbow Beach

Day 2 **E** Bermuda Aquarium, Museum and Zoo
F Village Pantry
G Shelley Bay

Day 3 **H** Crystal & Fantasy Caves
I Swizzle Inn
J Bailey's Bay Ice Cream Parlour
K Tobacco Bay

A Weekend for Romance

Friday 1 Hamilton Princess Hotel and Beach Club
2 Marcus'
Saturday 3 Guided Horseback Ride
4 Unfinished Church
5 Bermuda Perfumery
6 Grotto Bay Beach Resort
7 Blackbeard's
Sunday 8 Elbow Beach
9 Mickey's Beach Bistro
10 Lover's Lane
11 Paget Marsh Nature Reserve
12 Barracuda Grill

Saint George's Harbour · St. George's · Bailey's Bay · Castle Harbour · Harrington Sound · Hamilton · Great Sound · Little Sound · ATLANTIC OCEAN

0 — 3 mi
0 — 3 km

it. Steal a kiss, take a photo, and head for dinner at **Marcus'** (p. 131) just across the way. Created by Food Network star Marcus Samuelson, it is the island's best restaurant.

SATURDAY: Horseback Ride, Perfume Shopping, a Couples Massage & a Sunset Dinner

Sleep in and get breakfast in bed. Then head to St. George's for a guided horseback ride on the beach and to historic east end sites like the **Unfinished Church** (p. 110). A picnic and a bottle of Champagne are included. After lunch head back into town for some shopping (perhaps a purchase of his and her scents at the **Bermuda Perfumery** [p. 171]?). Gifts in hand, take a taxi to the **Grotto Bay Beach Resort** (p. 200) for a **couple's massage in its cave spa.** That's right: Treatment tables are set inside a subterranean cave, complete with stalactites and stalagmites. Afterward, catch the **sunset at Blackbeard's** (p. 148), a stunning cliffside restaurant on the east end.

SUNDAY: Hit the Beach, an Alfresco Lunch, a Quiet Walk & a Seafood Dinner

Start off by **renting a Twizy** (see p. 207)—a four-wheeled, electric-powered vehicle where you and your loved one will sit front-to-back in a low-to-the-ground, windowless cockpit—for a drive to **Elbow Beach.** You can relax on its rosy sands for free (if so, just park on the public-access road and walk down to the beach), but if you want the red-carpet treatment, pull in to the Elbow Beach Hotel, where $100 buys non-guests two chaise lounges, towels, an umbrella, and access to its changing rooms and showers. When hunger calls, grab fish sandwiches at **Mickey's Beach Bistro** (p. 126), an oceanfront restaurant with ace views of the turquoise coastline. Hop back in your Twizy and **drive to Lover's Lane,** an aptly named road where you can take a quiet walk through **Paget Marsh Nature Reserve,** a 25-acre woodland that's home to dozens of resident and migratory birds. For a final meal, pick **Barracuda Grill** (p. 128) in the City of Hamilton, the seafood restaurant Catherine Zeta-Jones and Michael Douglas used to canoodle in, when they lived on the island (ask for the "snug corner," which is out of sight of other diners).

BERMUDA FOR FAMILIES

The following itinerary does require travel around Bermuda. Because car rentals are not permitted in Bermuda, getting around the island with a family will likely be expensive. Yes, there are buses, but they don't always stay true to published schedules (if you plan to get around by bus, bring exact change). Taxi fares, the other option, add up quickly, especially if you've got more than four people in your party (one to four passengers pay $7.90 for the first mile and then $2.75 for each additional mile, while five to seven passengers pay $9.95 for the first mile and then $3.50 for each additional mile). So do budget for the cost of transportation when planning your trip. *Tip:* If you've got a smart phone download an app called Hitch, which is similar to Uber, but for licensed taxi drivers.

Day 1: Underwater Without Getting Wet, a Garden & the Beach

Since beach visits get everyone sandy and a bit sun-dazed, we're leaving that to the end of the day. But this *is* Bermuda—you don't want to stray too far from the ocean—so you'll start the day at the **Bermuda Underwater Exploration Institute** (p. 101). It's a whizbang museum with highly interactive exhibits that let the little ones get a taste of what it would be like to scuba dive, while gently teaching them science lessons about the undersea world. Some kids spend hours here, but if yours get antsy, grab a taxi to **Bermuda Botanical Gardens** (p. 96). It has a highly imaginative playground (created for the recent America's Cup) along with gardens for the blind, where the kids can use their non-visual senses to explore; a hedge maze; and a grove of banyan trees with hanging vines, perfect for Tarzan swings. At the main entrance to the Gardens is the Masterworks Museum of Bermuda Art where you'll duck in for lunch at **Homer's Café** (p. 128). After lunch, head to the beach, **Elbow Beach** to be precise, which is 5 minutes away by taxi. Spend the rest of the day in the surf and on the sand.

Day 2: See the Critters, Hit the Beach

Seals, flocks of flamingoes, lemurs from Madagascar, birds, reptiles, fish and more are the potent lures at the **Bermuda Aquarium, Museum & Zoo,** your starting place on day two. Pace yourself! There's a lot to see and do here: Toddlers will love the Discovery Centre—an indoor play-room where little visitors can look at picture books and crawl on a cozy rug—and bigger kids get their wiggles out at the zoo playground. For lunch, you can stay on-site, but if you're ready to move on, just a 5-minute walk away is the fab **Village Pantry** (p. 145), where the kids can play chef and make their own pizzas. After lunch? What could be better than a lazy afternoon on the beach. Shake it up by heading to **Shelly Bay.**

Day 3: An Underground Adventure & the Beach

If you'd like to get your kids jazzed about touring the underground net-work of caves called **Crystal & Fantasy Caves** (p. 105), watch a few episodes of the Jim Henson series *Fraggle Rock* before your trip; these caverns were the real-life inspiration for the whimsical world where Henson's creatures lived. These subterranean lagoons, with their centu-ries-old stalactites and stalagmites (all eerily illuminated by well-placed lights) should capture the imagination of your children. From here it's about a 7-minute walk to the **Swizzle Inn** (p. 147) for lunch (parents might want to indulge in the iconic rum punch). Don't order dessert here! That you're going to get across the street at **Bailey's Bay Ice Cream Parlour** (p. 147), which crafts 30 flavors on-site, some of which you'll only find here. Then, finish up your Bermuda adventure with more beach time, this go-round at **Tobacco Bay** (p. 69).

THE PARISHES OF BERMUDA

Bermuda is divided into nine parishes, all named for shareholders of the Ber-muda Company, which was formed by English investors in the early 1600s to develop the island as a profit-making enterprise. From west to east, the par-ishes are listed below.

Sandys Parish

In the far western part of the archipelago, Sandys (pronounced *Sands*) Parish encompasses the islands of **Ireland, Boaz,** and **Somerset** and is most notably home of **the Royal Naval Dockyard**—a former outpost for the British Navy, which is now a bustling cruise port with shops, restaurants and attractions. Named for Sir Edwin Sandys, this sleepy parish is centered in **Somerset**

Village—a quiet hamlet with a traditional English pub and a handful of small shops—and features a pair of picture-perfect bridges: **Watford Bridge,** where you'll have a sweeping view of Mangrove Bay and **Somerset Bridge,** known as the world's smallest drawbridge since a single, 32-inch plank slides out to allow the passage of a sailboat's mast.

Some visitors to Bermuda head directly for Sandys Parish and spend their entire time here; they feel that the far western tip, with its rolling hills, lush countryside, and tranquil bays, is something special and unique. (This area has always stood apart from the rest of Bermuda: During the U.S. Civil War, when most Bermudians sympathized with the Confederates, Sandys Parish supported the Union.) Sandys Parish has areas of great natural beauty, including **Somerset Long Bay,** the biggest and best public beach in the West End (which the Bermuda Audubon Society has developed into a nature preserve), and **Mangrove Bay,** a protected beach in the heart of Somerset Village that's popular with local boaters on weekends.

The parish boasts some of the most luxurious places to stay in Bermuda but if you want to be near the shops, restaurants and pubs of the City of Hamilton, you may want to stay in a more central location and visit Sandys Parish on a day trip. You can commute to the City of Hamilton by ferry, but it's a bit time-consuming. Those who prefer tranquility and unspoiled nature to shopping or lingering over an extra pint in a pub will be happy here. Another advantage of staying here is that Sandys has several embarkation points for various types of sea excursions, such as jet-skiing and glass bottom boat trips.

Southampton Parish

If dining at waterfront restaurants, staying at big resorts and lazing on endless pink sand beaches is part of your Bermuda dream, then Southampton is your parish. Named for the third earl of Southampton, it's the site of such famed resorts as the **Fairmont Southampton, The Reefs Resort & Club,** and **Pompano Beach Club.** The parish is also the best place to stay if you plan to spend a great deal of time on the island's fabled pink sand beaches. Among Southampton's jewels is **Horseshoe Bay**—consistently rated among the world's finest beaches—and **Church Bay,** a small southwestern cove that's one of the best spots in Bermuda to go snorkeling.

Southampton lacks the intimacy and romance of Sandys, but it has a lot of razzle-dazzle going for it. It's the top choice for a golfing vacation. If you like to sightsee, you can easily occupy 2 days just exploring the parish's many attractions. It also has more nightlife than Sandys—although not as much as the City of Hamilton.

Warwick Parish

Named in honor of the second earl of Warwick (pronounced War-ick), this parish lies in the heart of Great Bermuda Island. Like Southampton, it is known for its long stretches of rosy sand, chiefly **Warwick Long Bay,** a picture-perfect beach that's popular for lengthy walks and **Jobson's Cove,** a well-protected bay that's ideal for families with young children. Warwick also

Bermuda's Parishes

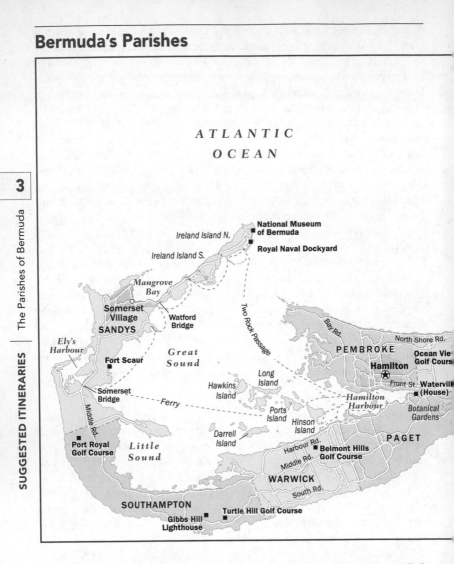

offers sprawling parklands bordering the sea, winding country roads and **Belmont Hills Golf Club,** a public course that features one of the island's top restaurants—**Blû** (p. 125).

Warwick is a great choice for visitors seeking cottage or apartment rentals, where you can do some of your own cooking to cut down on the outrageous expense of food (try **Lindo's** on Middle Road if you'd like to buy your own groceries). It's also where you can find a number of affordable inns and B&B's like **Granaway Guest House & Cottage** (p. 193). This being a mainly residential parish, you won't find much nightlife or even many restaurants, for that matter.

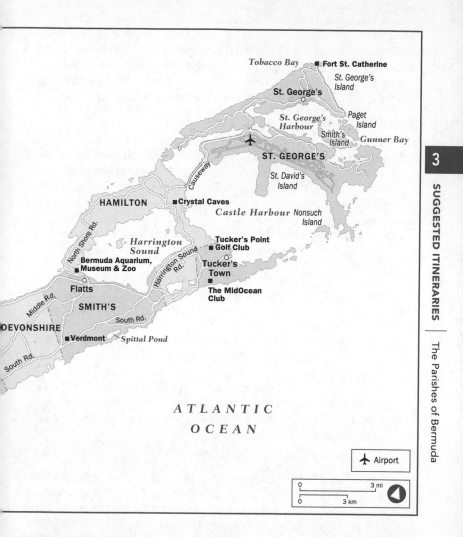

Paget Parish

Paget Parish lies directly south of the capital City of Hamilton, which is separated from it by Hamilton Harbour, itself a bustling body of water with daily ferries and boats bobbing in the breeze. Named after the fourth Lord Paget, it has many residences and historic estates, but is most notably the site of the **Bermuda Botanical Gardens,** a 36-acre park. The Botanical Gardens is also home to the **Masterworks Museum of Bermuda Art** and its collection of island-inspired paintings. But make no mistake: Paget's south shore beaches—namely **Elbow Beach,** a 1-mile-long slice of sand that's perfect for long walks—are what draw visitors here in droves.

Beyond its natural attractions, Paget is also one of the best parishes to stay in given its proximity to the City of Hamilton (depending on where you're staying, it's less than a 10-min. taxi ride to town). You'll also have your choice of many excellent accommodations, including **Elbow Beach Hotel** and **Newstead Belmont Hills Golf Resort & Spa.** Because public transportation is all-important (you can't rent a car in Bermuda), Paget is a good place to situate yourself; it has some of the best and most convenient ferry connections and bus schedules.

Pembroke Parish

This parish (named after the third earl of Pembroke) houses one-quarter of Bermuda's population. It is home to the **City of Hamilton,** Bermuda's capital and its only full-fledged city. The parish opens at its northern rim onto the vast Atlantic Ocean and on its southern side onto Hamilton Harbour; its western border is on Great Sound. The City of Hamilton is the first destination that some cruise-ship passengers will see.

This parish is not ideal for those seeking a tranquil vacation. Pembroke Parish, already packed with the island's greatest population density, also attracts the most visitors. The little city is especially crowded when cruise ships are in the harbor and travelers pour into the stores and restaurants. Yet for those who like to pub-crawl English style, shop until they drop, and have access to the largest concentration of dining choices, Pembroke—the City of Hamilton, in particular—is without equal on Bermuda.

Whether or not you stay in Pembroke, try to fit a shopping (or window-shopping) stroll along Front Street into your itinerary. The area also boasts several sightseeing attractions, most of which are easily accessible on foot (a plus because you don't have to depend on taxis, buses, or scooters—which can get to be a bit of a bore after a while). Nightlife is the finest on the island. Don't expect splashy Las Vegas–type revues, however; instead, think restaurants, pubs, and small clubs.

Devonshire Parish

Lying east of Paget and Pembroke parishes, near the geographic center of the archipelago, Devonshire Parish (named for the first earl of Devonshire and pronounced *Devon-shur*) is green, hilly and primarily residential. It has a handful of privately owned apartments and cottages, many of which are rented on websites like Airbnb, but for the most part, Devonshire is where you'll pass through to get to east or westward parishes. Three of Bermuda's major roads traverse through Devonshire: the aptly named South Road (also unofficially referred to as South Shore Rd.), Middle Road, and North Shore Road. As you wander its narrow lanes, you can, with some imagination, picture yourself in the parish's namesake county of Devon, England—especially while exploring sites like the **Old Devonshire Parish Church,** one of Bermuda's oldest churches, which dates from 1716.

Devonshire is also home to several unspoiled nature areas. The **arboretum** on Montpelier Road is one of the most tranquil oases on Bermuda. This 22-acre open space, created by the Department of Agriculture, Fisheries, and

Parks, is home to a wide range of Bermudian plant and tree life, especially conifers, palms, and other subtropical trees (runners love its shady trails with 20 exercise stations tucked in scenic spots). Another picturesque spot, **Edmund Gibbons Nature Reserve,** is located just off South Road and west of the junction with Collector's Hill. This portion of marshland provides living space for several birds and rare species of Bermuda flora.

While most of Bermuda's finest golf courses are located in the outer parishes, Devonshire also boasts a popular 9-hole course the **Ocean View Golf Course** which has sweeping views of Bermuda's north shore. Nearby is **Devonshire Dock,** long a seafarer's haven on North Shore Road where British soldiers came to be entertained by local women during the War of 1812. Today, its where local fishermen bring in grouper and rockfish, so if you're staying in a cottage that has a kitchen, head there to buy your fresh catch for dinner.

In short, Devonshire is one of Bermuda's quietest parishes, known for its hilly interior, beautiful landscape and fabulous estates bordering the sea. There's little sightseeing here. But the parish is right in Bermuda's geographic center, so it's an ideal place to base yourself.

Smith's Parish

Named for Sir Thomas Smith, this parish faces the open sea to the north and south. To the east is Harrington Sound; to the west, bucolic Devonshire Parish.

The parish encompasses **Flatts Village,** one of the island's most charming parish towns (take bus no. 10 or 11 from the City of Hamilton). It was a smugglers' port for about 200 years and served as the center of power for a coterie of successful politicians and landowners. Flatts Village's government was second in importance to that of St. George's, which was once Bermuda's capital. People gathered at the rickety Flatts Bridge to "enjoy" such public entertainment as hangings; if the offense was serious enough, victims were drawn and quartered here. In a distinct turn of irony, Flatts is now one of the best locations for families, since it's home to the **Bermuda, Aquarium, Museum & Zoo.**

In Smith's Parish, you can expect rolling hills and open green spaces. Most notably, the 64-acre **Spittal Pond Nature Reserve,** the largest reserve in Bermuda, which is home to a wide variety of land critters and waterfowl. Like Devonshire, Smith's is quiet and mostly residential, however it does boast one of the newest, and most exciting resorts in Bermuda: **The Loren at Pink Beach.**

Hamilton Parish

Not to be confused with the City of Hamilton (which is in Pembroke Parish), Hamilton Parish lies directly north of Harrington Sound, opening onto the Atlantic. It's bordered on the east by St. George and on the southwest by Smith's Parish. Named for the second marquis of Hamilton, the parish surrounds Harrington Sound, a saltwater lake stretching some 10km (6¼ miles). On its eastern periphery, the parish opens onto Castle Harbour.

The big attractions here are the **Bermuda Aquarium** and the **Crystal Caves.** Scuba diving and other watersports are also very popular in the area.

ISLAND-HOPPING ON your own

Most first-time visitors think of Bermuda as one island, but in fact it's an archipelago made up of more than 180 islets and cays. If you're a bit of a skipper, you can explore them on your own by renting a self-drive motorboat. With a little guidance and the proper maps, you can discover uninhabited islands, out-of-the-way coral reefs, and hidden coves that seem straight out of the Tom Hanks movie *Castaway.*

For this boating adventure, rent a Boston Whaler with an outboard engine. The name of these small but sturdy boats reveals their origins: New Englanders once used similar boats in their pursuit of whales. It's important to exercise caution, remembering that the English found Bermuda in 1612 only after the *Sea Venture,* en route to the Jamestown Colony, was wrecked off the Bermuda coast.

In the East End, you can explore Castle Harbour, which is almost completely surrounded by islands, forming a protected lake. To avoid the often-powerful swells, drop anchor on the west side of Castle Harbour, near Tucker's Point Golf Club. After a swim head across Tucker's Town Bay to Castle Island and Castle Island Nature Reserve. In 1612, Governor Moore ordered the construction of a fort on Castle Island, the ruins of which you can see today.

In the West End, begin your exploration by going under Watford Bridge into well-protected Mangrove Bay. On weekends, this cove fills with locals who raft up near King's Point to swim in its turquoise waters. When you're done, head around the point and drop anchor in front of Cambridge Beaches Resort & Spa, where you can spot schools of sea turtles swimming below.

And from the City of Hamilton, sail to Paradise Lakes, a large body of water at the mouth of the Great Sound that's home to dozens of inhabited and uninhabited islands (like Long Island, which was once where prisoners of the Boer War in 1901–02 were kept). Spot gorgeous coastal scenery including million-dollar homes, anchored sailboats and low-flying longtails.

You can rent a 13- or 16-foot Boston Whaler—and pick up some local guidance—at **KS Watersports,** with locations in Southampton, St. George's and the City of Hamilton (www.kswatersports.bm; *©* **441/232-4155**). Prices begin at $185 for 4 hours, $350 for 8 hours. Rates include a large cooler with ice, waterproof map and all safety gear, but do not include gas.

The waterfront section of **Railway Trail** in Bailey's Bay, featuring a 740-foot-long footbridge and amazing views of the coast, is also here.

Around **Harrington Sound,** the sights differ greatly from those of nearby St. George (see below). You'll find such activities as fishing, swimming, sunfish sailing, and kayaking at Harrington Sound, but it doesn't offer the historical exploration that St. George does. Some experts believe that Harrington Sound was a prehistoric cave that fell in. Harrington Sound's known gateway to the ocean is an inlet at Flatts Village (see "Smith's Parish," above). However, evidence suggests that there are underwater passages as well—several deep-sea fish have been caught in the sound.

For the best panoramic view of the north shore, head for **Crawl Hill,** the highest place in Hamilton Parish, just before you come to Bailey's Bay. "Crawl" is a corruption of the word *kraal,* which is where turtles were kept before slaughter. **Shelly Bay,** named for one of the passengers of the British ship *Sea Venture* that foundered on Bermuda's reefs in 1609, is the longest beach along the north shore.

Although the parish has some major resorts, such as Grotto Bay Beach Hotel, most visitors come here for sightseeing only. We must agree: Hamilton is a good place to go exploring for a day or half-day, but you're better off staying elsewhere. If you stay here, you'll spend a great deal of your vacation time commuting into the City of Hamilton or St. George. Bus no. 1 or 3 from the City of Hamilton gets you here in about an hour.

St. George's Parish

At Bermuda's extreme eastern end, this historic parish encompasses several islands. The parish borders Castle Harbour on its western and southern edges; St. George's Harbour divides it into two major parts, **St. George's Island** and **St. David's Island.** A causeway links St. David's Island to the rest of Bermuda, and St. George's is also linked by a road. Many parish residents are longtime sailors and fishers. St. George's Parish also includes **Tucker's Town** (founded in 1616 by Gov. Daniel Tucker), on the opposite shore of Castle Harbour.

Settled in 1612, the **Town of St. George's** was once the capital of Bermuda; the City of Hamilton succeeded it in 1815. The town was settled 3 years after Sir George Somers and his shipwrecked party of English sailors came ashore in 1609. (After Admiral Somers died in Bermuda in 1610, his heart was buried in the St. George area, while the rest of his body was taken home to England for burial.) Founded by Richard Moore, of the newly created Bermuda Company, and a band of 60 colonists, St. George was the second English settlement in the New World, after Jamestown, Virginia. Its coat of arms depicts St. George (England's patron saint) and a dragon.

Almost 4 centuries of history come alive here. Generations of sailors have set forth from its sheltered harbor. St. George even played a role in the American Revolution: Bermuda depended on the American colonies for food, and when war came, supplies grew dangerously low. Although Bermuda was a British colony, the loyalties of its people were divided because many Bermudians had relatives living on the American mainland. A delegation headed by Col. Henry Tucker went to Philadelphia to petition the Continental Congress to trade food and supplies for salt. George Washington had a different idea. He needed gunpowder, and several kegs of it were stored at St. George. Without the approval of the British Bermudian governor, the parties struck a deal. The gunpowder was trundled aboard American warships waiting in the harbor of Tobacco Bay under cover of darkness. In return, the grateful colonies supplied Bermuda with food.

Although St. George still evokes a feeling of the past, it's actively inhabited. When cruise ships are in port, it's likely to be overrun with visitors. Many people prefer to visit St. George at night, when they can walk around and enjoy it in relative peace and quiet. After dark, a mood of enchantment settles over the place: It's like a storybook village.

FUN ON & OFF THE BEACH

Although people visit Bermuda mainly to relax on its spectacular pink sand beaches, the island also offers a wealth of activities, both onshore and off. In fact, Bermuda's sports facilities are better than those on most Caribbean and Bahamian islands. The island recently hosted major international sporting events like the PGA Grand Slam of Golf, the ITU World Triathlon, and the 35th America's Cup.

BEACHES

Bermuda is one of the world's leading beach resorts. It boasts miles of pink shoreline, broken only now and then by cliffs that form sheltered coves. As you may have heard, the sand is uncommonly soft and blissfully pink—a rosy hue created by single celled organisms called foraminifera, which shed their red outer shells that in turn get pulverized into grains of sand. And no two beaches are alike. Some stretches have shallow, sandy bottoms perfect for families with young children, while others feature powerful surf and endless coastlines great for long walks. Some beaches (usually the larger ones) have lifeguards; others do not. Hotels and private clubs often have their own beaches and facilities. Even if you're not registered at a hotel or resort, you can often use their beach and facilities if you become a customer by having lunch there (just don't make it obvious that you're not a hotel guest, since this is very much an unwritten rule).

Here's a list of the island's most famous sands, arranged clockwise beginning with the south-shore beaches closest to the City of Hamilton.

Elbow Beach ★★★

One of the most popular beaches in Bermuda, this Paget Parish stretch features nearly 1 mile of pink sand and is flanked by three mid-sized resorts—**Coral Beach Club, Coco Beach Resort** and the **Elbow Beach Hotel.** You don't have to pay a dime to enjoy this spectacular slice of sand. Simply enter through the access lane off South Road and find your own little piece of paradise. Or you can splash out. For $100, you can rent an umbrella and a pair of chaise lounges while being served by a team of waiters who'll bring you food and drinks from nearby Mickey's Beach Bistro. Because protective coral reefs surround it, Elbow Beach is one of the safest on the island, so you'll see families enjoying the calm waves and pedestrians walking its long coastline.

Astwood Cove ★

This Warwick Parish public beach has no problem with overcrowding during most of the year; it's in a remote location, at the bottom of a steep, winding road that intersects with South Road. Many single travelers and couples head here to escape the families that tend to overrun beaches, such as Elbow Beach, in the high season. We prefer this beach for many reasons, one of them being that its cliffs are home to nesting Bermuda longtails, also known as white-tailed tropic birds. Astwood Beach has public restrooms but not many other facilities. Astwood Park, a favorite picnic and hiking area, is nearby. If you prefer your beaches small and secluded, head here.

Warwick Long Bay ★★★

Like Astwood Cove, this is one of the best places for people who want to find solitude. True to its name, it features the longest uninterrupted stretch of pink sand on the island. This expanse offers plenty of space to escape the crowds. Against a backdrop of scrubland and low grasses, the beach lies on the southern side of South Shore Park, in Warwick Parish. Despite the frequent winds, the waves are surprisingly small thanks to an offshore reef. Have your camera ready: Jutting above the water less than 60m (200 ft.) from the shore is a jagged coral island that, because of its contoured shape, appears to be floating above the water's foam. You'll find restrooms near the parking area but little else, so make sure you bring everything you need to enjoy the day. *Important:* There are no lifeguards on duty so be sure that your swimming skills are up to par—riptides are common in summer.

Jobson's Cove ★★★

Directly adjacent to Warwick Long Bay is this calm, secluded cove, perfect for families with young children. Thanks to a protective horseshoe of volcanic rock, this quiet bay features serene, standing water—akin to a natural, saltwater pool. In fact, it isn't much more than 6-feet-deep, making it ideal for little swimmers. Fish like it, too, and snorkelers will encounter schools of colorful parrotfish at the back of the bay. To get here, enter the beach at Warwick Long Bay and head west over the sand dunes; it's no more than a 5-minute walk. For one of the very best views, swim to the back of the cove and climb the natural rock stairs carved out of the cliff. Once at the top you'll be treated to a sweeping panorama of Bermuda's stunning south shore. There are no facilities here, but it's close enough to Warwick Long Bay to walk over and use its restrooms.

Stonehole Bay ★

Near Jobson's Cove in Warwick Parish, Stonehole Bay is more open and less sheltered than Jobson's, with a sandy shoreline that's studded with big rocks.

Bermuda Beaches

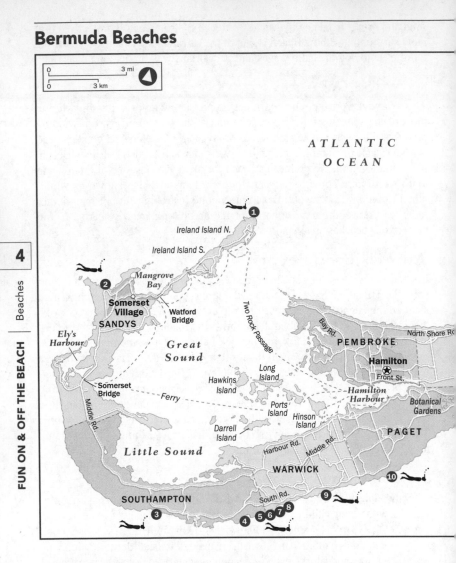

It's almost never crowded, and wading is safe even though strong waves sometimes make the waters cloudy—so they're less than ideal for snorkeling. There are no facilities at Stonehole Bay.

Chaplin Bay ★

Straddling the boundary between Warwick and Southampton parishes, this small but secluded beach disappears almost completely during storms and exceptionally high tides. Geologists come here to admire the open-air coral barrier that partially separates one half of the beach from the other. Chaplin Bay, like its more famous neighbor, Horseshoe Bay (see below), lies at the

Achilles Bay **14**	Long Bay **18**
Astwood Cove **9**	Shelly Bay **11**
Chaplin Bay **5**	Snorkel Park **1**
Church Bay **3**	Somerset Long Bay **2**
Clearwater Beach **16**	St. Catherine's Beach **15**
Elbow Beach **10**	Stonehole Bay **6**
Horseshoe Bay **4**	Tobacco Bay Beach **13**
Jobson's Cove **7**	Turtle Bay **17**
John Smith's Bay **12**	Warwick Long Bay **8**

southern extremity of South Shore Park. From Chaplin, you can walk over to use the facilities and equipment at Horseshoe, but you'll enjoy more solitude here than at the more active Horseshoe Bay.

Horseshoe Bay Beach ★★★

With its quarter-mile-long curved strip of pink sand, Horseshoe Bay, on South Road in Southampton Parish, is Bermuda's most famous beach. That means it's likely to be crowded, especially if cruise ships are in port. Most tourists congregate near its main entrance, so our advice is to walk to the eastern edge of the beach to avoid the cruise ship crowds. On the plus side, the beach has

If you're headed to popular west end beaches including Elbow Beach, Astwood Cove, Warwick Long Bay, Jobson's Cove, Stonehole Bay, Chaplin Bay, Horseshoe Bay and Church Bay take bus number 7, which runs along South Road. Beaches west of those, including Somerset Long Bay and Snorkel Park Beach are served by buses 7 and 8, which make their final stops at the Royal Naval Dockyard. Unsure where to get off? Simply tell your driver where you're headed when you step onboard—just make sure that you've got pre-purchased tickets or exact change in coins, since drivers cannot make change and do not accept bills.

a lot of useful facilities like bathrooms, showers and changing facilities (at the main entrance); a lunch counter and concession area for souvenirs and sundry items; a full-service restaurant with a full bar; and a beach stand where you can rent chaise lounges and umbrellas. Unlike most beaches in Bermuda, Horseshoe also boasts a team of lifeguards who keep a watchful eye on its waters from May through September, an important service: The bay is known for powerful riptides and Portuguese man-of-war, venomous jellyfish that sting and occasionally wash up on the beach. Families head to Baby Beach, a calm lagoon of still saltwater on Horseshoe's far west end.

Church Bay ★★★

Located in Southampton Parish at the west end of South Road, this picturesque cove has Bermuda's very best snorkeling. Simply enter the beach via the wooden stairway, then walk to the west end of the bay. There you'll find the beginnings of a natural coral trail that leads to two massive coral boilers, about 100 yards offshore teeming with parrotfish, angelfish, sergeant majors and more. Swim around the rocks and hug the eastern edge of the bay upon your return to shore to spot healthy elk horn and brain coral, plus large schools of colorful reef fish in this aquarium-like cove. You'll need to bring your own gear since there's nothing more than public bathrooms at this national park.

Somerset Long Bay ★

Thanks to offshore storms, which stir up the waters northwest of Bermuda, the bottom of this beach isn't always sandy or of a consistent depth. For that reason, many people find Somerset Long Bay better suited to beachcombing or long walks than to swimming. Nevertheless, many favor this beach when they're looking for seclusion since it's tucked away in sleepy Sandys Parish. The undeveloped neighboring parkland shelters it from the rest of the island, and the beach's crescent shape and length—about one-third of a mile—make it unusual by Bermudian standards. Bird-watchers will love its proximity to the **Bermuda Audubon Society Nature Reserve** (www.audubon.bm), where you can go for long walks and enjoy moments of solitude—except on weekends, when family picnics abound.

Snorkel Park Beach

You won't find many locals at this bustling white sand beach located within the Royal Naval Dockyard on Bermuda's west end; this is where the bulk of cruise ship passengers descend after exiting their mega ship at King's Wharf, a short walk away. With loud reggae music, water sports rentals and a full-service restaurant serving lunch and stiff drinks, Snorkel Park has a cheesy vibe. That being said, the snorkeling here is pretty good (www.snorkelpark beach.com; ℂ **441/234-6989;** $5 for adults, free for kids 12 and under).

Shelly Bay ★★

Because it's located on the calm north shore in Hamilton Parish, this shady beach is best for families with small children—waves are virtually nonexistent and the shoreline remains shallow for several yards out to sea. There's also a playground directly adjacent to it, so when your little one's tire of building sand castles, they can swing, climb and run alongside local kids. Buses from the City of Hamilton heading east along the north shore, primarily no. 11, stop here.

Tobacco Bay ★★

Less than a ten-minute taxi ride from the Town of St. George's, this tiny cove is popular with cruise shippers since it's the only east end beach that has a full-service restaurant, free Wi-Fi and a hut that rents chairs, umbrellas and water-sports equipment (kayaks, hydro-bikes, and snorkel gear). For that reason, in addition to its small size, Tobacco Bay can get crowded quickly. But on days when there are no big ships in town its calm, crystal clear waters are one of Bermuda's best snorkeling spots (www.tobaccobay.bm; ℂ **441/705-2582**).

St. Catherine's Beach & Achilles Bay

Directly adjacent to the massive stone fortress for which it is named, this large north shore beach on the outskirts of the Town of St. George's is popular with locals who comb it for beach glass and swim in its deep, calm waters. In 2020 a massive hotel called the The Residences at St. Regis Bermuda is set to open along its shoreline in the second quarter of that year—an event that will definitely affect the beach's ambiance. About a 5-minute walk east, on the opposite side of Fort St. Catherine is Achilles Bay, a tiny beach not far from where the *Sea Venture* originally wrecked on a reef just offshore in 1609.

John Smith's Bay ★★

This is the only public beach in Smith's Parish and one of the few in Bermuda with lifeguards from May to September. It's more popular with residents of Bermuda's eastern end than with visitors, but if you've rented a private home on that side of the island, this long stretch of pale pink sand couldn't be more ideal.

Clearwater Beach, Turtle Bay & Long Bay ★★

This trio of family-friendly pink sank beaches is located on St. David's Island, one of the two main islands that make up the Parish of St. George's on

Bermuda's far east end. Of the three, Clearwater is the most popular since its waters are shallow and still—all the better to spot sea turtles, which are often seen popping their heads up and swimming down below.

SNORKELING

Bermuda is well known for the crystal-clear purity of its waters and for its vast array of coral reefs, many of which are home to shallow shipwrecks waiting to be explored. If you're ready to dive in, all you need are a snorkel, mask, and fins—and if you've forgotten yours at home, many resorts rent them by the day. For offshore sites, a handful of companies can take you on half- or full-day excursions to popular locations (see below); otherwise, the best places to go snorkeling are public beaches.

Die-hard snorkelers prefer **Church Bay ★★★** above all other snorkeling spots on Bermuda. It lies on the south shore, just west of the Fairmont Southampton and Gibbs Hill Lighthouse. The little cove, which seems to be waiting for a movie camera, features a natural coral trail leading to two semi-submerged boiler reefs about 100 yards offshore (so named because the waves that continuously break on the surface of the reef make the water appear as if its boiling). Except on the roughest of days (that is, when storms churn up the south Atlantic), this bay is fairly calm, well protected, and filled with snug little nooks, all worth exploring.

At the eastern end of the south shore is **John Smith's Bay,** which is just east of Spittal Pond Nature Reserve. Like Church Bay, this beach has several coral reefs close to shore. Also on the east end is **Tobacco Bay ★★**, a small, protected cove about a ten-minute taxi ride from the Town of St. George's where you can rent snorkel gear, among other water sports equipment (like kayaks and hydro bikes). Due to its small size, this beach gets crowded quickly—especially if there's a cruise ship in town—but if you hop in the water, you'll likely see nothing more than the schools of reef fish.

Although snorkeling is a year-round pursuit, it's best from May to October. Snorkelers usually wear wet suits in winter, when the water temperature dips into the 60s Fahrenheit (15–20°C). The waters of the Atlantic, which can be tempestuous at any time of the year, can be especially rough in winter.

Some of Bermuda's best snorkeling locations are accessible only by boat. If you want to head out on your own and you have some knowledge of Bermuda's waters, rent a self-drive motor boat from **KS Watersports** with locations in the City of Hamilton, Southampton, St. George's, and the Royal Naval Dockyard (www.kswatersports.com; ✆ 441/232-4155). The rental company will provide a map of popular shallow water shipwrecks and advise on where to go and more importantly, where not to go. If you're not familiar with Bermuda's waters and you'd like to explore its outer reefs and wrecks, then it's best to let the professionals do the work. For a list of outfitters than run snorkeling excursions aboard motor boats, see our list below (the use of snorkeling equipment is included in the prices listed). And for snorkeling excursions aboard sailing vessels including catamarans and monohulls, see "Boating & Sailing" (p. 76).

A LOOK UNDER BERMUDA'S waters

For a glimpse of Bermuda's dynamic marine environment that doesn't involve bathing suits, head to **Bermuda Underwater Exploration Institute** (www.buei. org; ✆ **441/292-7219**). The highlight of a visit is a simulated dive 3,600m (12,000 ft.) to the bottom of the Atlantic. You'll learn about newly discovered ocean animals that live in the murky depths. Displays include artifacts rescued from long-sunken vessels off the coast, and even a scale model of a ship that wrecked centuries ago. Admission is $15 for adults; $8 for children 6 to 17, free for children 5 and under; open from 10am to 5pm, 7 days a week (last admission is at 4pm).

Bermuda Reef Explorer ★★   This double-decker, glass-bottomed boat provides a window on the island's reefs, sea turtles and even an 18th-century wreck. Captain Mike Gladwin often anchors his 75-foot boat in hard-to-reach coves (like King's Point in Mangrove Bay); patrons then snorkel from the boat in waist-deep waters or explore uninhabited islets. This is a good tour for guests who'd rather depart from Hamilton, since most others leave from the Royal Naval Dockyard.

Ste. 251, 48 Par-la-Ville Rd. www.bermudareefexplorer.com. ✆ **441/535-7333.**

Captain Kirk's Coral Reef Adventures ★   This outfitter operates three motorboats of varying sizes, in addition to a catamaran. All take snorkelers to shipwrecks and coral beds both inside and outside of Bermuda's barrier reef. Of the trio, its 31-foot, glass-bottom RIB *Jesse James* is the fastest, offering a two-stop reef and wreck tour in a mere 2½ hours.

17B West Side Rd., Sandys. www.kirksadventures.com. ✆ **441/747-2204.**

Fantasea Bermuda ★★   In addition to seasonal whale watching tours, kayaking excursions and pontoon boat rentals, this one-stop-shop in the Royal Naval Dockyard operates snorkeling excursions on its fleet of glass-bottomed and double decker motor boats, all of which depart from the west end. Where you'll go is completely weather dependent, but you're guaranteed to spot healthy coral and marine life of all kinds on its 3½-hour tour. In addition to all gear, a complimentary rum swizzle is included (there's a cash bar aboard).

Royal Naval Dockyard. www.fantasea.bm. ✆ **441/236-3483.**

SCUBA DIVING

Bermuda is a world-class dive site, known for its evocative and often eerie shipwrecks, teeming with marine life. Most scuba diving outfitters go to all sites. If you're diving, talk to the dive master about what you'd like to see, including any or all the various wrecks that are accessible off the coast and not viewed as dangerous. For the locations of many of these sites, see the map on p. 66.

The Diving Sites

CONSTELLATION When Peter Benchley was writing *The Deep* (later made into a film), he came here to study the wreck of the *Constellation* for inspiration. Lying in 9m (30 ft.) of water, this wreck is 13km (8 miles) northwest of the Royal Naval Dockyard. Built in 1918, the *Constellation* was a four-masted, wooden-hulled schooner. During World War II, it was the last wooden cargo vessel to leave New York harbor. It wrecked off the coast of Bermuda on July 31, 1943, and all the crew survived. Today, the hull, broken apart, can be seen on a coral and sand bottom. You can see the 36,300kg (80,000 lb.) of cement it was carrying, and morphine ampoules are still found at this site. Large populations of parrotfish, trumpet fish, barracuda, grouper, speckled eels, and octopus inhabit the wreck today.

CRISTÓBAL COLÓN Bermuda's largest shipwreck, the *Cristóbal Colón* was a Spanish luxury liner that went down on October 25, 1936, between North Rock and North Breaker. A transatlantic liner, it weighed in excess of 10,000 tons. The ship was traveling to Mexico to load arms for the Spanish Civil War when it crashed into a coral reef at a speed of 15 knots. During World War II, the U.S. Air Force used the ship as target practice before it eventually settled beneath the waves. Its wreckage is scattered over a wide area on both sides of the reef. It is recommended that you take two dives to see this wreck. Most of the wreck is in 9 to 17m (30–56 ft.) of water, but the depth range actually varies from 4.5m (15 ft.) at the ship's bow to 24m (79 ft.) at its stern.

HERMES This 1984 American freighter rests in some 24m (79 ft.) of water about 1.5km (1 mile) off Warwick Long Bay on the south shore. The 825-ton, 50m (164-ft.) freighter is popular with divers because its U.S. Coast Guard buoy tender is almost intact. The crew abandoned this vessel (they hadn't been paid in 6 months), and the Bermuda government claimed it for $1, letting the dive association deliberately sink it to make a colorful wreck. The visibility at the wreck is generally the finest in Bermuda, and you can see its galley, cargo hold, propeller, and engines.

L'HERMINIE This 1838 French frigate lies in 6 to 9m (20–30 ft.) of water off the west side of Bermuda, with 25 of its cannons still visible. A large wooden keel remains, but the wreck has rotted badly. However, the marine life here is among the most spectacular of any shipwreck off Bermuda's coast: brittle starfish, spiny lobster, crabs, grouper, banded coral shrimp, queen angels, and tons of sponges.

MARY CELESTE This is one of the most historic wrecks in the Atlantic, a 207-ton paddle-wheel steamer from the Confederacy. The steamer was a blockade runner during the Civil War. In exchange for guns, this vessel would return to Bermuda with cotton and cash. Evading capture throughout most of the war, it was wrecked off the coast of Bermuda on September 25, 1864. The ship sank in 17m (56 ft.) of water, where its ruins lie like a skeleton today. This is not a great dive site for observing marine life, but the wreck is evocative and offers many caves and tunnels to explore.

NORTH CAROLINA This iron-hulled English bark lies in 7.5 to 12m (25–39 ft.) of water off Bermuda's western coast. While en route to England, it went down on New Year's Day in 1879 when it struck the reefs. The bow and stern remain fairly intact. There is often poor visibility here, making the wreck appear almost like a ghost ship. Hogfish, often reaching huge sizes, inhabit the site, along with schools of porgies and snapper.

RITA ZOVETTA This Italian cargo steamer was built in 1919 in Glasgow and went aground off St. David's Island in 1924. The ship lies in 6 to 21m (21–69 ft.) of water just off St. David's Head. The wreck measures 120m long (395 ft.), and its stern is relatively intact. Divers go through the shaft housings to see the large boilers. Stunning schools of rainbow-hued fish inhabit the site.

SOUTH WEST BREAKER Some 2.5km (1½ miles) off Church Bay, this was the location chosen for the famous Jacqueline Bisset scene in Peter Benchley's movie *The Deep*. The breaker was supposed to be a hideout for a man-eating squid. In reality, the breaker was created from fossilized prehistoric worms. It has an average depth of 8.5m (28 ft.) and on most days a visibility of 30m (98 ft.). New divers prefer this site because it's not considered dangerous and it has a large variety of hard and soft coral. It's also a good place for snorkelers. A large tunnel split through the center of the breaker provides a protective cover for green moray eels, spiny lobsters and schools of barracuda.

TARPON HOLE This series of large breakers lies directly off the western extremity of Elbow Beach. The site is named Tarpon Hole because of the large schools of tarpon that often cluster here, some in excess of 2m (6½ ft.) long. It is a sea world of lush fans and soft corals, made all the more intriguing with its tunnels, caves, and overhangs.

TAUTON This Norwegian coastal steamer ran afoul on Bermuda's treacherous reefs on November 24, 1920. The 68m (228-ft.) steel-hulled vessel sank in 3 to 12m (10–39 ft.) of water off the northern end of Bermuda. Its boilers and steam engines are still visible. This is a favorite dive for beginners, as the wreck lies in shallow water. Because of its breathtaking varieties of fish, it's a favorite site for photographers.

Diving Schools & Outfitters

Diving in Bermuda is great for novices, who can learn the fundamentals and go diving in 6 to 7.5m (20–25 ft.) of water on the same day as their first lesson. Thanks to strict protective laws, Bermuda's reefs are among the world's healthiest, so expect to find thriving elk horn, brain and fan coral among thick schools of rainbow-hued fish. Although scuba fanatics dive year-round, the best diving months are May through October when the sea is the most tranquil and the water temperature is moderate (it averages 62°F [17°C] in the spring and fall, 83°F [28°C] in the summer).

Weather permitting, scuba schools function daily, but many are closed in winter—so be sure to bring your own gear from November through April. Fully licensed scuba instructors oversee all dives, and most are conducted from large boats that visit a pair of sites in one trip (typically called a two-tank

THAR SHE blows!

If you're visiting Bermuda in March or April treat yourself to an experience of a lifetime by joining a **whale-watching excursion** off the South Shore. During those months, pods of majestic humpback whales pass Bermuda as they migrate to North Atlantic feeding grounds. And while these giant mammals can occasionally be spotted coming up for air from land, they're best viewed from a boat at sea, where you can get a better view of them breaching and slapping their huge tail fins on the ocean. The Royal Naval Dockyard-based **Island** **Tour Centre** (www.islandtourcentre.com; ℂ **441/236-1300**) represents several charter operations that organize 5- to 6-hour whale-watching tours. The most exciting tours are those aboard local research vessels. Run by the **Bermuda Zoological Society** (www.bamz.org; ℂ **441/293-4014**) and the **Bermuda Underwater Exploration Institute** (www.buei.bm; ℂ **441/292-7219**), these cruises feature local scientists who answer questions and narrate what you're seeing. Most tours costs around $100 for a full-day outing.

dive). Although Bermuda boasts hundreds of known shipwrecks, about 40 of them function as regular dive sites (the oldest of which dates from the 17th c.). Dive depths at these sites run 7.5 to 26m (25–85 ft.) however inexperienced divers may want to stick to the wrecks just off the western coast, which tend to be in shallower waters—about 9.5m (31 ft.) or less.

Note: Spearfishing is not allowed within 1.5km (1 mile) of any shore, and spear guns are not permitted in Bermuda.

While one can easily find small dive outfits and private charter boats that organize scuba excursions, the three most reputable dive operations are **Dive Bermuda** (at Fairmont Southampton; 101 South Rd., Southampton Parish; www.bermudascuba.com; ℂ 441/238-2332), **Blue Water Divers & Watersports Ltd.** (Robinson's Marina, Sandys Parish; www.divebermuda.com; ℂ **441/234-1034**), and **Dive Bermuda** (at Grotto Bay Beach Resort, 11 Blue Hill, Bailey's Bay, Hamilton Parish; www.bermudascubagrottobay.com; ℂ **441/293-7319**). All three offer introductory dives for non-certified divers, specialty dives for PADI-certified participants, and feature well-trained staffs with hundreds of combined underwater hours. The major difference among this trio are the reef and wreck sites they visit most, since one is based on the west end of the island (Blue Water Divers), the central south shore (Dive Bermuda at Fairmont Southampton), and Bermuda's east end (Dive Bermuda at Grotto Bay). Determine which one is right for you by targeting what wreck or reef you'd like to explore or simply choose the operation that's nearest to your hotel.

MORE FUN IN THE WATER
Fishing

Bermuda is one of the world's finest destinations for anglers, especially in light-tackle fishing. In fact, anglers from around the world descend upon the island every July for the Bermuda Triple Crown Billfish Championships, a trio of deep-sea fishing tournaments featuring hefty cash purses. But you don't have to be a professional to catch the big one. Blue marlin catches have increased dramatically in recent years, and Bermuda can add billfishing (for marlin, swordfish, and sailfish) to its already enviable reputation. Although fishing is a year-round sport, its best between May and November, when the seas are calmest and big fish like wahoo, tuna and mahi-mahi run in large schools just off Bermuda's shores. Even novice anglers can spend a day at sea, just don't expect to bring home all of your catch, since many charter captains supplement their income by selling the day's bounty to local restaurants and markets.

REEF & DEEP-SEA FISHING

Three major reef banks lie off Bermuda: the Inner System, which begins about 1km (⅔ mile) offshore and stretches for nearly 8km (5 miles); the Challenger Bank, about 23km (14 miles) offshore; and the Argus Bank, which is about 50km (31 miles) from the shoreline. As a rule of thumb, the farther out you go, the more likely you are to turn up larger fish. In the Inner System you'll find amberjack, chub and snapper; at Challenger you'll see wahoo, tuna, mahi-mahi and barracuda; and at the Argus Bank is where you'll find the biggest of boats searching for the biggest of fish including marlin, swordfish and sailfish. There are dozens of qualified operators to choose from, but below is a list of our favorites, most of which offer half- or full-day charters.

Paradise One **Sports Fishing Charters** ★★★ *Paradise One* is a 54-foot sport fishing catamaran owned and operated by brothers Allan and Delvin Bean, who have over 35 years of combined experience fishing in Bermuda's waters. With space for up to 25 passengers, this luxurious boat features a large, air-conditioned cabin and can be chartered for half-, three-quarters-, and full-day excursions, with half-day rates starting at $1,150.

7 Colony Valley, Southampton. www.paradiseone-fishingcharters.com. ✆ **441/734-9409.**

Wound Up ★★ You'll be fishing with winners on this 37-foot custom Duffy sportfish, captained by James Robinson. *Wound Up* has the all-time Bermuda record for catching the most wahoo in 1 day (51), the all-time Bermuda record for catching marlin in one season (57) and has reeled in two Blue Marlins over 1,000 pounds. Half-day (4-hr.) charters are $1,000 and can include up to 6 anglers.

Albuoys Point, City of Hamilton, Pembroke. www.woundupbermuda.com. ✆ **441/737-9985.**

Mako Charters ★★ Captained by Allen DeSilva since 1976, this charter business is one of the most reputable in Bermuda. Its boat—a 65-foot, 2004 Hatteras called *El Mucho!*—is also one of the most luxurious, since the vessel boasts a spacious air-conditioned cabin, a large eat-in galley and four en suite staterooms. Half-day excursions are not an option on this boat, the starter is a full-day, 9-hour trip, which costs $3,000 for up to six people. "Live aboard" rates are also available.

11 Abri Lane, Spanish Point, Pembroke. http://fishbermuda.com. ✆ **441/295-0835.**

FUN ON & OFF THE BEACH

More Fun in the Water

Reel Addiction ★★   Winner of the 2016 Bermuda Triple Crown Billfish Championship, this 48-foot, custom Carolina is outfitted with a full complement of Shimano and Penn reels and features a tall bridge for picture-perfect views of the fighting chair and beyond. Captain by Cragin "Curly" Curtis, this boat can be chartered for half-, three-quarters-, and full-day excursions for up to six people, and all prices include beer, soda and water (half-day trips cost $1,150).

1 Cavello Lane, Sandys. www.reeladdictionbermuda.com. © **441/799-9927.**

SHORE FISHING

Shore fishing turns up such catches as bonefish, pompano, snapper and barracuda, most of which can be found in Bermuda's shallow bays and coves. Locals prefer shore fishing at Spring Benny's Bay in Sandys Parish or West Whale Bay in Southampton; and on the east end, St. George's Harbour. Another popular spot is Daniel's Head Beach Park near Somerset Village. Many of the island's tackle shops have closed so it's best to bring your own gear if you're planning to fish along Bermuda's shoreline (for bait, try any gas station or grocery store).

Boating & Sailing

Bermuda is one of the world's sailing capitals. Sail-yourself boats are available to rent for 2, 4 (half-day), and 8 (full-day) hours. Several places charter yachts with licensed skippers. *Tip:* Beyond the outfits recommended below, www.getmyboat.com is worth visiting. This popular marketplace site lists over 60 private charters in Bermuda, and rates are competitively priced (in fact, we'd say the fact that there *is* now an online boat marketplace is helping to drive down daily rates).

Sail Bermuda ★★★   Captain Caleb Zuill operates two sailing yachts, both of which are available for private, 3- to 6-hour cruises: *Shekynah*, a 51-foot catamaran; and *Wyuna*, a 47-foot monohull. Unlike most private charter operations, which depart from the east or west ends of the island, Sail Bermuda typically shoves off from the City of Hamilton (however, passengers can also be picked up from points west like Belmont Dock, Jew's Bay, and the Royal Naval Dockyard). Complimentary snacks are served aboard *Wyuna* and alcohol can be purchased at the cash bar aboard both vessels (you can BYOB, but a corkage fee will be charged). Charters aboard *Wyuna* for up to 12 people range from $1,300 for a 3-hour jaunt to $2,500 for a 6-hour trip; and excursions on *Sheyknah* for up to 25 people range from $800 for 3 hours to $1,400 for 6 hours.

71 Harbour Rd., Paget Parish. www.sailbermuda.com. © **441/737-2993.**

***Ana Luna* Adventures** ★★   Based at the Grotto Bay Beach Resort on the island's east end, *Ana Luna* is a 45-foot catamaran owned and operated by Captain Nathan Worswick—a seasoned sailor who'll regale you in stories of his world travels. Excursions include a half-day swim and snorkel ($79), champagne sunset cruises ($79), boutique scuba diving trips, private "live aboard" experiences and glow worm cruises—seasonal nighttime sails when you can view bioluminescent organisms swimming down below.

Grotto Bay Beach Resort, 11 Blue Hole Hill, Hamilton Parish. www.analunaadventures. bm. ℂ **441/504-23780.**

Restless Native ★★   If you sail aboard this bright pink, 48-foot Bermudian built catamaran, you'll sail with purpose: Portions of the proceeds are donated to the Bermuda Cancer & Health Centre. Group excursions consist of a 3½-hour sail and snorkel, which includes unlimited rum swizzle, chocolate chip cookies and use of their standup paddleboards and kayaks (adults $70, kids $60). Its 90-minute sunset cruise also includes unlimited rum swizzle and gorgeous sunset views (adults $50, kids $40). All trips depart from the Royal Naval Dockyard and private charters are available.

Royal Naval Dockyard. www.restlessnative.bm. ℂ **441/531-8149.**

Rising Son Cruises ★★   One of Bermuda's most reputable charter operations, featuring a boisterous crew that keeps the party going, Rising Son Cruises operates two catamarans for public group trips and private excursions. Its flagship vessel is the 60-foot *Rising Son* (with free Wi-Fi aboard); and the newest member of the fleet is *Filante*, a 62-foot, open-style converted racing catamaran that was brought to the island in 2017. Choices include a 3-hour snorkel trip, which includes a complimentary rum swizzle and use of its standup paddleboards and kayaks (adults $75, kids $55); and a 2-hour sunset cruise in the Great Sound, where guests are treated to a complimentary glass of champagne or rum swizzle (a cash bar is available on all cruises). Trips depart from the Royal Naval Dockyard and the City of Hamilton.

Island Tour Centre, Royal Naval Dockyard. www.risingsoncruises.bm. ℂ **441/236-1300.**

KS Watersports ★★★   With locations in the City of Hamilton, Dockyard, Southampton and St. George's, this one-stop-shop for everything on the water is the biggest rental agency on the island. Kayaks, standup paddleboards and snorkel equipment are all available as are jet ski safaris, parasailing excursions and Wild Cat adventure cruises on its 50-passenger speed boat. Or rent a boat: Options include a 55-foot luxury Viking yacht for up to 15 passengers; 23-foot pontoon boats for up to 10 passengers; and 13- and 16-foot Boston

---

Dolphin Encounters

As people learn more about the habits of dolphins, and their need for vast terrains in which to swim, swimming with dolphins attractions are increasingly controversial. Those who support them point out that many of the organizations that do them are active in protecting the ecology of the ocean. You'll have to make your own call. But if you'd like to learn more about opportunities on Bermuda, look at the programs of **Dolphin Quest** (www. dolphinquest.org; ℂ **441/234-4464**).

Whalers, self-drive motor boats with 30hp and 40hp engines, which include large shaded canopies (4-hr. rentals from $185).

76 Pitts Bay Rd., Pembroke. www.kswatersports.com. ℂ **441/232-4155.**

Somerset Bridge Watersports ★★   In addition to kayak rentals and jet ski tours, this west end watersports facility also rents self-drive, 13- and 15-foot Boston Whalers for island-hopping. Boats include retractable canopies, floatation noodles and a bag of bread, which you can use to feed the Bermuda chub that congregate around the wreck of the Vixen (a nearby shipwreck). You can rent a snorkel and fins ($8) or even fishing gear, which includes a rod and reel, tackle box and bait for $18. Boat rentals range from $95 for 2 hours to $280 for 8 hours, and licenses are not required.

Robinson's Marina, Somerset Bridge, Ely's Harbour, Sandys Parish. www.bdawater sports.com. ℂ **441/234-3145.**

H2O Sports ★   If you're staying on the west end of the island, this watersports facility will be the most convenient. In addition to jet skis and kayaks, this is the only outfitter in Bermuda that rents Hobie Cats. These two-person boats are best for experienced sailors—knowledge of waves, water and wind are a necessity for these high-performance catamarans (prices range from $60 for 1 hr. to $130 for 8 hr.). If you'd prefer an engine, then rent one of its Twin V, 17-foot, self-drive motor boats, which come with 40hp engines (rentals range from $100 for 1 hr. to $310 for 9 hr.).

2 Cambridge Rd., Sandys Parish. www.h2osportsbermuda.com. ℂ **441/234-3082.**

Wakeboarding

Like most watersports in Bermuda, the best time of year to go is May through September when the ocean is warm and calm, but weather pending, guides can organize excursions year-round. **Axis Adrenaline Projects** (Flatt's Village, Hamilton Parish; www.axisbermuda.com; ℂ **441/537-1114**) offers daily excursions, in season, on Harrington Sound, a calm, protected body of water that's completely encircled by land. One-hour excursions depart from the "T" dock in Flatt's Village (across from the Bermuda, Aquarium, Museum & Zoo) and cost $230. No experience necessary and all gear is included. Rather get towed while lying on your belly? Then request a white-knuckle ride on its inflatable high-performance tube, which is suitable for adults and children alike.

Windsurfing

Thanks to Bermuda's strong off shore breezes, windsurfing is an increasingly popular sport on Bermuda. For up-to-the-hour wind reports log onto **Wind Guru (www.windguru.cz)**, which specializes in gust speeds and directions.

Upwind Sports ★★   This mobile windsurfing school goes where the wind is. That means on any given day, owner and certified windsurfing instructor Jay Riihiluoma meets students at a destination of his choosing given the conditions of the day. Two-hour lessons are available for up to three surfers per session and rates include all gear and safety equipment (one person

$150; two people $125 each; three people $100 each; four 2-hr. lessons can be purchased for $395).

www.upwindsports.com. ✆ **441/505-5297.**

Blue Hole Watersports ★ Located at Grotto Bay Beach Resort in Hamilton Parish, this full-service water sports facility rents windsurfers for beginner and advanced riders in addition to motorboats, paddleboards and kayaks. Because the facility is situated on protected Castle Harbour, you can expect smooth seas on most days. Rentals cost $30 per hour ($20 for each additional hour).

11 Blue Hole Hill, Hamilton Parish. www.blueholebermuda.com. ✆ **441/293-2915.**

GOLF

Ever since British Army officers first brought their clubs to the island in the late 1800s, golf has been a way of life in Bermuda. One can play year-round—the temperature never drops below a balmy 55 degrees Fahrenheit. Bermuda's courses—many of which feature rolling, oceanview fairways—are among the prettiest and most challenging in the world. No matter where you play make sure to bring your "A" game: Strong coastal breezes are prevalent, so balls run fast on firm fairways. Care to join a tournament? Then contact the **Bermuda Golf Association,** which organizes professional and amateur events throughout the year (www.bermudagolf.org; ✆ **441/295-9972**).

Belmont Hills Golf Club ★★ This course, one of the most respected in Bermuda, was originally designed by Scotsman Emmett Devereux in 1923. In 2002, California-based designer Algie M. Pulley, Jr., radically reconfigured its layout as a means of adding a series of golf features that brought the standards and allure of this course up to the demands of modern-day golf pros. Since its reopening there has been endless discussion about the peculiar features of this relatively short (6,017 yards) but challenging course. Despite the fact that some of the undulations in its terrain were flattened during the 2002 overhaul, an interconnected network of caves beneath the turf sometimes cause the ball to roll unpredictably. Another odd feature involves exceptionally narrow fairways. But despite these quirky disadvantages, golf pros recommend Belmont for beginners as well as seasoned pros. Although the first hole is said to be "confidence building," holes 2, 6, and 12 are all only relatively difficult (each

---

Rain Delay? No Problem!

If rain is threatening to wash out your tee time and you'd still like to practice your swing, then head to **Island Kaddy** on Reid Street in the City of Hamilton. Featuring high-tech indoor golf simulators, it allows clients to "play" some of the world's top courses. In addition to three simulators, Island Kaddy also has billiards, video games, and a full bar serving typical pub grub to keep your duo, trio or foursome happy. (94 Reid St.; www.islandkaddy.com; ✆ **441/293-4653**.)

with a par of 5). Likewise, the 17th and 18th holes, arguably the most difficult on the course, reward golfers with some of the best ocean views. Except for the above-mentioned 17th and 18th holes, most of the course is inland, so unlike other golf courses in Bermuda, this one provides few views of the Atlantic. Greens fees, which include golf carts are $50 on Monday, Wednesday and Friday; $115 on Tuesday, Thursday, Friday, Saturday and Sunday. Clubs rent for $50.

Btw. Harbour and Middle rds., Warwick Parish. www.newsteadbelmonthills.com. © **441/236-6060.** Daily 7am–5pm. Holes: 18. Par: 70. Length: 5,501m (6,017 yards). Ferry from the City of Hamilton. Bus: 8.

Mid Ocean Club ★★★ Originally designed by Charles Blair McDonald in 1921 then rearchitected by Robert Trent Jones in 1953, this ocean-hugging, 6,548-yd course is commonly ranked among the top 100 golf courses outside the U.S. It's also one of the most difficult to play since the elite private club only allows member to tee off on weekends (non-members can play anytime on Mon, Wed, and Fri; and on Tues and Thurs after 10:30am). Expect picturesque inland lakes, green undulating fairways and sweeping ocean views from many holes. Greens fees for 18 holes cost $275 ($314 with a cart) and club rentals cost $75. Caddies, who are paid in cash, can also be arranged ($65 for singles; $50 per bag for doubles).

1 Mid Ocean Dr., Tucker's Town, Hamilton Parish. www.themidoceanclub.com. © **441/293-1215.** Daily 7:30am–6pm. Holes: 18. Par: 71. Length: 5,987m (6,548 yards).

Ocean View Golf Course ★ Featuring views of Bermuda's north shore in Devonshire Parish, this 9-hole, 2,940-yard course is one of Bermuda's two government-owned courses (the other being the championship caliber Port Royal in Southampton). With panoramic views of the Atlantic Ocean from many of its elevated tees, local golfers consider the terrain unpredictable; that, combined with rambling hills and winds from the Great Sound, makes the course more challenging than it appears. Because some holes have as many as six tees boxes, many golfers switch tees on their second loop of the 9 holes, to make a par of 70. But no matter how many holes you play, expect windy coastal conditions—club choice will be crucial. Greens fees are $50, including cart and club rentals cost $15.

2 Barkers Hill Rd., Devonshire Parish. © **441/295-9092.** Daily 7:30am–6:30pm. Holes: 9 (18 tee positions). Par: 35. Length: 2,688m (2,940 yards). Bus: 2, 10, or 11.

Port Royal Golf Course ★★★ Originally architected by Robert Trent Jones Sr. in 1970, then redesigned by original design team member Roger Rulewich in 2009, this 6,842-yard course is one of Bermuda's finest. Once the home of the prestigious PGA Grand Slam of Golf, this professional-length course was completely overhauled in advance of the event, which was played in Bermuda from 2009-2014. Irrigation was added, tee boxes were rebuilt, greens were returfed, and dozens of invasive casuarina trees were cut to create sweeping ocean views from most of the back nine and some of the front. Indeed, over $14.5 million was spent to revamp this world-class government-owned course, which features some of the most challenging, and picturesque holes in all of golf. Bring your camera on the par-three 16th, a 235-yard cliff-hugging crescent where there's nothing but the turquoise Atlantic between the tee and the pin; and try not to be distracted by the unparalleled views on 7, 8, and 9 where you'll also be challenged by strong coastal winds. Greens fees for 18 holes cost $180 including cart; after 3pm, fees are $110 including cart. Rent Taylor Made Burners for $50 or Taylor Made M2's for $65.

Tip: If you don't have time for a full round or you'd rather just practice your swing and grab lunch, buy a bucket of balls and head to its oceanview driving range. Since it's the longest of any course in Bermuda you can use every club in the bag (including your driver), plus it's conveniently located next to Port Royal's clubhouse restaurant, where you can grab an alfresco table with views of the Atlantic Ocean.

5 Middle Rd., Southampton Parish. www.portroyalgolf.bm. ℭ **441/234-0974.** Daily 7:30am–6pm. Holes: 18. Par: 71. Length: 6,256m (6,842 yards). Bus: 7 or 8.

Tucker's Point Golf Club ★★★ Once known as the Castle Harbour Golf Club, this 6,500-yard course was totally revamped in 2002 by Roger Rulewich, the acclaimed architect who studied under Robert Trent Jones Sr. What he created is now one of the island's premier courses with steep elevation changes, challenging blind doglegs and gorgeous views of Castle Harbour (like the par-four, 315-yard 17th hole, featuring a raised tee box with bird's-eye views of the water and beyond). In addition to a short driving range where drivers are not permitted, the course also features a 10,000-square-feet practice area where you can warm up your short game and a handsome clubhouse for drinks and a meal when you're done. Greens fees for 18 holes costs $210 including cart ($130 for 9 holes, including cart). Club rentals cost $75 for 18 holes and $40 for 9 holes.

60 Tucker's Point Dr., Hamilton Parish. www.tuckerspoint.com. ℭ **441/298-6970.** Daily 7:30am–6pm. Holes: 18. Par: 70. Length: 5,943m (6,500 yards).

Turtle Hill Golf Club ★★ On the grounds of the Fairmont Southampton, this par-three course occupies not only the loftiest but also one of the most scenic settings on the island—chiefly why it annually hosts the Grey Goose Par 3 World Championships. Elevated tees, strategically placed bunkers and plenty of water hazards make it a challenge, and golfers have been known to use every club in their bag when the wind blows in from the Atlantic. Highlights include the 16th hole, which sits against the backdrop of picturesque Gibbs Hill Lighthouse and the scenic 1st and 2nd holes, where you're greeted by the ocean and a vertical drop of almost 200 feet. Even experienced golfers like to break in on this course before taking on some of Bermuda's more challenging ones. *A bonus:* This well-irrigated course is often green when some other courses suffer a summer brownout. Its 18 holes are usually completed in 2½ to 3 hours (as opposed to around 5 hr. at most of the others). Greens fees for 18 holes cost $99 and include cart. From noon onward, greens fees

Big Legends Mini Golf-Style

Bermuda Fun Golf at the Royal Naval Dockyard (www.fungolf.bm; ℭ **441/400-7888**) features 18 miniature versions of the world's most iconic holes—like The Road Hole from St. Andrews Old Course and Augusta National's Golden Bell. All in all, the course has six legendary holes from Bermuda, six from the United States, and six from Scotland. Well designed, and with a lovely oceanfront setting, this mini course is true test of putting acumen. Play during the day for gorgeous views of the south shore or tee up at sunset, when solar-powered lights illuminate the course. Open from 10am until 10pm when a cruise ship is in port; call ahead for availability (adults $15, kids $12).

cost $69 (including cart); and after 3pm, you can walk the course for $45. Club rentals cost $40.

101 South Rd., Southampton Parish. www.fairmont.com/southampton. ℭ **441/238-8000.** Daily 7am–sunset. Holes: 18. Par: 3. Length: 2,454m (2,684 yards). Bus: 7 or 8.

OTHER OUTDOOR PURSUITS

Bicycling

With a year-round average temperature of 70°F (21°C), Bermuda offers ideal weather for cycling—but don't go calling your two-wheeler a "bike." That term is reserved for motorized scooters. In Bermuda, a bicycle is referred to as a "push bike" or "pedal bike."

Much of the island's terrain is easy for biking, consisting of flat stretches (although there are some hills, especially along South Road through Southampton and Warwick parishes). That being said, roads that are shared with motorists can get congested (this is very true during the morning and evening rush hour to and from the City of Hamilton), and there are a number that are narrow, winding and/or lacking any shoulder. Most drivers are considerate of cyclists, but some have grown impatient of the island's growing tourist population on motorized scooters and two-wheelers of any kind, so use caution when riding on Bermuda's roads. We don't encourage families to rent bikes for their children for these reasons.

Those interested in joining a group cycle or race should contact the **Bermuda Bicycle Association** (www.bermudabicycle.org), and another good source of information for local cycling is the island's top bike shop, Winner's Edge, located on Front Street in the City of Hamilton (www.winnersedge.bm; ℭ **441/295-6012**).

RENTING A BICYCLE

A handful of cycle liveries and specialty shops rent bicycles in Bermuda and most can be rented by the day or for the week (just make sure to inquire about a push bike or pedal bike, since Bermudians use the word "bike" for motorized scooters). For information about bicycle and scooter rentals, see "Getting Around," in chapter 10. Bicycle rentals generally cost $40 for 1 day or $175 for 1 week for an 18-speed mountain bike. Some hotels, including the Hamilton Princess, offer complimentary bicycles for guests' use. It's always a smart idea to reserve as far in advance as possible, to either your hotel or a bike shop, because demand is great especially from April to October.

WHERE TO BIKE ON BERMUDA

Only the hardiest of cyclists set out to traverse the complete 34km (21-mile) length of Bermuda in 1 day. Most focus on smaller sections at different times. So, decide what interests you parish by parish, and proceed from there. To save time, you can take your bike aboard various public ferries (they're free) and then begin cycling.

A safe choice for beginning riders is the **Bermuda Railway Trail** (see below); another good stretch is the length of South Road between **Warwick** and **Southampton parishes**, since it tends to be wider than most others and has spectacular ocean views for most of the ride. If you're searching for steep climbs head to **Devonshire** and **Smith's parishes,** where you'll be treated to a pair of monsters: **Collector's Hill** and **Knapton Hill,** both of which afford riders bird's-eye views from their apex. Another is **Lighthouse Road** in Southampton, which leads to **Gibbs Hill Lighthouse,** the oldest cast-iron lighthouse in the world. Finally, for a scenic cycle that's far less exhausting, try **Spittal Pond** in Paget Parish, a wildlife sanctuary with bike paths running along seaside cliffs; and the pleasant stretch of South Road through **Sandys Parish,** where you'll cross Somerset Bridge—the smallest drawbridge in the world—then pedal along Somerset Road to Fort Scaur Park. There you can relax and admire the view of Ely's Harbour while enjoying a picnic.

THE BERMUDA RAILWAY TRAIL By far the island's finest bicycle path is the **Bermuda Railway Trail** (see the box "Rattle & Shake: The Bermuda Railway Trail," on p. 43), an 18-mile-long, noncontiguous pedestrian and bicycle path. The Railway Trail consists of seven sections, each with its own character: Some sections pass over oceanside bridges, while others meander through shady forests. Our favorite stretch is in Bailey's Bay since it includes a brand new, 740-feet bridge that connects Coney Island to Crawl Hill. This section of the trail hugs Bermuda's north shore, so you'll be treated to blissful water views as you amble through shady coastal scenery. You can decide how much of the trail you'd like to cover in 1 day, and which sections to focus on. There's no official map for the Railway Trail but staffers at the Visitor Services Centre in the City of Hamilton and the Royal Naval Dockyard can help plan your route.

Horseback Riding

Moran Meadows (9 Cut Rd., St. George's; www.bermudahorsetrailride.com; **✆ 441/537-0400;** May–Oct) is the only place to saddle up on a horse in Bermuda. Its 1-hour Scenic Coast Ride trots along the beach near historic sites like Alexandra Battery and Fort St. Catherine ($130); a 90-minute Sunrise Beach Ride with much of the same terrain allows guests to ride in the water (doable because of the hour; $190). It also offers a 2-hour tour of St. George's

($240) and a private two-person ride that includes a picnic lunch with champagne (call for pricing). No experience necessary.

Tennis

It was Bermudian Mary Outerbridge who introduced tennis to the United States when she set up America's first tennis court on the grounds of the Staten Island Cricket & Baseball Club in New York in 1872. The sport is even more popular today on island, and most of Bermuda's big hotels (and some of the smaller ones) have courts; many are lit for night play. Expect mostly Har-Tru, Plexipave, and clay courts, and be sure to pack your tennis clothes, since non-marking sneakers and proper attire are required at most clubs. *Tip:* Save cash by bringing your own balls since cans cost up to $10 each.

Elbow Beach Hotel ★★   The Elbow Beach Hotel in Paget Parish has five hardcourts, three of which are lit for nighttime play. Rates are $15 per hour during the day and $20 per hour at night. Lessons cost $60 for 30 minutes, $75 for 45 minutes and $95 for 1 hour. Racquets can be rented for $10 per hour, and balls are $9 per can of three.

60 South Rd., Paget Parish. www.elbowtennisbda.com. ℂ **441/236-3535.** Daily 9am–7pm.

Pomander Gate Tennis Club ★★   A stone's throw from the City of Hamilton, this private club is among the least pretentious in all of Bermuda. Its welcoming, family-friendly vibe makes it perfect for children, teenagers, seniors and adults of all skill levels. To play, join as a temporary member ($40 for a family, $30 for singles) then pay $6 per hour for a court. Nighttime play is available for $7 more per hour. In addition to tennis, the club also offers pickleball—a low-impact version of badminton played with hard paddles and a hollow plastic ball—playable on Monday and Wednesday for $5 cash (no membership necessary).

21 Pomander Rd., Pembroke Parish. www.pgct.bm. ℂ **441/236-5400.** Daily.

The Fairmont Southampton ★★   Of Bermuda's resorts this Southampton facility on the water's edge has the island's largest tennis court layout with six Plexipave courts, three of which are lit for night play. Guests of the resort play for free and non-guests can play for $25 per hour (for more than two players, add $10 per player per hour). Rackets rent for $10 per hour, balls cost $10 per can. Lessons from club pros cost $110 for 1 hour.

101 South Rd., Southampton Parish. www.fairmont.com/southampton. ℂ **441/238-8000.** Daily 8am–7pm (until 6pm in winter). Bus: 7 or 8.

W. E. R. Joell Tennis Stadium ★   Because this government-run facility is centrally located near the City of Hamilton this is one of the busiest clubs on the island. Here you'll find five Plexicushion courts and three Har-Tru courts (three are lit for night play). $12 per hour for adults, $10 per hour for seniors (60 and over) and $8 per hour for juniors (18 and under). Playing at

Other Outdoor Pursuits

FUN ON & OFF THE BEACH

EXPLORING BERMUDA'S natural wonderlands

The **Bermuda National Trust** has wisely protected the island's nature reserves. If you abide by the rules—that is, don't disturb animal life or take plant life as a souvenir—you can explore many of these natural wonderlands on your own. The superb nature trails are a rewarding reason to visit Bermuda.

The best and largest sanctuary is **Spittal Pond Nature Reserve** in Smith's Parish. Birders visit the reserve—especially from September to April—to see herons, ducks, terns, and many migratory fowl, which can't be seen after March. This 64-acre untamed seaside park is always open to the public with no admission charge. Other popular nature reserves are run by the **Bermuda Audubon Society,** which operates 16 nature reserves totaling over 60 acres including **Vesey Reserve** in Southampton, **Somerset Long Bay Nature Reserve** in Sandys and the **Alfred B. Smith** reserve in Paget—a nearly 9-acre coastal reserve open to Audubon Society Members and guests of Coral Beach Club (others may contact the club to visit; www.audubon.bm; © **441/238-8628**).

Hidden Gems, an eco-tour company, takes guests to some of the most wild and well-preserved natural attractions in Bermuda. The cost is $180 for a 7-hour excursion; children 6 and under are not permitted (www.bermudahiddengems.com; © **441/236-1300**).

night costs $10 extra. Racquets rent for $5 per hour for adults; $2.50 per hour for kids; balls cost $7.

Cedar Ave., Pembroke Parish. © **441/292-0105.** Mon–Fri 8am–9pm; Sat–Sun 9am–6pm. Bus: 1, 2, 10, or 11.

Grotto Bay Beach Resort ★   This all-inclusive resort across from L. F. Wade International Airport has four Plexipave courts, two of which are well-lit for night games. Guests play for $10 per hour and non-guests can play for $15 per hour. The hotel rents rackets for $5 and private lessons can also be arranged.

11 Blue Hole Hill, Hamilton Parish. www.grottobay.com. © **441/293-8333.** Daily 24 hr.

SPECTATOR SPORTS

In this tradition-bound British colony, the most popular spectator sports are cricket, golf, rugby and soccer—better known in Bermuda, and the world over for that matter, as "football." There's also a small, but dedicated, population of islanders who compete in beach volleyball tournaments on Horseshoe Bay each summer (to watch those, check scheduling at the Bermuda Volleyball Association: www.bva.bm). But the big-ticket sports in Bermuda are not surprisingly the same as those in Britain. This being an island nation, sailing regattas are also quite popular, especially when the biggest of the bunch—i.e. the biannual Newport-Bermuda Race—bring with it dockside parties and rum-fueled events galore (see the "Bermuda Calendar of Events," in chapter 3).

Cricket

In Bermuda, cricket is king. This international sport, with its deep British roots and genteel traditions, is played in private clubs across the island from April through September and the island's top players have status equal to the stars of the NBA in the United States. These cricketeers can be seen competing in the island's premier tournament—**Cup Match,** a 2-day extravaganza held in late July or early August when players from the **St. George's Cricket Club** square off against those from the **Somerset Cricket Club.** In baseball terms, it's a hotly contested Yankees-Red Sox game with boisterous island flair and should not be missed if you're visiting during the summer months. Come to watch the match and join the crowds who mingle in the spectator tents, many of which throw dice and bet cash at the Crown & Anchor tables since it's the only day of the year when gambling is permitted (buy tickets at the gate on the day of each event and expect to pay between $18 and $20 per ticket for entrance to this long-standing Bermuda tradition). Of course, you don't have to wait until Cup Match to watch cricketers face off, just head to a handful of local clubs that host games throughout the summer. Across from the entrance to Horseshoe Bay Beach is the **Southampton Rangers Sports Club** (1 Middle Rd.; ✆ **441/238-0058**); and in St. David's, watch matches at the Lord's Oval at the **St. David's County Cricket Club** (52 Great Bay Rd.; ✆ **441/297-0449**). Weekend matches are also held at the aforementioned **St. George's** and **Somerset Cricket Clubs,** but for information about all events and tournaments, contact the **Bermuda Cricket Board** (www.cricket.bm; ✆ **441/292-8958**).

Golf Tournaments

Bermuda attracts some of the finest players in the world, making local tournaments exciting spectator experiences. These days the two biggest tournaments are the **Grey Goose World Par 3 Championship,** an annual event held in March at the Turtle Hill Golf Club in Southampton, which draws former PGA professionals and amateurs alike; and the **Goodwill Golf Tournament,** the longest running pro-am in golf, which is played at Port Royal, Tucker's Point, and the Mid Ocean Club (www.bermudagoodwillgolf.com). For more information about tournaments and events, contact the **Bermuda Golf Association** (www.bermudagolf.org; ✆ **441/295-9972**).

Soccer

Better known as football, soccer is one of Bermuda's two national sporting pastimes—second only to cricket, as discussed above. In fact, Bermuda is so serious about its soccer that most kids start playing at the age of 4, and the competition in local clubs can be fierce. Because of this, you can watch spirited games kick off on the pitch of the **Bermuda Athletic Association** (www.baa.bm; ✆ **441/292-3161**) in the City of Hamilton, or you can catch the occasional national team match, typically held at the **Bermuda National Sports Centre** (www.bermudanationalsportscentre.com; ✆ **441/295-8085**) in Devonshire. Since national team matches are infrequent, your best bet for watching live action is by going to a Bermuda Premier League game. Comprising ten teams made up of athletes who represent the highest level of professional soccer in Bermuda, these games are played on Sunday afternoons, September through April, on fields across the island. For more info, contact the **Bermuda Football Association** (www.bermudafa.com; ✆ **441/295-2199**).

Rugby

In addition to several club teams that play on public fields from September through April, Bermuda is chiefly known for the **World Rugby Classic**—an annual tournament in November when the world's top players (who are mostly retired from the sport) compete at the National Stadium in Devonshire. Seats in the general admission grandstands are at the 50-yard line ($25); in the VIP Members Tent ticket (from $275), you'll rub elbows with the island's moneyed expatriates who come for the unlimited food and drinks as much as they do for the zone views (www.worldrugby.bm; ✆ **441/295-6574**).

Yachting

Bermuda has long capitalized on its geographical position in the mid-Atlantic to lure the yachting crowd. The racing season runs from March to November, with most races scheduled on weekends in the relatively calm waters of Bermuda's Great Sound. The best land vantage points include Spanish Point, the islands northeast of Somerset, and Hamilton Harbour (although shifting sightlines can make it confusing to watch races from land). Better views are available from the decks of privately owned boats that anchor near the edge of the racecourse, so it's good to befriend a private boat owner or rent one for yourself (see "Boating & Sailing," earlier in this chapter). Although the carefully choreographed regattas might be confusing to newcomers, the sight of a fleet of racing craft with spinnakers and pennants aloft is always exciting.

Bermuda is the final destination in two of the most important annual yacht races: the **Annapolis-Bermuda Race** (www.bermudaoceanrace.com) and the even more prestigious **Newport-Bermuda Race** (www.bermudarace.com), both held in late June during alternate years. Both provide enough visual distraction and maritime pageantry to keep audiences enthralled. Participating yachts range from 9 to 30m (30–98 ft.) in length, and their skippers among the most dedicated in the world. Another world class regatta is the **Argo Gold Cup** when international one design yachts race from Hamilton Harbour to Bermuda's Great Sound, all vying to win the coveted King Edward VII cup, indeed the oldest trophy in match racing (www.argogroupgoldcup.com).

SEEING THE SIGHTS

B ecause of Bermuda's small size, it's easy to get to know the island parish by parish. There's much to see, whether you travel by bike, ferry, bus, or taxi.

You'll need plenty of time, however, because the pace is slow. Cars and other motorized vehicles, such as scooters, must observe the maximum speed of 25kmph (15 mph) in the City of Hamilton and St. George, and 35kmph (23 mph) in the countryside. The speed limits are rigidly enforced, and there are severe penalties for violations.

The smartest strategy is to focus your sightseeing on the three distinct sections of the island: the Town of St. George's and the east end, the City of Hamilton, and the Royal Naval Dockyard and the west end. By tackling one at a time, you won't waste your precious vacation days commuting.

5

If you're visiting for the first time, you may want to follow the traditional tourist route. The Dockyard, Crystal Caves, and cruise-boat outings are all popular for first-time visitors. For travelers on a second, third, or fourth visit to Bermuda, a different experience unfolds. Once you've done all the "must-sees," you'll want to walk around and make discoveries on your own. The best parishes for walking are Somerset and St. George's, and the City of Hamilton.

But don't fill your days with too much structured sightseeing. You'll want time to lounge on the beach, play in the water, or hit the links; and to enjoy moments such as sitting by the harbor in the late afternoon, enjoying the views as the yachts glide by. Absorbing Bermuda's beauty at your own pace and stopping to chat with the occasional islander will give you a real taste of Bermuda.

SANDYS PARISH

Sandys Parish is one of the island's real beauty spots. If you're looking for a place to just wander about on a summer day, this sleepy parish is well worth your time. Fort Scaur and the Royal Naval Dockyard on Ireland Island are the major attractions; however, **Gilbert Nature Reserve** and **St. James' Anglican Church** are also pleasant spots for quiet moments (you can skip them if you're pressed for time).

To explore this tip of the fishhook that is Bermuda, it's best to take a ferry from the City of Hamilton to Dockyard (the fare is $5). The 20-minute nonstop trip departs every 90 minutes and you can

Many locals contend that you can't get lost in Bermuda. But as you begin to travel along Bermuda's narrow, winding roads, most of which were originally designed for horse and carriage, it's likely you'll eventually go astray—especially if you're looking for an obscure guesthouse on some long-forgotten lane. But have no fear: You won't stay lost for long.

Bermuda is so narrow—only about 1¾ miles wide at its broadest point—that if you keep going east or west, you'll eventually come to a main road. The principal arteries are North Shore Road, Middle Road, and South Road (also unofficially referred to as South Shore Rd.), so you'll usually have at least some sense of what part of the island you're in.

bring bicycles onboard for free (there's an additional $4.50 charge for scooters). Hours and schedules change seasonally, but generally the Hamilton Ferry Terminal is open Monday to Friday, 6:30am to 8pm; Saturday 7:30am to 6pm; Sunday and holidays 8:30am to 6pm. For detailed scheduling information, look at the info from **Visitors Services Centre** at the Royal Naval Dockyard (www.rccbermuda.bm; ✆ **441/799-4842**).

Gilbert Nature Reserve ★ NATURE RESERVE   In the center of the island lies the Gilbert Nature Reserve, 5 acres of unspoiled woodland. It bears the name of the family that owned the property from the early 18th century until 1973, when the Bermuda National Trust acquired it in conjunction with the Bermuda Audubon Society. The reserve is one of the best places on the island for bird-watching, and it is riddled with paths that connect to the Railway Trail, which crosses Bermuda. In the northeastern corner of the reserve are the finest examples of mature Bermuda cedars on the island.

Springfield, 29 Somerset Rd. www.bnt.bm. ✆ **441/236-6483.** Free admission. Daily dawn–dusk. Organized tours available. Bus: 7 or 8 from the City of Hamilton.

Scaur Hill Fort Park ★ HISTORIC SITE   On the highest hill in Sandys Parish, Fort Scaur was part of a ring of fortifications constructed in the 19th century during a period of troubled relations between Britain and the United States. Intended as a last-ditch defense for the Royal Naval Dockyard, the fort was skillfully constructed, taking advantage of the land contours to camouflage its presence from detection at sea. The fort has subterranean passages, a dry moat that stretches across the land from Ely's Harbour to Great Sound, and panoramic views; using the free telescope, you'll see such faraway points as St. David's Lighthouse and Fort St. Catherine. The fort sits on 22 acres of parkland filled with interesting trails, picnic areas, a rocky shoreline for fishing, and a public dock. Picnic tables, benches, and restrooms are available.

Ely's Harbour, Somerset Rd. Free admission. Daily sunrise–sunset. Bus: 7 or 8 from the City of Hamilton.

St. James' Anglican ★ CHURCH   This is one of the most beautiful churches on Bermuda. It was constructed on the site of a structure that was destroyed by a hurricane in 1780. The present church was built 9 years later.

Bermuda Attractions

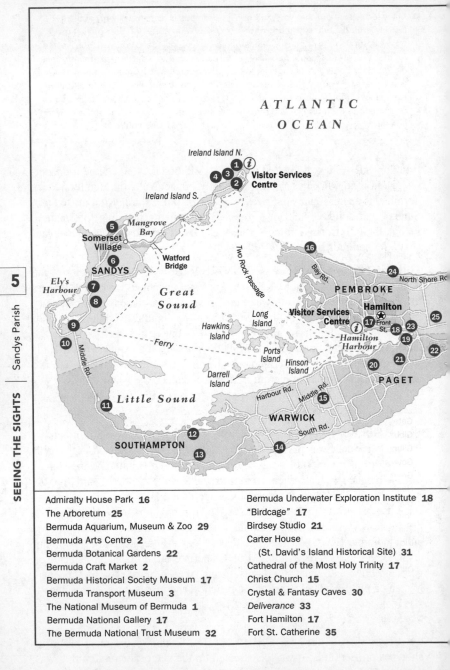

ATLANTIC OCEAN

Ireland Island N.

ⓘ
1
3
4
2

Visitor Services Centre

Ireland Island S.

Mangrove Bay
5
Somerset Village

Two Rock Passage

16

Bay Rd.

24
North Shore Rd

PEMBROKE

Watford Bridge

6
SANDYS

Great Sound

Hamilton

Ely's Harbour
7
8

Visitor Services Centre
ⓘ

17 Front St.

Hamilton Harbour

18 **23** **25**
19

Long Island

9

Hawkins Island

22

10
Middle Rd.

Ferry

Ports Island

Hinson Island

20
21

PAGET

Darrell Island

Little Sound

Harbour Rd.
Middle Rd.

11

WARWICK

15

12

South Rd.

SOUTHAMPTON

13
14

Parish 5

SEEING THE SIGHTS | Sandys Parish

Admiralty House Park **16**
The Arboretum **25**
Bermuda Aquarium, Museum & Zoo **29**
Bermuda Arts Centre **2**
Bermuda Botanical Gardens **22**
Bermuda Craft Market **2**
Bermuda Historical Society Museum **17**
Bermuda Transport Museum **3**
The National Museum of Bermuda **1**
Bermuda National Gallery **17**
The Bermuda National Trust Museum **32**

Bermuda Underwater Exploration Institute **18**
"Birdcage" **17**
Birdsey Studio **21**
Carter House
  (St. David's Island Historical Site) **31**
Cathedral of the Most Holy Trinity **17**
Christ Church **15**
Crystal & Fantasy Caves **30**
Deliverance **33**
Fort Hamilton **17**
Fort St. Catherine **35**

90

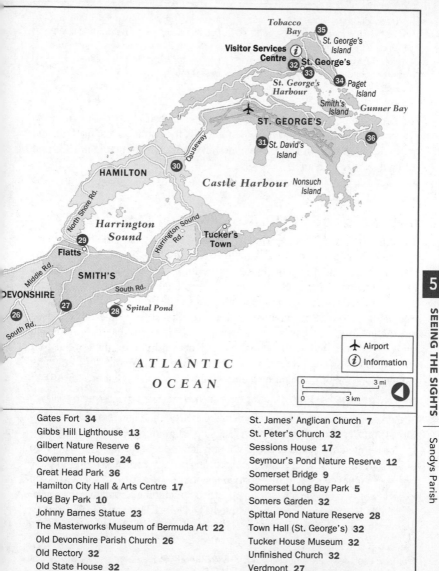

Airport
Information

ATLANTIC
OCEAN

The World's Smallest Drawbridge

After leaving Fort Scaur, you can continue over the much-photographed 17th-century **Somerset Bridge,** which is widely regarded as the world's smallest drawbridge. During the very rare moments when it's open for marine traffic, the space between the spans is a mere 32 inches at road level—just large enough for the mast of a sailboat to pass through.

A unique feature is the altar, which faces west instead of the customary east. The north and south aisles were added in 1836, the entrance gate in 1872, and the spire and chancel in 1880. The church was struck by lightning in 1939 and restored shortly thereafter.

90 Somerset Rd. ℂ **441/234-0834.** Free admission. Daily 8am–5pm. Bus: 7 or 8 from the City of Hamilton.

Ireland Island & the Royal Naval Dockyard

The American War of Independence created a crisis for Britain's military planners: Ports along the U.S. Atlantic seaboard were closed to British warships for repairs and replenishments. And during the Napoleonic Wars with France, the need for a British-controlled stronghold in the mid-Atlantic became something approaching an obsession with Britain's military leaders. Beginning in 1809, foundations for a massive naval fortress evolved, based mostly on enforced labor from slaves (and later freed slaves), prisoners, and prisoners-of-war. Today, the Royal Naval Dockyard is a bustling cruise port that's also one of the premier attractions of Bermuda. Within the sprawling compound are shops, restaurants, and the attractions listed below.

Bermuda Arts Centre ★★★ COMMERCIAL ART GALLERY One of the largest collections of locally painted artwork and handcrafted sculpture for sale on Bermuda is shown here. But stop by even if you're not in the market for Bermudiana because you'll not only get to see some lovely art, but also the creators at work. Every day, local artisans paint, weave, and sculpt in three open-art studios here. Exhibits change about every 4 to 6 weeks, but you can expect works from dozens of local artists (including Graham Foster, the acclaimed Bermudian artist who painted The Hall of History, a 1,000-square-foot wall mural that hangs in the National Museum of Bermuda across the street).

Maritime Lane. www.artbermuda.com. ℂ **441/234-2809.** Free admission. Daily 10am–5pm. Bus 7 or 8 or ferry from the City of Hamilton.

Bermuda Craft Market ★★ MARKET This is another prime place to watch local artists at work and to buy their wares, some of which make swell souvenirs. Established in 1987 within the shadowy, thick-walled premises of what was originally conceived as a warehouse and boat repair yard, this market offers items made from Bermuda cedar, candles, clothing, banana leaf dolls, fabrics, hand-painted goods, sea glass jewelry, needlework, quilts, shell art, antique glass bottles, and woven-cane goods, among other things.

In the Cooperage Bldg., 4 Freeport Rd. www.bermudacraftmarket.com. ✆ **441/234-3208.** Free admission. Mon–Sat 10am–4pm; Sun 11am–4pm. Bus 7 or 8 or ferry from the City of Hamilton.

Bermuda Transport Museum ★ MUSEUM   Located just beyond the main gates of the Royal Naval Dockyard where the hull of an ORACLE TEAM USA foiling catamaran is on display, this transportation museum features a large collection of antique cars and vintage Bermuda motorcycles. These include beautifully restored and heavily modified Mobylettes and Cyruses—prized collectors' items among Bermudian scooter lovers—plus classic sports cars, like a 1966 candy-apple red MGB GT and several VW bugs.

2 Smithery Row. ✆ **441/799-2886.** Adults $5, free for children 12 and under. Tues–Thurs and Sat–Sun 10am–4pm. Bus 7 or 8 or ferry from the City of Hamilton.

The National Museum of Bermuda ★★★ MUSEUM   Housed in a 19th-century fortress built by convict labor, this museum exhibits artifacts, models, and maps pertaining to Bermuda's nautical heritage. The fortress's massive buildings of fitted stone, with their vaulted ceilings of English brick, would be worth visiting even if they weren't crammed with artifacts and exhibits. So are the 9m (30-ft.) defensive ramparts; the underground tunnels, gun ports, and magazines; and the water gate and pond designed for boats entering from the sea. Exhibits in six large halls illustrate the island's long, intimate connection with the sea—from Spanish exploration to 20th-century ocean liners, from racing dinghies to practical fishing boats, from shipbuilding and privateering to naval exploits.

The compound's most impressive component is the **Commissioner's House,** dating from around 1834. The world's first cast-iron building has a grand Victorian design, meant to demonstrate Britain's architectural might. Left derelict in the 1950s, the house went through a 20-year restoration and is

A park OF YOUR OWN

Bermuda is very much like the onions it was once known so well for: Keep peeling back its layers and you're bound to uncover something new—like **Hog Bay Park** in Sandys Parish. Named for the wild hogs that once roamed the island in the 17th century, this 38-acre park is one of Bermuda's hidden gems. To reach it, take the number 7 or 8 bus, which operates between Hamilton and Dockyard (ask your driver for the correct stop), and prepare for a short hike through dirt trails and lush spice trees. You'll pass ruins of kilns once used for making lime to paint the whitewashed roofs of island homes, and the ruins of old abandoned cottages. Eventually the trail will lead to **Sugar Loaf Hill** and the aptly named **Look Out Point,** where you'll be rewarded with one of the greatest panoramic views on Bermuda. *Tip:* Bring your bathing suit. At low tide (typically in the late afternoon), the sea unveils a perfect spot for swimming and sunbathing that's easily reachable once deep inside the park.

now the crown jewel of an already impressive collection of historical buildings and artifacts. Today, glistening with a richly restored sense of Imperial Britain at the height of the Victorian age, it contains exhibits associated with slavery and the slave trade, antique maps, a collection of 19th- and 20th-century maritime paintings, watercolors with maritime themes painted in Bermuda, exhibits linking Bermuda's trade and emigration patterns to the Azores and the West Indies, and testimonials to the cooperative efforts of the British and U.S. Navies. Its highlight: the **Hall of History,** an impressive 1,000-square-foot mural painted by Bermudian artist Graham Foster depicting 500 years of Bermuda's history. The whimsical painting took Foster over 3 years to complete.

Don't omit a visit to the half-dozen stone and masonry buildings surrounding the Commissioner's House, most of which feature exhibits dedicated to Bermuda's maritime history. The best of the bunch is the **Queens Exhibition Hall** in the 1850 Ordnance Building that once used 19th-century bomb-proof technology to house 4,860 kegs of gunpowder. This vaulted-ceiling magazine is home to *Shipwreck Island: Sunken Clues to Bermuda's Past,* which explores the early history of Bermuda through shipwreck artifacts (including Spanish gold, Danish pottery, and tools used by early settlers). Nearby is the **Boatloft,** which houses part of the museum's boat collections including the champion fitted racing dinghy *Victory,* which was built in 1886; the St. David's dinghy *Magic,* that was used for turtle fishing until the practice was banned in 1973; and the 15-foot sloop *Spirit of Bermuda,* which was sailed by two Bermudian cousins on an 18-day voyage from Bermuda to New York in 1935.

Around the corner from these buildings you'll find **The Keep,** which is home to **Dolphin Quest** (p. 77) in addition to two adjacent spaces perfect for visitors with small children: **the Museum Playground,** featuring a 70-foot moray eel that kids can crawl through; and **The Playhouse,** a whimsical children's museum with interactive exhibits. On your way out snap a photo next to the giant statue of King Neptune, a limestone replica of the one recovered from HMS *Irresistible,* which sunk in 1891.

Royal Naval Dockyard. www.nmb.bm. © **441/234-1418.** Admission $15 adults, $12 seniors, free for children 16 and under. Weekdays 9am–5pm (last ticket sold at 4pm); weekends and holidays 9:30am–5pm. Closed Dec 25. Bus 7 or 8 leaves the City of Hamilton for the Royal Naval Dockyard Mon–Sat every 15 min. 6:45am–11:45pm. The trip takes 1 hr. and costs $4 for adults, $2 for children 5–16, free for children 4 and under.

The Royal Naval Dockyard ★★★ HISTORIC SITE   Home of the **National Museum of Bermuda,** the island's largest cruise piers, and dozens of shops, restaurants, galleries and attractions, the Royal Naval Dockyard is Bermuda's most visited tourist attraction. Even if you plan to spend all of your time on Bermuda's pink sand beaches, try to schedule at least a half day to check it out. Once a working boatyard for the British Royal Navy (its purchase by the Bermudian government in 1953 marked the end of British naval might in the western Atlantic), this bustling west end village has been transformed into a 24-acre pedestrian-friendly park. Simply called "Dockyard" by locals, the area has a place to swim, **Snorkel Park Beach** (www.snorkelparkbeach.com;

Bermuda has one of the highest concentrations of limestone caves in the world. Most began forming during the Pleistocene Ice Age. As early as 1623, the adventurer Capt. John Smith wrote that he had encountered "vary strange, darke, cumbersome caves."

In Bermuda, nature's patient, relentless underground sculpting has left behind a dream world for even the casual spelunker. Deep in the majestic silence of the earth's interior, you can roam in caverns full of stalactites and stalagmites of Gothic grandeur, delicacy, and beauty. This awesome underground has been the inspiration for creative achievements as diverse as Shakespeare's *The Tempest* and Henson Associates' *Fraggle Rock*. To see them for yourself visit the **Crystal & Fantasy Caves** along Harrington Sound Road in Hamilton Parish (p. 105).

C 441/234-6989); outposts of popular Hamilton shops at the **Clocktower Shopping Mall;** a mini-golf course called **Bermuda Fun Golf** (p. 82); a Segway tour operator (www.segway.bm; *C* 441/236-1300); the **Bermuda Craft Market** and **Bermuda Arts Centre;** the **Neptune Cinema** (www.liberty theatre.com; *C* 441/292-7296); and the **Bermuda Transport Museum,** as described above. Like most everything in Bermuda, Dockyard is closed on Good Friday, Christmas Day, and Boxing Day (Dec 26).

www.dockyardbermuda.com. Nonstop ferries from the City of Hamilton to Dockyard depart every 90 min. Mon–Fri 6:30am–8pm, Sat 7:30am–6pm, and Sun and holidays 8:30am–6pm, with additional evening routes added during midsummer, based on demand and during special events. Fare $5 each way. Ferry schedule at www.rcc bermuda.bm. *C* **441/295-4506.** Bus 7 or 8 leaves the City of Hamilton for the Royal Naval Dockyard Mon–Sat every 15 min. 6:45am–11:45pm. The trip takes 1 hr. and costs $4 for adults, $2 for children 5–16, free for children 4 and under.

SOUTHAMPTON PARISH

Most visitors stop by Southampton for the beaches if for no other reason. If you're not staying here, it's worth a journey to see the view from **Gibbs Hill Lighthouse**—indeed, there's no finer panorama in all of Bermuda—and golfers should book a tee time at **Port Royal Golf Course** (p. 80).

Gibbs Hill Lighthouse ★★★ HISTORIC SITE Southampton's main attraction is this completely restored lighthouse, built in 1846. It's the oldest cast-iron lighthouse in the world, and although it is a 185-step climb to the top, the panoramic view of Bermuda and its shoreline is spectacular. You can also view the same panorama that Queen Elizabeth II gazed on in 1953; just find the commemoration plaque across the street from the entrance to the lighthouse. The lighthouse keeper will explain the workings of the machinery and if you visit in the spring, you may spot migrating whales.

Gibbs Hill, Lighthouse Rd. (btw. South and Middle rds.). https://bermudalighthouse. com. *C* **441/238-8069.** Admission $2.50, free for children 4 and under. Daily 9am–5pm. Closed Feb. Bus: 7 or 8 from the City of Hamilton.

WARWICK PARISH

This parish has few sightseeing attractions, but it is a place of great natural beauty. Visitors come here mostly for the sandy beach, **Warwick Long Bay** on South Road (see "Beaches," in chapter 4, for details), and nearby, **Christ Church** on Middle Road. Built in 1719, it's one of the oldest Scottish Presbyterian churches in the New World. Also in Warwick Parish is the top-rated **Belmont Hills Golf Club** (p. 80).

PAGET PARISH

Bermuda Botanical Gardens ★★★ PARK/GARDEN Serenity embodied! This 36-acre green space was founded in 1898 to protect endemic Bermuda species like cedar and palmetto trees. Today the sprawling park has those, and a plethora of other attractions, including a sensory garden for the blind; a Japanese Zen garden; and maze gardens with 7-foot-tall Tudor-style hedges arranged in winding crisscross patterns. For children, a nautically inspired playground that was once part of the America's Cup Village is the draw. The Botanical Gardens is also home to **Camden House**—the official residence of Bermuda's Premier, which is not open to visitors—and the **Masterworks Museum of Bermuda Art** (see below for details; the museum also features an excellent cafe for breakfast and lunch).

Point Finger Rd. (at South Rd.). ⓒ **441/236-4201.** Free admission. Daily sunrise–sunset. Bus: 1, 2, 7, or 8. By scooter, turn left off Middle Rd. onto Tee St.; at Berry Hill Rd., go right; about 1km (⅔ mile) farther on the left is the signposted turnoff to the gardens.

The Masterworks Museum of Bermuda Art ★★★ ART MUSEUM Bermuda's first purpose-built art museum was the subject of island-wide patriotic fervor when it opened early in 2008, and the crowds pouring in haven't abated since. It's housed within the much-altered, much-expanded premises of what functioned in 1900 as an arrowroot processing plant. As part of a skillful recycling of the once-decrepit building, it now boasts a state-of-the-art security system, sophisticated lighting, air-conditioning, preservation facilities, floors crafted from wide planks of exotic Brazilian hardwood, and a constantly shifting exposition of Bermuda-inspired artworks. Only about 5% of the total number of artworks within this museum's collection can be exhibited at any time making it an ideal gallery for return visits since you'll likely see something new each time. A visit to this collection will certainly impress upon you the artistic power of Bermuda as muse to an array of radically different artists. You'll see many paintings by artists you might never have heard of (many of whom are locals), as well as works by 19th-century masters such as Winslow Homer and Georgia O'Keeffe, both of whom responded to Bermuda with artistic zeal.

On your way into the museum, note the stately 18th-century mansion, **Camden House,** that's immediately adjacent: Closed to the public, it's the official residence of the premier of Bermuda who rented the premises of what's now the museum to its curators for a fee of $1 a year. And on your way *out* don't miss the steel sculpture *Double Fantasy* from Bermudian artist Graham Foster. The impressive

A Beatle Visits Bermuda

After stepping away from his career in 1975 to spend time raising his son Julian, John Lennon experienced a creative draught. Searching for inspiration, he decided to sail to Bermuda from Newport, Rhode Island in the summer of 1980. The 700-mile journey was a harrowing one, his small boat pounded by rough seas and high winds. Lennon arrived on shore a changed man, and after renting a small cottage in Bermuda's Fairylands district, he began to write once again. "I was so centered after the experience at sea that I was tuned in, or whatever, to the cosmos," Lennon famously said of his time on the island, "and all these songs came!" One place where he sought inspiration was the Bermuda Botanical Gardens, where he would take long walks and admire the lush flowerbeds. In fact, it's where he got the name for his acclaimed final album. Called *Double Fantasy*, the double-album was named for a multi-petaled freesia found in the park and features classics such as "Woman" and "(Just Like) Starting Over." By the end of his 2-month stay, Lennon had written more than 25 songs. A sculpture by local artist Graham Foster (see above) commemorates the musician's time on the island. Lennon's impact can still be very much felt on Bermuda.

work is a tribute to John Lennon; the musician wrote several songs in Bermuda after being inspired by his walks through the Botanical Gardens in June 1980.

The museum has a terrific restaurant, **Homer's Café,** serving salads, small bites and Mexican favorites.

The Arrowroot Bldg. in the Botanical Gardens, 183 South Rd. www.bermudamaster works.com. ℂ **441/236-2950.** Admission $5. Mon–Sat 10am–4pm; closed Sun and public holidays. Bus: 1, 2, 7, or 8.

Paget Marsh ★★ NATURE RESERVE Maintained by the Bermuda National Trust and the Bermuda Audubon Society, this 25-acre nature reserve features stands of centuries-old cedar and palmetto—two endemic species of trees that are home to hundreds of native and migratory birds including great egrets, kingfishers and night herons. Visitors can tour on their own but must stay on the reserve's wooden boardwalk, which winds under the reserve's natural canopy and features signs describing the area's mangrove forests and unspoiled marshlands. One-hour guided tours ($75) with the Bermuda National Trust are available but must be booked well in advance.

Middle Rd. ℂ **441/236-6483.** Free admission. Mon–Fri dawn–dusk. Bus: 2, 7, or 8.

Waterville ★ HISTORIC HOME Built in 1725, Waterville is one of the oldest houses on Bermuda, and served as home to seven generations of the prominent Trimingham family. From the house's cellar storage rooms in 1842, James Harvey Trimingham started the business that was to become Trimingham Brothers—one of Bermuda's finest Front Street department stores until it closed in 2005. Major renovations were undertaken in 1811 and the house has been restored in that period's style. The two rooms that are open to the public hold period furnishings, mainly Trimingham family heirlooms. Frankly, we think Tucker's House in St. George's (p. 109) and Verdmont in

Devonshire parish (p. 104) make for more interesting visits, but those with a deep interest in Bermuda history will enjoy their time here. Waterville is just west of the Trimingham roundabout, near the City of Hamilton.

29 The Lane (Harbour Rd.), at Pomander Rd. www.bnt.bm. © **441/236-6483.** Free admission. Mon–Fri 9am–5pm. Closed on holidays. Bus: 7 or 8 from the City of Hamilton.

PEMBROKE PARISH & THE CITY OF HAMILTON

Pembroke parish, home to the **City of Hamilton,** is where most of Bermuda's shops, galleries, and restaurants can be found and where several of the island's most important historic buildings are located. You can spend an entire day in this colorful metropolis, but don't ignore the rest of the parish, which also features public parks and impressive architectural sites.

One of those is **Government House,** which is the home of Bermuda's resident British governor. Located on North Shore Road and Langton Hill, this stately Victorian residence has housed many notable guests, including Queen Elizabeth II and Prince Philip, Prince Charles, Sir Winston Churchill, and President John F. Kennedy. Since it's a private home, Government House is not open to the public, but you can view its manicured lawns and gardens, which quite tragically is where Gov. Sir Richard Sharples and his aide, Capt. Hugh Sayers, were assassinated in 1973.

Nearby is **Black Watch Pass,** a soaring limestone tunnel that was hand carved by hundreds of Bermudian workers in the 1930s. Over 2.5 million cubic feet of solid limestone rock had to be removed in order to create this roadway, which connects North Shore Road to the City of Hamilton. To this day it exemplifies the ingenuity of Bermudian engineering.

Another choice spot is **Admiralty House Park,** off North Shore Road at Spanish Point Road. In 1816 a house was erected here, which was where the commanding British admiralty lived when not working at the Royal Naval Dockyard. Over the years, the house was rebuilt several times. In the 1850s, it gained a series of subterranean tunnels, plus a number of galleries and caves carved into the cliffs above the sea. By 1951, the Royal Navy withdrew, and most of the house was torn down—except for a ballroom, which survives but is off limits to visitors. Today, you can explore the parklike grounds or watch adventurous islanders hurl themselves into the ocean: The adjacent Deep Bay is a popular spot for **cliff-jumping.**

The City of Hamilton

Once known as the "show window of the British Empire," the City of Hamilton was named after its former governor, Henry Hamilton and was originally incorporated in 1793. Because of its central location and its large, protected harbor, it replaced St. George's as the island's capital in 1815 and was once a major outlet for the export of fresh vegetables and Bermuda cedar. In 1852, the cornerstone was laid for the Hamilton Hotel, the island's only until the Hamilton Princess was built in 1887. After a fire destroyed the original Hamilton

Hotel in 1955, the Hamilton Princess—better known as "The Pink Palace"—quickly became the city's most recognizable landmark and a new age of tourism in Bermuda was born.

Today, the City of Hamilton is home to several major insurance companies and financial institutions that have set up shop in Bermuda (to benefit from the island's favorable tax incentives). Tourists really won't notice their presence, however, as most are captured by the city's candy-colored charm. For a fun half-day walking tour, turn to "Iconic Bermuda in 3 Days," in chapter 3. The only sights that are worth in-depth visits are **Fort Hamilton,** the **Bermuda Historical Society Museum,** the **Bermuda Underwater Exploration Institute,** and the **Bermuda National Gallery.** You can skip the rest if you're pressed for time.

A stroll along **Front Street ★** will take you by some of the City of Hamilton's most elegant stores, but you'll also want to branch off into the little alleyways to check out the shops and boutiques. On the shores of Hamilton Harbour is the brand-spanking-new, and architecturally intriguing **Visitor Services Center** (it's built from nearly 30 shipping containers). The helpful folks there will load you down with maps and advice.

This being Bermuda's capital city, all buses and ferries operate to and from its main ferry and bus terminals, so getting there is a breeze. Ferries back to Paget, Warwick, and Sandys parishes leave daily between 6:40am and 8pm (on Sat and Sun, there are fewer departures), and buses run frequently to all points east and west from the main terminal on Church Street. For ferry schedules and fares, go to www.rccbermuda.bm, and for bus routes, visit www.gov.bm.

AFRICAN DIASPORA heritage trail

Bermuda's African Diaspora Heritage Trail commemorates the role African slaves played in the formation of the island nation. Thirteen sites have been identified across the island, including the site of the slave ship *Enterprise* incident, which, like the better-known *Amistad* affair, involved the rescue of slaves seeking refuge and freedom, and the historic **Slave Graveyard** at St. Peter's Church (ca. 1612), both located in the Town of St. George's; **Crow Lane** where slave revolt leader Sally Bassett was executed by being burned to death; and sites associated with Mary Prince, the Bermudian slave who wrote the first known account of slavery actually authored by a slave. Published in London in 1831, it played a key role in the struggle to abolish slavery. Another important site is Cobb's Hill **Wesleyan Methodist**

Church, built by slaves by moonlight. The 13 sites can be collectively visited through a combination of bus and fast ferry routes, and as such, require a full day. Their densest concentration is in St. George's, where five of them lie within easy walking distance of one another. Some of the other sites are part of major attractions (for example, the **Commissioner's House** at the Royal Dockyard), which you might have otherwise visited independently. Even if you opt not to visit every single site, you'll learn a lot about the sociology of Bermuda during its sometimes-tormented formative years. Unfortunately, the pamphlet the tourist board created about these sites is now out of print. But the folks at the Visitor's Center (see above) should be able to recreate a doable itinerary. Ask.

Bermuda Historical Society Museum & Par-la-Ville Park ★★

MUSEUM This delightful little museum has artifacts both expected (old cedar furniture, antique silver, early Bermudian coins called "hogge money," and ceramics imported by early sea captains) and not (tools crafted by the Boer War prisoners who were sent here in the early 1900s). The museum's "Mona Lisa" is the sea chest and navigating lodestone of Sir George Somers, whose flagship, the *Sea Venture,* became stranded on Bermuda's reefs in 1609, resulting in Bermuda's first European settlers. Also on hand and of interest: models of *Patience, Deliverance,* and the ill-fated *Sea Venture.* The museum occupies part of the premises of the Bermuda National Library. It was originally the home of William Bennett Perot, the City of Hamilton's first postmaster (1818–62; see p. 102 for more on him).

Adjacent to the museum, Par-la-Ville Park is historically important in its own right, with gardens modeled on those originally planted in the 19th century by William Perot, Bermuda's first postmaster. It's also just a lovely spot to unwind, with koi ponds, sculptures, and an engaging poetry walk for kids.

13 Queen St., Par-la-Ville Park. © **441/295-2905.** Free admission. Mon–Thurs 8:30am–7pm; Fri 10am–5pm; Sat 9am–5pm; Sun 1–5pm.

Bermuda National Gallery ★★ ART MUSEUM Located on the second floor of City Hall in the heart of the City of Hamilton, this is the home of the island nation's art collection, showing Bermudian and world art alike. The museum displays a diverse permanent collection as well as changing exhibitions. Both past and contemporary works from local and international painters not only tell the story of Bermuda's history, but also reflect its heritage. The gallery opened in 1992 with a core collection of European masters, including Gainsborough, Reynolds, and Murillo. The collection was bequeathed to Bermuda by the Hon. Hereward T. Watlington. In addition to the Watlington

---

Pop Art at the Princess

Thanks to its collector-owners, the **Hamilton Princess Hotel** (p. 197) holds the most impressive contemporary art collection on Bermuda. Stroll through the marble-clad ground floor and you'll find *Divina Proportione,* a huali wood sculpture from Chinese activist and artist Ai Wei Wei; Nelson Mandela's *Struggle Series,* the South African leader's sketches of hands breaking free from chains; and several portraits from Andy Warhol, including Queen Elizabeth (hanging behind the reception desk) and Mick Jagger (located inside the private dining room of **Marcus'** (p. 131) and signed by both the artist and his muse). There are also works by Damien Hirst and famed graffiti artist Banksy, among others. Outside are several compelling sculptures, the most imposing of which is the nearly 19-foot-tall hardwood statue by contemporary artist KAWS titled *At This Time, Companion Series,* a Mickey Mouse–like figure that wows adults and children alike. Ask for a copy of the hotel's *Little Book of Art* to conduct your own self-guided tour or arrive on a Saturday morning, when free guided tours are led at 10am (or by special appointment).

Collection, the museum has an African collection (African figures, masks, and royal regalia), a Bermuda collection (which ranges from 17th-c. decorative arts to contemporary Bermudian work), and a wide range of Bermudian and international photographs, prints, and modern art.

City Hall, 17 Church St. www.bermudanationalgallery.com. © **441/295-9428.** Free admission. Mon–Fri 10am–4pm; Sat 10am–2pm.

Bermuda Underwater Exploration Institute ★★★ MUSEUM This blockbuster attraction is a glitzy, metallic, and electronic counterpart to the rich patina and genuine historicity of the Commissioner's House at the Royal Dockyard, with which it is sometimes compared. The force behind it was the late Teddy Tucker, considered to be the patriarch of Bermuda's underwater wreck explorations, who discovered more than 100 shipwrecks in its waters (including the treasure ship *San Pedro,* which contained the gold and emerald Tucker Cross, a replica of which is on display). There's something very akin to a museum of science and industry within this glistening, multimedia extravaganza. Various rooms are devoted to the underwater geology of Bermuda; one of the world's largest collections of seashells, bioluminescence, and the creatures that produce it; and a showcase of the treasure that Tucker salvaged from underwater wrecks. It also features interactive exhibits galore, including an "underwater shark cage", which rattles every time a Great White bangs its nose, and a theater-like dive simulator (a 7-min. ride that encounters underwater creatures of all kinds). The science and technology driving the America's Cup are also explored, in compelling fashion: Visitors don VR goggles that recreate high-speed sailing aboard a foiling catamaran. Both children and adults will love this innovative attraction.

40 Crow Lane, Pembroke Parish. www.buei.org. © **441/292-7219.** Admission $15 adults, $12 seniors, $8 ages 6–16, free for kids 5 and under. Daily 10am–5pm. Last ticket sold at 4pm.

Cathedral of the Most Holy Trinity (Bermuda Cathedral) ★★ CATHEDRAL This is the mother church of the Anglican diocese in Bermuda. It became a cathedral in 1894 and was formally consecrated in 1911. The building features a reredos (ornamental partition), stained-glass windows, and ornate carvings. If you have the stamina, climb the 155 steps to the top of the tower for a panoramic view of the City of Hamilton and the harbor.

Church St. www.anglican.bm. © **441/292-4033.** Free admission to cathedral; admission to cathedral tower $3 adults, $2 children 6 and under and seniors 65 and over. Cathedral Mon–Fri 9:30am–4:30pm and Sun services; tower Mon–Fri 10am–3pm.

Fort Hamilton ★★ HISTORIC SITE For one of the very best views of the City of Hamilton and beyond, head to this historic fortification on the outskirts of town. Perched high upon a hill and built in the 1870s to defend against attacks on Spanish Point and the Royal Naval Dockyard, this polygonal Victorian fort is open for self-guided tours daily. Explore its dark, limestone dungeons, cross its moat, and view massive cannons, none of which ever had to be fired. In addition to other seasonal events, the fort hosts a cacophonous skirling ceremony on Mondays at noon from November to March, when kilted bagpipers blow their horns from atop the ramparts—a tradition that dates to 1955 when the Island Pipe Band formed to celebrate Bermudians of Scottish heritage.

Happy Valley Rd. ℂ **441/292-1234.** Free admission. Daily sunrise–sunset.

Hamilton City Hall & Arts Centre ★ CULTURAL INSTITUTION The City Hall is an imposing white structure with a giant weather vane to tell maritime-minded Bermudians which way the wind is blowing (it's a replica of the *Sea Venture,* which crashed on Bermuda's shores in 1609). Completed in 1960, the building is the seat of the City of Hamilton's municipal government. The Earl Cameron Theatre on the ground floor hosts stage, music, and dance productions throughout the year, and is the main venue of the Bermuda Festival of the Performing Arts. The **Bermuda National Gallery** is also here. Since 1956, the Bermuda Society of Arts has encouraged and provided a forum for contemporary artists, sculptors, and photographers. Its gallery, with ever-changing exhibitions, displays the work of local and visiting artists.

17 Church St. ℂ **441/292-1234** or 441/292-3824. Free admission to City Hall and Bermuda Society of Arts. City Hall Mon–Fri 9am–5pm, Sat 9am–noon; Bermuda Society of Arts Mon–Sat 10am–4pm.

Perot Post Office ★ GOVERNMENT BUILDING Bermuda's first stamp was printed in this landmark building, which was run by Bermuda's first postmaster, William Bennett Perot, from 1818 to 1862. Beloved by international stamp collectors, Perot stamps are extremely rare and some of the most valuable in the world: Only 11 are known to exist, and the last time one came on the market in 2011, it fetched $205,000. It's said that Perot and his friend J. B. Heyl, who ran an apothecary, conceived of the first postage stamp to protect the post office from cheaters. People used to stop off at the post office and leave letters, but not enough pennies to send them. These days, philatelists can purchase contemporary Bermuda stamps here. The inventory of Bermuda-inspired postage changes seasonally, but one can often peruse its collection which includes stamps saluting the arrival of the tall ships to Bermuda's shores, another honoring the reign of Queen Elizabeth II and those commemorating the 50th anniversary of a local turtle conservation project.

Queen St., at the entrance to Par-la-Ville Park. ℂ **441/292-9052** or 441/295-5151. Free admission. Mon–Fri 9am–5pm.

Sessions House ★ ARCHITECTURE/GOVERNMENT BUILDING This Italian Renaissance–style structure was originally built in 1819. Its clock tower, added in 1893, commemorates the Golden Jubilee of Queen Victoria. The **House of Assembly** meets on the second floor from November to May, and visitors are permitted in the gallery. On the lower level, the chief justice presides over the **Supreme Court** to hear important cases.

21 Parliament St. ℂ **441/292-7408.** Free admission. Daily 9am–12:30pm and 2–6pm. Tours, if demand warrants, Mon–Thurs at 10:30am and 2:30pm.

No one person personified love and brotherhood more than Johnny Barnes, a gray-bearded Bermudian who greeted morning motorists at the Crow Lane roundabout for more than 40 years. With big smiles, boisterous blown kisses, and repeated shouts of "I love ya, I love ya, I love ya," the retired bus driver delighted all who entered the City of Hamilton. Sadly, Barnes died in 2016 at the age of 93. Commemorating him, and called "Spirit of Bermuda," is a life-size bronze statue of Johnny, standing in the roundabout since 1998. "I don't want a statue when I'm dead," Johnny would always say, so Bermuda paid homage to its very own Mr. Happy Man—the title of a documentary film about Barnes—with one of its highest honors while he could still enjoy it. The film is available on YouTube.

DEVONSHIRE PARISH

Known for its hilly interior, beautiful landscapes and million-dollar estates bordering the sea, Devonshire is a residential parish with limited sightseeing attractions. Pronounced *Devon-shur* (as opposed to *Devon-shyer*), it's where you'll find a handful of churches, open green parks and most notably, the **National Sports Centre,** where major sporting events like the World Rugby Classic and matches by Bermuda's national soccer team are held. Devonshire is also home to **Ocean View Golf Course,** a public 9-hole course with stunning views of the coastline.

Old Devonshire Parish Church ★ CHURCH   The Old Devonshire Parish Church is believed to have been built on this site in 1624, although the present foundation dates from 1716. A fire virtually destroyed the church in 1970, but it was reconstructed. Today, the tiny structure looks more like a vicarage than a church. Some of the church's contents survived the blaze, including silver dating from 1590, which may be the oldest on the island. The Old Devonshire Parish Church is about a 15-minute walk northwest of the "new" Devonshire Parish Church, which dates from 1846.

Middle Rd. © **441/236-3671.** Free admission. Daily 9am–5:30pm. Bus: 2.

The Arboretum ★★ PARK/GARDEN   Featuring saplings obtained from Japan, New Guinea and Canada, plus horticultural specimens from the Royal Botanic Gardens in Kew, England (that were once sent by Queen Elizabeth II), this 22-acre park is one of the most tranquil oases in Bermuda. Beloved by runners who come for its shady trails and exercise stations, this park is home to wide range of Bermudian plant and tree life, including conifers, palms and other subtropical trees.

Montpelier Rd. Free admission. Daily sunrise–sunset.

SMITH'S PARISH

Bordered on its north shore by Harrington Sound—a 3-square-mile inland lake that's popular among boaters who enter via Flatt's inlet—Smith's Parish is best known for its natural attractions. Chiefly, the 64-acre **Spittal Pond**

Nature Reserve and nearby **John Smith's Bay,** a gorgeous slice of pink sand that's great for families with small children since the beach boasts lifeguards in season. History buffs will enjoy a visit to the **Verdmont Museum**—a restored early-1700s house filled with ghost stories and period antiques—and ecclesiastical architecture buffs should brake for **St. Mark's Church** on South Road. Built in 1847, its mighty gray spire set against a sprawling green field is one of Smith's picture-perfect views.

Spittal Pond Nature Reserve ★★★ NATURE RESERVE Spread across 64 acres and teeming with wildlife, this is the largest nature preserve in Bermuda. It's also a bird-watchers' paradise. The reserve is home to dozens of species of resident and migratory waterfowl which congregate near its freshwater ponds and surrounding marshlands. The best months for spotting birds are November through March, when it's possible to see more species in a single day than at any other time of year (since 1974, more than 250 species have been recorded). But don't let that stop you from ambling its winding pathways and scenic trails the rest of the year, when you can spot finches, sandpipers, black warblers, white egrets, blue herons and Bermuda's ubiquitous longtail tropic birds. Spittal Pond is also known for the oceanside bluff that's home to **Portuguese Rock**—a historic carving believed to have been left by shipwrecked sailors from Portugal. Now cast in bronze, the inscription includes the initial "RP" (a reference to Rex Portugaline, the King of Portugal), along with the date 1543. Historians believe the castaways eventually sailed off in a new vessel they constructed from cedar timber.

South Rd. ℭ **441/236-6483.** Free admission. Daily sunrise–sunset. Bus: 1 or 3.

Verdmont ★★ HISTORIC HOME One of the best-preserved homes outside of St. George's, this mansion was originally built in 1710 and, unlike many of Bermuda's colonial structures, has gone virtually unchanged since it was erected. Now a museum displaying period artwork and antiques (furnishings brought in by early sea captains), the home is a preeminent example of how the island's upper class once lived. Chinese porcelain and handmade Bermuda cedar woodwork are viewable throughout. To the delight—or chagrin—of many local historians, the house is said to have several resident ghosts. It's believed that an adolescent girl who died of typhoid in 1844 still lives there, in addition to the ghost of 1930s resident Spencer Joell, who has reportedly appeared in photos snapped by visitors.

6 Verdmont Lane, Collector's Hill. www.bnt.bm. ℭ **441/236-7369.** Admission $5 adults, $2 ages 6–18, free for children 5 and under. Combination ticket to all 3 Trust Museums (Bermuda National Trust Museum, Tucker House, Verdmont) $10. Tues–Wed 11am–2pm; Fri 10am–4pm.

HAMILTON PARISH

Home to many of Bermuda's family-friendly attractions, Hamilton Parish is not to be confused with the City of Hamilton, which is in Pembroke Parish. It has many top-drawer attractions (see below). If golf is your game then

Hamilton Parish is where you'll likely spend much of your time since it's home to two of the island's finest courses: the **Mid Ocean Club** and **Tucker's Point Golf Club,** both of which provide gorgeous ocean views.

Bermuda Aquarium, Museum & Zoo ★★★ AQUARIUM/ZOO   Plan to spend at least a half-day exploring this superb complex, which feature fish and land animals from Bermuda and around the globe, plus an extensive natural history museum devoted to the island's cultural traditions and geological beginnings. The highlight of the aquarium is the **North Rock Exhibit,** a display that's modeled after an actual geological formation off Bermuda's north shore. It occupies a 529,958-liter (140,000-gal.) tank and allows visitors to experience a coral reef washed by ocean surge. The tank houses a living coral reef, as well as reef and pelagic fish species. It was the first living coral exhibit on this scale in the world. The **zoo**'s open-air exhibits star lemurs and fossa from Madagascar, kangaroos and wallabies from Australia, and other handsome critters. In the **natural history museum,** visitors learn how the volcanic creation of the island, as well as the techniques Bermudians have implemented over the centuries to survive on an island with limited natural resources. If you've got little ones in tow, there's a fantastic **playground** with a replica pirate ship.

40 North Shore Rd. (in Flatts Village). www.bamz.org.© **441/293-2727.** Admission $10 adults, $5 seniors and children 5–12, free for children 4 and under. Daily 9am–5pm. Closed Dec 25. Bus: 10 or 11 from the City of Hamilton or St. George's.

Crystal & Fantasy Caves ★★★ NATURAL ATTRACTION   Originally discovered by a pair of Bermudian boys trying to retrieve a lost ball in 1907, this network of subterranean lakes, caves, and caverns houses translucent formations of stalagmites and stalactites. All tours are guided and lead down steep stairwells carved into the rock and across a floating pontoon bridge that spans 55-foot-deep crystal-clear subterranean lake. Using the lighting system, the guides make shadow puppets on walls covered in thick calcite mineral deposits and are fond of pointing out the similarity to the skyline of Manhattan. *Note:* If you suffer claustrophobia, you may want to skip this one, as some passages are quite tight.

8 Crystal Caves Rd., off Wilkinson Ave., Bailey's Bay. www.caves.bm. © **441/293-0640.** Admission to either Crystal or Fantasy Cave $20 adults, $10 children 6–12, free for children 5 and under. For a guided tour that incorporates visits to each of the 2 caves, adults $30, children 6–12 $12, free for children 5 and under. Daily 9am–5pm. Closed Jan 1, Good Friday, Dec 24–25, and Boxing Day. Bus: 1, 3, 10, or 11.

ST. GEORGE'S PARISH

Composed of several islands, the two largest of which are St. George's Island and St. David's Island, St. George's Parish is by far Bermuda's most historic. Here the *Sea Venture* first crashed upon the island's shores in 1609 and it is where its colonial capital was first established 3 years later. That capital, the **Town of St. George's** is a treasure trove of historical sites and attractions. Also worth a visit: neighboring St. David's, with its eponymous red-and-white striped lighthouse, and **Cooper's Island Nature Preserve,** home of **Clearwater Beach** and **Turtle Bay,** two handsome slices of sand.

The Town of St. George's

A smart way to see St. George's beauty spots is to follow our walking tour (see p. 44, in chapter 3). We recommend beginning the visit in King's Square, which is also where you'll find the St. George's branch of the **Visitor Services Centre,** open Monday through Saturday from 10am to 4pm.

Note: If you're pressed for time, don't worry about skipping interior visits to the sights listed below. The entire Town of St. George's, with its quaint streets and old buildings, *is* the attraction. If you have time to visit only one attraction, make it **St. Peter's Church,** which is the oldest Anglican house of worship in the Western Hemisphere. Otherwise, wander around, do a little shopping in the boutiques along **Water Street** and soak in the historic atmosphere. To reach these attractions, take bus no. 1, 3, 10, or 11 from the City of Hamilton.

Bermuda National Trust Museum ★ MUSEUM Important U.S. Civil War history was made here. When this building was the Globe Hotel, it was the headquarters of Maj. Norman Walker, the Confederate arms runner. It was his job to sneak cotton out of the American South, to trade to England for much needed munitions. His story, and the story of those who got rich running the Union blockade, is described in great detail in the Museum's permanent exhibit: "Rogues and Runners: Bermuda and the American Civil War."

At the Globe Hotel, King's Sq. www.bnt.bm. © **441/297-1423.** Admission $5 adults, $2 children 6–18, free for children 5 and under. Combination ticket to all 3 Trust Museums (Bermuda National Trust Museum, Tucker House, Verdmont) $10. Mon–Fri 11am–3pm; Sat. 11am–2pm. Closed public holidays.

Carter House (St. David's Island Historical Site) ★★ HISTORIC HOME/MUSEUM Set on a hillside about 1 mile east of Swing Bridge, Carter House is believed to be the oldest dwelling place on St. David's Island, at least 350 years old. It's now a museum dedicated to the life and values of the people of St. David's, one of the most rugged and hardy districts of Bermuda. The museum houses exhibitions on the history of whaling, piloting, fishing, and farming and various artifacts of Bermudian life are displayed here, including a 13-foot dinghy once used for turtle fishing, dolls and children's toys crafted from palmetto leaves, and artifacts and paneling crafted from Bermuda cedar. Whatever you do, don't miss the "Settler's Cabben," an exact replica of a 1612-era Bermuda home, which was built with the very same tools and techniques that settlers would've used in the 17th century.

34 Southside Rd. (St. David's). © **441/293-5960.** Free admission (donations accepted). Nov–Apr Wed and Sat 10am–4pm; May–Oct Tues–Thurs 10am–4pm.

Deliverance ★★ SHIP Across from St. George's town square and over a bridge is Ordnance Island, where visitors can see a full-scale replica of *Deliverance.* The shipwrecked survivors of the *Sea Venture* built the pinnace (small sailing ship) in 1610 to carry them on to Virginia—arguably, a journey that saved the U.S. colony from famine. Alongside the vessel is a ducking stool, a

SPECIAL PLACES WHERE YOU CAN BE alone

Bermuda is not a large island and its natural attractions can get overrun with tourists and cruise passengers (we're looking at you, Horseshoe Beach). That doesn't mean one can't escape the crowds, though. Serene nature is available in the following spots:

o **Walsingham Nature Reserve:** Set in **Hamilton Parish,** this pleasant spot is often called "Tom Moore's Jungle" by locals since the famed Irish poet wrote some of his most celebrated work in a house nearby. Accessible through **Blue Hole Park,** which itself features walking trails and a wooden deck for viewing of a water-filled sunken cave, the reserve has Surinam cherry forests and shady mangrove trees and is easily explored on foot.

o **Somerset Long Bay West Nature Reserve:** Located in Sandys Parish where Daniel's Head Road meets Cambridge Road, this quiet park has groves of Bermuda cedar and palmetto replanted by the Bermuda Audubon Society; white-eyed vireos, and other local birds, sing from a grove of fiddlewood trees. When you're done enjoying the sounds of silence, take a swim in **Somerset Long Bay Park,** an adjacent beach that's as shallow as it is calm.

o **Seymour's Pond Nature Reserve:** Near the Barnes Corner junction of Middle and South Shore Roads in Southampton, this half-acre park attracts birders and nature-lovers alike—its natural freshwater pond is a popular spot for migrant and resident waterfowl. It's an ideal spot for a quiet stroll.

o **Vesey Nature Reserve:** Featuring limestone quarries and woodland valleys, this 8-acre reserve is among the island's most well-maintained, with pleasant walking trails and wooden boardwalks. It is a half-mile west of Seymour's Pond.

o **St. David's Island:** For a true taste of the quiet life, head to the east end of Bermuda. You can begin your walk at **Great Head Park,** which is southeast of the cricket fields. At the end of the parking lot, follow the trail into a wooded area filled with cherry trees and palmettos where eventually you'll spot **St. David's Lighthouse,** an octagonal red-and-white tower in the distance to the southwest (the working lighthouse is open to the public May–Sept 8am–4pm; free). The trail forks left until you come to a ruined garrison with a panoramic sea view. It's one of the remotest, loveliest spots on the island—and chances are, you'll have it all to yourself.

contraption used in 17th-century witch trials to punish the wicked, and across the street is a bronze statue of Sir George Somers, captain of the *Sea Venture*.

Ordnance Island. ℂ **441/297-5791.** Free admission (donations accepted). Mon–Sat 10am–4pm.

Old Rectory ★ HISTORIC HOME   Built by a reformed pirate in 1705, this charming old cottage was later home to Parson Richardson, who was nicknamed "the Little Bishop." Now a private home, it's open only during the St. George's Christmas Walkabout, usually held the first Friday of December.

At the head of Broad Alley, behind St. Peter's Church. www.stgeorgesfoundation.org. ℂ **441/297-8043.**

Short for United Nations Educational, Scientific and Cultural Organization, UNESCO chooses its honorees based on a long list of cultural, historic and scientific criteria, most important of which are that the site be of outstanding universal value. Considering this architecturally rich 400-year-old town is the oldest continuously inhabited town of English origin in the Western Hemisphere, **St. George's** was an easy choice (it was inscribed on the list in 2000). Today, the town and its surrounding fortifications are part of an elite group of historic sites that will be preserved for generations to come—in fact, just over 1,000 in all located in 20 countries worldwide. Think about that the next time you're atop the Eiffel Tower.

Old State House ★ ARCHITECTURE/GOVERNMENT BUILDING Behind the Town Hall is Bermuda's oldest stone building, constructed with turtle oil and lime mortar in 1620. Unless there's a special event, the landmark building doesn't offer much to see—you might settle for a look at the exterior, then continue with your sightseeing. The Old State House, where meetings of the legislative council once took place, was eventually turned over to the Freemasons of St. George's. The government asked the annual rent of one peppercorn and insisted on the right to hold meetings here upon demand. The Masonic Lodge members, in a ceremony filled with pageantry, still turn over one peppercorn in rent to the Bermuda government every April. Known as the **Peppercorn Ceremony,** this 45-minute ceremony begins around 11am with the gathering of the Bermuda Regiment on King's Square. Then the premier, mayor, and other dignitaries arrive, amid the bellowing introductions of the town crier. As soon as all the principals have taken their places, a 17-gun salute is fired as the governor and his wife make a grand entrance. His Excellency inspects a military guard of honor while the Bermuda Regiment Band plays. The stage is now set for the presentation of the peppercorn, which sits on a silver plate atop a velvet cushion. Payment is made in a grand and formal manner, after which the Old State House is immediately used for a meeting of Her Majesty's Council.

4 Princess St. www.stgeorgesfoundation.org. ✆ **441/297-8043.**

Somers Garden ★ PARK/GARDEN The heart of Sir George Somers was buried here in 1610; a stone column perpetuates the memory of Bermuda's founder. The garden was opened in 1920 by the Prince of Wales (later King Edward VIII, and then the Duke of Windsor). A large fountain has been built in the middle of the garden to enhance its beauty.

Duke of York St. www.stgeorgesfoundation.org. ✆ **441/297-8043.** Free admission. Daily sunrise–sunset.

St. George's Historical Society Museum ★★ MUSEUM With its traditional "welcoming arms" staircase, antique cedar furnishings and period artifacts throughout, this living history museum is fashioned to resemble a working Bermudian home in the early 1700s. On display: centuries-old cooking tools in the original stone kitchen, a working replica of the printing press invented by Johannes Gutenberg in Germany in the 1450s, a letter from George Washington, and Native American ax heads (some early settlers on St. David's Island were Native Americans, mainly Pequot). Particularly lovely: the fragrant herb gardens in the backyard.

Duke of Kent St. www.stgeorgesfoundation.org. ℂ **441/297-8043.** Admission $5 adults, $2 children 12 and under. Hours change seasonally; call for schedule.

St. Peter's, Their Majesties Chappell ★★★ CHURCH   Although it was granted the Royal designation of "Their Majesties Chappell" in 2012 by Her Majesty the Queen to celebrate its 400th anniversary, most Bermudians simply know this historic landmark as St. Peter's Church. And while it has the distinction of being the oldest Anglican place of worship in the Western Hemisphere, the building is not the original church to stand on the site. Originally constructed in 1612, the first church was built by early colonists and constructed of cedar beams and palmetto leaves. Following a hurricane in 1712, that structure was almost completely destroyed, although some of its interior, including the original wooden altar, was incorporated into a new stone church, which was built in 1713. Since then, St. Peter's has been restored many times, which is why architectural styles of the 17th, 18th, and 19th centuries can be viewed throughout.

Inside, the church is brimming with history. Top sights: the three-decker wooden pulpit, which was hand-carved in 1660; a collection of fine Communion silver from the 1600s that's kept in the vestry; and a 1594 Geneva Bible. Because its pews and exposed beams are made of Bermuda cedar, the church is also home to pleasant aromas wherever you may go. This also holds true for its historic graveyard—with flowering plants and lush trees, it has tombstones more than 3 centuries old (like the grave of Midshipman Richard Dale, an American who was the last victim of the War of 1812). The churchyard also holds the tombs of Gov. Sir Richard Sharples and his aide, Capt. Hugh Sayers, who were assassinated while strolling on the grounds of Government House in 1973. To the west is a separate churchyard for slaves and free blacks, a solemn reminder of the island's ugly past.

Duke of York St. www.stpeters.bm. ℂ **441/297-2459.** Free admission (donations appreciated). Daily 10am–4:30pm; Sun services 11am; guide available Mon–Sat.

Town Hall ★ GOVERNMENT BUILDING   Officers of the Corporation of St. George's, headed by a mayor, meet in the Town Hall, located near the Visitor Services Centre. There are three aldermen and five common councilors. The Town Hall holds a collection of Bermuda cedar furnishings, photographs of previous mayors and letters written by Queen Elizabeth II.

7 King's Sq. ℂ **441/297-1532.** Free admission. Mon–Sat 10am–4pm.

Tucker House Museum ★★ MUSEUM   This was the 1750s home of the well-known Tucker family of England, Bermuda, and Virginia. It displays a notable collection of Bermuda cedar furniture, Tucker family portraits, and sterling silver tableware. Also in the Tucker House is the Joseph Rainey Memorial Room, where Joseph Hayne Rainey (see p. 47) practiced

barbering. An exhibit on the ground floor traces the archaeological history of the site and the fully restored kitchen is an excellent window into the world of early cooks.

5 Water St. www.bnt.bm. ℰ **441/297-0545.** Admission $5 adults, $2 children 6–18, free for children 5 and under. Combination ticket to all 3 Trust Museums (Bermuda National Trust Museum, Tucker House, Verdmont) $10. Mon and Wed–Thurs 11am–3pm. Closed public holidays.

Unfinished Church ★★ CHURCH/RUIN   At the top of Government Hill Road in the northeast quadrant of town is this elegant edifice known as the "folly of St. George's." The cathedral, begun in 1874, was intended to replace St. Peter's after a hurricane damaged the historic church. But the planners ran into money problems, and a schism within the church developed. As if that weren't enough, a storm swept over the island, causing considerable damage to the structure. Result: this dreamy, roofless cathedral, which is now a popular venue for destination weddings.

Blockade Alley. www.bnt.bm. No phone. Free admission. Sunrise–sunset.

Historic Forts That Never Saw Much Action

From its earliest days, Bermuda has been a heavily fortified island. Once a strategic military outpost for Great Britain, the island was nicknamed "The Gibraltar of the West" since it had so many batteries and stone fortresses, many of which still exist to this day. And while they never saw much military action, reminders of that history are interesting to explore. **Fort Hamilton** (p. 101) in the City of Hamilton is an excellent spot for a sweeping view of the city; the giant stone fortress at the **Royal Naval Dockyard** (p. 94) was once the home to the largest outpost of the British Royal Navy outside of England; and the many forts of Bermuda's east end. Heading eastward out of the Town of St. George's, take Cut Road to reach **Gates Fort** (see below)—and **Alexandra Battery,** an 1860s fort that's well-known among sea glass collectors for the colorful pieces of worn-down glass that wash up around its adjacent beach (called Building Bay, it's where the shipwrecked victims of the *Sea Venture* built their vessel, the *Deliverance,* in 1610). Head further down Barry Road and you'll eventually reach imposing **Fort St. Catherine** (see below).

Fort St. Catherine ★★★ HISTORIC SITE   Towering above the beach where the shipwrecked crew of the *Sea Venture* came ashore in 1609 this fort was completed in 1614 and named for the patron saint of wheelwrights and carpenters. The fortifications have been upgraded over the years. The last major reconstruction took place from 1865 to 1878, so the fort's appearance today is largely the result of work done in the 19th century. In the museum, visitors first see a series of dioramas, "Highlights in Bermuda's History." Figures depict various activities that took place in the magazine of the fort, restored and refurnished as it was in the 1880s. In the keep, which served as living quarters, is information on local and overseas regiments that served in Bermuda. You'll also find a fine small-arms exhibit, replicas of England's crown jewels and gigantic muzzle-loading cannons—18-ton behemoths that could fire a 400-pound shell a half-mile to pierce 11 inches of solid steel.

15 Coot Pond Rd. (✆ **441/297-1920.** Admission $7 adults, $5 seniors, $3 children, free for children 5 and under. Mon–Fri 10am–4pm. Closed public holidays and weekends.

Gates Fort ★ HISTORIC SITE This small-scale, partially ruined two-story watchtower is capped with a cannon that once monitored the entrance to St. George's Harbour. With an interior of only two square and angular rooms, it was originally built in the 1620s by its namesake, Sir Thomas Gates. One of the original band of settlers from the *Sea Venture* who colonized Bermuda, Gates was later the governor-designate for the Colony of Virginia.

Cut Rd. No phone. Free admission. Daily 10am–4:30pm.

ESPECIALLY FOR KIDS

Bermuda is a top destination for the entire family. Most resorts offer children's activities, special family packages and babysitting services. More importantly, Bermuda offers many activities that will keep kids interested all day long, from sailing, water-skiing, snorkeling, and glass-bottom-boat trips to tennis, visits to museums and caves, and a wide array of walking tours. We've found that our kids have also enjoyed some not-so-obvious diversions, like feeding the birds at **Par-la-Ville Park** in the City of Hamilton (just pop into a City of Hamilton cafe, like Chatterbox [p. 140], to ask for some bread). Here are some of Bermuda's top sights and activities for kids:

Bermuda Aquarium, Museum & Zoo (p. 105): This trio of attractions in Flatts Village offers kids a wonderful introduction to Bermuda's underwater world, in addition to that of animals from other oceanic eco-systems. There's also a fantastic waterfront playground on-site and a playful Discovery Centre where little ones can crawl on plush carpeting and read picture books.

National Museum of Bermuda (p. 93): The whole family will enjoy exhibits dedicated to Bermuda's nautical history, all of which are housed in an authentic Victorian fort. Make time for the adjacent Children's Museum and nautically themed playground.

Bermuda Railway Trail (p. 43): This nature walk, with strolls overlooking the seashore and along quiet tree-lined alleyways, is suitable for kids on bicycles or little ones in strollers. You can pick up the 21-mile trail at many points and explore as many sections as you like.

Bermuda Fun Golf (p. 82): Located at the Royal Naval Dockyard near the entrance to Snorkel Park, this oceanfront mini-golf course features 18 miniature versions of the world's most iconic holes (like The Road Hole in St. Andrews or Augusta's Golden Bell).

Bermuda Underwater Exploration Institute (p. 101): It takes a good half-day to see everything in this 40,000-square foot discovery center devoted to Bermuda's underwater world. That includes a collection of more than 1,000 shells, a highly interactive exhibition about the America's Cup race (and sailboats in general), and an attraction that simulates a 12,000 feet "dive" inside a virtual submersible.

Bermuda Botanical Gardens (p. 96): This 36-acre park is Bermuda's largest, which makes it a perfect spot for shady picnics or long strolls through lush gardens. Kids love getting lost in the Tudor-style hedge maze; climbing on and hiding in a grove of giant banyan trees; and playing in the nautically inspired playground that was once in the America's Cup Village.

Crystal & Fantasy Caves (p. 105): Originally discovered by a pair of Bermudian boys trying to retrieve a lost ball in 1907, this network of subterranean lakes, caves, and caverns houses centuries-old stalagmites and stalactites—a whimsical underground world that was the real-life inspiration for the Jim Henson movie, *Fraggle Rock*.

ORGANIZED TOURS

It's relatively easy to explore Bermuda on your own. But if you prefer help from island-born and -bred residents, there are plenty of options available, depending on your interests.

The most adventurous of the bunch are tours from **Hidden Gems** ★★★ (www.bermudahiddengems.com; ℂ **441/236-1300;** $175 for a 7-hr. excursion; children 6 and under not permitted), an eco-tour company that takes guests to some of the most wild and well-preserved natural attractions in Bermuda. In summer that includes Tom Moore's jungle where you'll jump into blue hole lagoons and explore dry caves. In winter, ambles through the vines of Southlands Estate are a big draw, a thick grove of banyan trees surrounded by garden pools and limestone quarries.

If a slower, more historical pace is what you're after, then consider hiring a guide from the **Bermuda National Trust** ★ (www.bnt.com; ℂ **441/236-6483;** $75 per person), whose experts take groups on 1-hour tours of popular natural and cultural attractions, like Waterville—a historic residence in Paget—and various wildlife preserves including Paget Marsh, Spittal Pond and Vesey Nature Reserve.

Another popular option for visitors interested in architecture, natural history and island lore are the bespoke walking tours given by British transplant **Tim Rogers ★★** (90-min. tours for up to six people cost $100; $25 extra per additional person; ✆ **441/238-0344;** timrogers852@msn.com), who has lived in Bermuda for more than 2 decades. His walks tend to focus on the major hubs of the City of Hamilton, the Royal Naval Dockyard and the Town of St. George's, but depending on your interests, Tim can host a walking tour most anywhere on Bermuda.

And finally, there's **Segway Tours of Bermuda ★** (www.segway.bm; ✆ **441/236-1300**), which runs 90-minute guided tours of the Royal Naval Dockyard and the West End aboard electric-powered, two-wheeled Segways. These are the only motorized vehicles allowed inside the confines of the National Museum of Bermuda. Tours run year-round, cost $80, and start and end at the yellow double-decker bus in Dockyard.

SIGHTS & ATTRACTIONS BY THEME INDEX

Sights & Attractions by Theme Index

SEEING THE SIGHTS

WHERE TO EAT

The arrival of the 35th America's Cup in 2017 was a benchmark moment for the Bermuda food scene. With the eyes of the world on the island—and their taste buds, too—a number of exciting new restaurants opened, and many of Bermuda's old guard restaurants upped their game. Sure, you'll still find eateries serving typical "resort food" (run-of-the-mill international fare that satisfies most and thrills few), but a good number of the nation's restaurants and cafes have been reinvigorated with a new sense of culinary purpose.

Bermuda's cuisine is driven by the ocean. This is an island lacking any source of fresh water, so growing vegetables and raising animals is not only difficult, but prohibitively expensive. (That's also the reason for the overall high prices you'll encounter when dining out here.) Seafood specialties like mussel pie, shark hash and fish chowder were once Bermuda's defining dishes. These days, however, while seafood remains a focal point, it comes in a wider variety of preparations. That's thanks to the increasingly multicultural population, and a steady stream of visitors who expect variety. In the City of Hamilton alone are English pubs, French bistros, Italian cafes, barbeque joints, sushi bars, and Asian *teppanyaki* tables.

And while most of the food in these restaurants has been imported, a handful of eateries are making the move toward locally sourced vegetables. Still, seafood is king, so your best option on the menu will likely be the catch of the day, whether it be locally caught tuna, wahoo, mahi-mahi, rockfish and when in season, spiny Caribbean lobster.

As we noted earlier, eating out in Bermuda can be exorbitantly expensive. That includes beer, wine and spirits. Dining out here tends to be pricier, even, than in most major world cities (for example, it's not uncommon to pay around $18 for a hamburger or $11 for a pint of beer). Where you may save some money is when you're signing your bill, since most of Bermuda's restaurants include a 15%–17% gratuity. Of course, you can choose to add a few extra dollars, but an additional tip is not required, nor is it expected.

Unlike its sister isles to the south, Bermuda is a decidedly formal island nation—so forget any notions of "no shoes, no shirt, no problems." That being said, the days when men had to wear jackets and ties to dinner are long gone. When in doubt dress for dinner in a "smart casual" outfit, which means a collared shirt, closed-toe

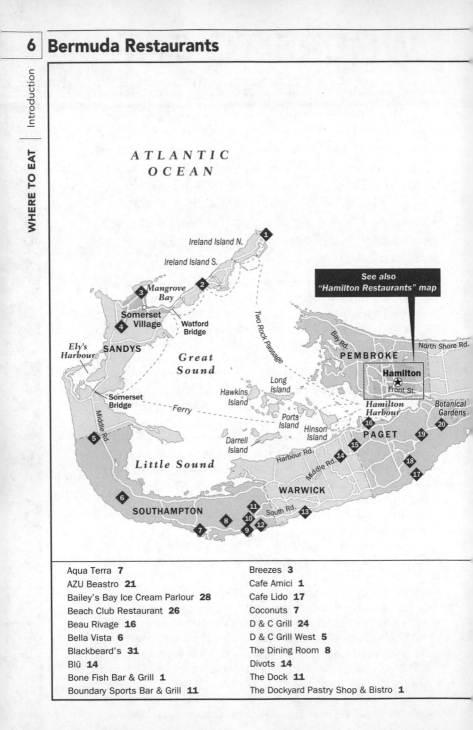

ATLANTIC
OCEAN

Ireland Island N.

Ireland Island S.

See also
"Hamilton Restaurants" map

Mangrove
Bay

Somerset
Village

Watford
Bridge

Two Rock Passage

Bay Rd.

North Shore Rd.

Ely's
Harbour

SANDYS

PEMBROKE

Great
Sound

Hamilton

Front St.

Somerset
Bridge

Ferry

Hawkins
Island

Long
Island

Hamilton
Harbour

Botanical
Gardens

Ports
Island

Hinson
Island

PAGET

Little Sound

Darrell
Island

Harbour Rd.

Middle Rd.

WARWICK

South Rd.

SOUTHAMPTON

Aqua Terra **7**	Breezes **3**
AZU Beastro **21**	Cafe Amici **1**
Bailey's Bay Ice Cream Parlour **28**	Cafe Lido **17**
Beach Club Restaurant **26**	Coconuts **7**
Beau Rivage **16**	D & C Grill **24**
Bella Vista **6**	D & C Grill West **5**
Blackbeard's **31**	The Dining Room **8**
Blû **14**	Divots **14**
Bone Fish Bar & Grill **1**	The Dock **11**
Boundary Sports Bar & Grill **11**	The Dockyard Pastry Shop & Bistro **1**

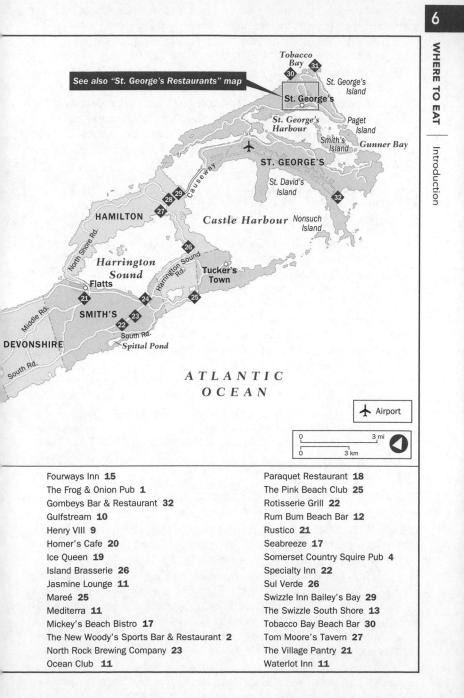

See also "St. George's Restaurants" map

Tobacco Bay

St. George's Island

St. George's

St. George's Harbour

Paget Island

Smith's Island

Gunner Bay

ST. GEORGE'S

St. David's Island

Castle Harbour Nonsuch Island

HAMILTON

North Shore Rd.

Harrington Sound

Flatts

Harrington Sound Rd.

Tucker's Town

Middle Rd.

SMITH'S

DEVONSHIRE

South Rd.

South Rd.

Spittal Pond

Causeway

ATLANTIC OCEAN

✈ Airport

0   3 mi
0   3 km

shoes and knee length shorts or slacks for men, and dresses, pants or Bermuda shorts for ladies. (Lunch, too, has rules, which means you can't show up in a bikini; cover-ups are required virtually everywhere, except if you're eating on the beach).

If you're visiting from May through September, reservations are recommended: The island's most popular restaurants fill up fast. And don't even think about hopping on a scooter after you've had a few Dark n' Stormy's. Not only is it wildly dangerous to navigate Bermuda's narrow, winding roads on a two-wheeler while impaired, but the Bermuda Police Service is cracks down on drunk drivers, so roadside checkpoints are not an uncommon sight on Friday and Saturday nights.

SANDYS PARISH

Expensive

Breezes ★★★ INTERNATIONAL   Getting one of the four tables right on the beach here is a two-step operation. First, you'll need to make a reservation. Then, plan to arrive at least half an hour before you're due—tables on the sand are strictly first-come, first seated (you can't request them in advance). All of this effort is worth it, though: You'll be treated to a view so blissfully tropical it could serve as an ad campaign for Bermuda. And, yes, the breezes are quite lovely, too. Complimenting the eye candy vistas is a parade of flavorful dishes that make use of local products (Bermuda onions, local goat cheese) when possible. This is the more casual of the two restos at this resort, making it an excellent choice when you want fine dining, but without the pomp and dress code.

30 King's Point Rd., at the Cambridge Beaches Resort and Spa, Somerset. www. cambridgebeaches.com. ℂ **441/234-0331.** Lunch main courses $12–$28; dinner main courses $24–$75. May-Oct lunch daily noon–3pm, dinner Mon and Wed–Sun 7–9pm. Bus: 7 or 8.

Moderate

Bone Fish Bar & Grill ★ INTERNATIONAL   Located on the west end of the Royal Naval Dockyard not far from the King's Wharf cruise piers, this is the first restaurant that most cruise passengers see after they depart their ship. Which means that the restaurant staff doesn't have to work too hard to stay busy—and they don't (service can be lackadaisical, and the food standard). But it *is* convenient, so if you do decide to dine here, opt for a Bermuda classic: Its fish sandwich, made with lightly breaded snapper served on thick cut raisin bread, is quite tasty. From May through October the restaurant features live music daily on its sprawling outdoor patio (like Spanish guitar music from local guitarist Randy Lambert or reggae, calypso, and soca from the Fire and Ice band).

Royal Naval Dockyard. www.bonefishbermuda.com. ℂ **441/234-5151.** Lunch main courses $8–$26; dinner main courses $16–$29. Daily 11:30am–10:30pm. Bar menu 10:30pm–midnight. Bus: 7 or 8 or ferry from the City of Hamilton.

Bermuda's two national drinks are both of which are made with **Goslings Black Seal Rum** (mmm mmm—molasses in color, with rich notes of vanilla and caramel). It's one of main ingredients in a **Dark n' Stormy**—a simple cocktail made with Black Seal rum and spicy ginger beer—and the **Bermuda Rum Swizzle.** Said to be invented at the Swizzle Inn in Bailey's Bay, where it's served in iced-down pitchers or by the glass, this potent rum punch is made with two types of Goslings (Black Seal Rum and Gold Seal Rum), orange and pineapple juices, a sweet simple syrup called falernum, and a dash of angostura bitters. Want to swizzle at home? Pop into any local grocery store and pick up a bottle of **Nine Parishes Authentic Rum Swizzle** (www.9parishes bda.com), handmade and bottled locally in small batches.

Café Amici ★★ ITALIAN   Located inside the Clocktower Mall within the Royal Naval Dockyard, this Italian restaurant has the best pizza in the west end (try the eponymously named Amici, with arugula, sliced Parma ham, and Parmesan shavings). It's also one of the few places in Dockyard where you can get a traditional Bermudian breakfast of codfish and potatoes—a classic you should try at least once before leaving the island that's served here on Sunday mornings from 9am to noon. Instead of sitting in its drab inside dining room grab a seat on its outside patio for a view of the boats docked in the adjacent marina.

Clocktower Bldg., Royal Naval Dockyard. www.amicibermuda.com. ✆ **441/234-5009.** Main courses $12–$38. Daily 9am–10pm. Bus: 7 or 8 or ferry from the City of Hamilton.

Somerset Country Squire ★ PUB GRUB   Overlooking Mangrove Bay in the heart of Somerset Village, this English pub specializes in traditional Brit favorites like fish & chips, bangers & mash and hearty Indian curries. Snap a photo under its Bermuda moongate entryway—said to grant enduring happiness to newlyweds who walk through them—then grab a table at its open-air patio. From there you can watch boats bob in the bay while you enjoy a reasonably priced lunch or dinner. In the mood for a beer? Buy a bucket of five for just $28, easily one of the best deals in pricey Bermuda. (*Note:* Beer by the pint is *not* a good deal here; in fact, you may end up paying as much as $15 for a freshly pulled glass.)

10 Mangrove Bay Rd., Somerset Village. www.fb.com/SomersetCountrySquire. ✆ **441/234-0105.** Lunch main courses $18–$26; dinner main courses $16–$35. Daily 10am–1am. Bus: 7 or 8.

The Frog & Onion Pub ★★★ PUB GRUB   Within the shadowy premises of the former 18th-century cooperage at the Royal Naval Dockyard, the Frog & Onion is the most traditional British pub in Bermuda. It's named for its founders, French-born Jean-Paul Magnin (the Frog) and Bermuda-born Carol West (the Onion). The place rambles on through at least three rock-sided dining rooms and two outdoor decks, so wander around to find a table

Check, Please! A Note on Service Charges

Don't make the mistake of tipping on top of your tip. On Bermuda, a service charge of 15%–17% is automatically added to most restaurant bills, so it's not necessary nor is it expected to leave something extra. You will, however, see a line for "extra tip" on most bills. If the service has been good, by all means, leave a few more dollars for your server, but don't get caught leaving an additional 15% since some restaurants include the basic service charge but leave the service charge line blank. Scrutinize your bill, and don't be shy about asking if you're not sure what's included.

that best suits your mood (for a memorable meal, reserve the one inside the cooperage's cavernous stone fireplace, where barrels were once forged and iron candelabras now stand). On offer is classic English pub grub like bangers & mash, Cornish pasties, shepherd's pie, and fish & chips though there's also a range of burgers, salads and sandwiches. The fish chowder is especially good. When cruise ships are in it often hosts live music. It's also one of the few places in Bermuda to drink locally brewed beers from the Dockyard Brewing Company, six of which are on tap.

The Cooperage, at the Royal Naval Dockyard. www.frogandonion.bm. © **441/234-2900.** Lunch $11–$24; dinner main courses $18–$34. Daily 11:30am–10pm. Bus: 7 or 8 or ferry from the City of Hamilton.

Inexpensive

The Dockyard Pastry Shop & Bistro ★★★ BAKERY/CAFE   Owned by Swiss pastry chef Joerg Rudolph, who has called Bermuda home for nearly 30 years, this Royal Naval Dockyard patisserie serves much more than the island's finest baked goods (think apple strudel, caramel eclairs, almond macaroons, and Paris-Brest cream puffs). The cozy sidewalk cafe, with its charming cobblestone patio and upstairs dining room, also has hearty salads, generously stacked sandwiches and hot-pressed paninis, making it one of the best places in the West End for lunch.

12 Dockyard Terrace, Royal Naval Dockyard. www.fb.com/The-Dockyard-Pastry-Shop-148693078535644. © **441/232-2253.** Lunch main courses $12–$21. Daily 9am–5pm. Bus: 7 or 8 or ferry from the City of Hamilton.

The New Woody's Sports Bar & Restaurant ★ PUB GRUB   The ultimate locals hangout, this waterside dive bar is where you'll find Bermudians inside watching soccer or congregated on the outdoor patio drinking beers and eating what many consider to be the best fish sandwich on Bermuda. Typically featuring crispy filets of fried grouper or wahoo, Woody's fish sandwiches are served in traditional Bermudian style: on raisin bread with cole slaw and tartar sauce. Delish!

1 Woody's Dr., Boaz Island, Sandys. © **441/234-2082.** Lunch $10–$20. Daily 11am–1am. Bus: 7 or 8.

SOUTHAMPTON PARISH

Expensive

Aqua Terra ★ INTERNATIONAL   The food is hit or miss, and the service can be slow, at this, the most formal restaurant of the Reefs Hotel and Club. But if you reserve a table next to the windows you may not mind, as you'll be treated to blissful Atlantic Ocean views. It is a 180-degree panorama and it is killer. The dining room is handsome, too, with vaulted ceilings, exposed cedar beams, and a pianist often tickling the ivories in the nearby cocktail lounge many nights.

In the Reefs Hotel, 56 S. Shore Rd. www.thereefs.com. ✆ **441/238-0222.** Main courses $28–$38. Daily 6–10pm. Bus: 7 or 8.

Coconuts ★ INTERNATIONAL   And here's another one with a stunning beachfront location but food that is inconsistent at best. Still, this seasonally open spot at the Reefs Hotel and Club draws a crowd in summer, when hotel guests and off-site diners alike fill its covered wooden veranda for calm ocean breezes and endless views of the turquoise coastline. *Note:* This restaurant is not recommended for mobility impaired travelers since it requires a walk down (and back up) a steep hill to reach its beachside tables.

The Reefs Hotel & Club, 56 South Rd. www.thereefs.com. ✆ **441/238-0222.** Lunch main courses $12–$26; dinner main courses $28–$40. Daily lunch noon–4pm, dinner 6:30–10pm. Closed Dec–Mar. Bus 7 or 8.

Ocean Club ★★★ SEAFOOD   Set atop a low cliff overlooking rocks and pink sands, the Ocean Club is the top place for seafood in Southampton—and one of the best on the island for it, too. We especially like their Bermuda-style rockfish served with torched local banana and toasted almond gremolata, but it's unlikely you'll go wrong with anything you order here. The cooking is expert and the fish extremely fresh. Kudos, too, to the friendly and professional waitstaff, who make all guests feel like VIPs. *Tip:* When reserving a table, ask to be seated outside on the romantic veranda.

Fairmont Southampton, 101 South Rd. www.fairmont.com. ✆ **441/238-8000.** Main courses $32–$49. Daily 6–10pm. Closed Nov–Mar. Bus: 7 or 8.

Waterlot Inn ★★★ STEAK & SEAFOOD   Housed in a 1670s-era Bermuda cottage, where merchant sailors once unloaded their cargo into the basement, the Waterlot Inn is the island's premier steakhouse. Situated on picturesque Jew's Bay in Southampton, the high-end restaurant no longer requires that gentlemen wear jackets, but men should don one anyway, as its white tableclothed dining room, complete with tall Windsor chairs, nautical oil paintings and exposed dark wood flickered with candlelight, is awash in five-star formality—and you wouldn't want to spoil the mood. Choose from an impeccably executed menu of steakhouse classics such as oysters Rockefeller, seared foie gras and escargots; on- and off-the-bone cuts of USDA Angus beef, including an imperial American Wagyu striploin or a 20-ounce porterhouse. Not into steak? There's Bermuda cedar plank salmon, jumbo scallops or seared yellowfin tuna for the red meat-averse. A final bit of theater comes at the end of the meal if you order bananas foster flambé for two (highly recommended), prepared tableside with brown sugar, dark rum, and vanilla ice cream. When you're done with dinner, have a drink or a cigar at The Dock, the Waterlot's waterside outdoor cocktail lounge that also serves small plates and hosts live music seasonally.

101 S. Shore Rd. www.waterlotinn.com. © **441/238-8000.** Reservations recommended. Main courses $34–$68. Daily 6–9pm. Closed Oct–Mar Mon. Bus: 7.

Moderate

Henry VIII ★★ PUB GRUB/SUSHI   Henry VIII shouldn't be as good as it is. It's set walking distance from two Southampton resorts (the Fairmont and the Reefs), all but guaranteeing it clientele. Its menu is all over the place. And its "Ye Olde" Tudor styling, with portraits of former English kings, dark wood and brass finishings could have been heavy-handed. But somehow it all works, and it works to such an extent that you'll be competing for reservations with locals, who keep this place busy place year-round (particularly at the all-you-can-eat Sunday brunch). Why so popular? The service is kindly, the ambiance fun, and all the food is quite tasty, high quality, and not exorbitantly priced (well, by Bermuda standards). That goes for the pub grub (burgers, fish and chips, and the like), as well as such international dishes as rockfish almondine, rack of lamb or grilled ribeye steak. There's also a small, Japanese-styled dining room where creative maki rolls are prepared by affable and talented Filipino chefs. On Friday, Saturday and Sunday nights, the restaurant typically hosts live music.

52 S. Shore Rd. www.henrys.bm. © **441/238-1977.** Lunch main courses $14–$36; dinner main courses $21–$42; sushi rolls $18. Sun brunch $42 per person. Mon–Sat lunch noon–5pm, daily dinner 6–10pm, Sun brunch noon–3pm. Bus: 7 or 8.

Putting Together the Perfect Picnic

In Bermuda, eating and drinking on public beaches and parks is a prized pastime. Locals pack a picnic to "sit off" with friends, a term used among islanders to denote socializing outdoors with food and drinks. Where to shop for supplies? If you're near the City of Hamilton make a beeline for **Miles Market,** a specialty food shop that sells international cheeses, fine wines and prepared foods of all kinds (96 Pitts Bay Rd.; www.miles.bm; © **441/295-1234**). On the east end, the choice is **Harrington Hundreds,** another high-end grocer in Smiths that sells fresh produce, sandwiches, and baked goods galore (99 South Rd.; www.harringtonhundreds.bm; © **441/293-1635**). There are also grocery stores islandwide, most prominently **Lindo's Family Foods** (www.lindos.bm), with stores in Devonshire and Warwick parishes. And if you'd prefer that your wine, beer, and select gourmet foods be brought to your doorstep, then place an order with **Two Rock Wines,** which offers free same-day delivery on orders over $200; $10 fee for smaller orders (8 Harvey Rd., Paget; www.tworockwines.com; © **441/232-2325**).

Boundary Sports Bar and Grille ★★ BARBECUE   Low and slow—that's the key to good BBQ, and that's how they do it here. Every day, Boundary's Texas-trained chef, and his assistants, pack their industrial smoker with a mix of mesquite, cherry wood, maple and hickory. Fine brisket (from Wagyu beef) is put in first, since it will cook for 24 hours. It's followed by St. Louis ribs, local wahoo, and (often) Bermuda-grown carrots. Eventually, it's all served in the laid-back dining room, which is a gamers paradise. Not only are there a dozen high-def TV's tuned to sports, but Boundary has billiards, table shuffleboard and Jenga to keep diners busy until their food arrives. (That makes this a primo choice for families with kids.) In addition to 'cue, they serve finger foods and burgers.

In the golf clubhouse of the Fairmont Southampton, 101 S. Shore Rd. www.fairmont. com. ℭ **441/238-8000.** Mon–Fri 5pm–midnight; Sat–Sun 11am–midnight. Bus: 7 or 8.

Bella Vista ★★ ITALIAN   Set within the airy and rambling pink-sided clubhouse of the Port Royal Golf Course, Bella Vista's restaurant's hilltop location provides excellent views of the back nine and the Atlantic Ocean. At lunch, a roster of salads, tacos, sandwiches and burgers is served. Dinner is devoted to traditional Italian favorites, say meat lasagna or chicken parmesan, plus a handful of hearty meat dishes, like New Zealand rack of lamb, striploin steak and a Brazilian churrasco platter for two with steak, lamb chops, chorizo and more. Service is warm, the food is toothsome, and it's fun watching the duffers do their stuff as you dine.

On the grounds of the Port Royal Golf Course, 5 Port Royal Dr., Southampton. www. bellavistagrill.com. ℭ **441/232-0100.** Lunch main courses $12–$32; dinner main courses $24–$39. Daily 11am–10pm. Bus: 7 or 8.

Gulfstream ★★ SEAFOOD/PIZZERIA   This roadside restaurant is located directly across the street from the entrance to Horseshoe Bay Beach, making it a perfect stop for lunch before you take a dip or for an early dinner after you're done swimming (just make sure to cover up before you head over). Since it's owned by an Italian expat originally from Lake Como, the food is authentically Italy and quite good: thin crust pizzas and specialties from northern Italy, like veal Milanese, a fried veal cutlet over arugula. Also on offer: simple preparations of fresh local fish (wahoo with soy, ginger, and lime was a recent special). *Tip:* If you've rented a Twizy (see p. 207), Gulfstream has two electric power stations where you can plug in and charge up.

117 South Rd., Horseshoe Bay. www.bermuda-dining.com. ℭ **441/238-1897.** Main courses $22–$44. Daily 11:30am–10pm. Bus 7 or 8.

The Dining Room ★★ ITALIAN   Housed in a former lighthouse keeper's cottage adjacent to Gibb's Hill Lighthouse, this restaurant is home to one of Bermuda's most memorable dining experiences. From May through September, it places its tables outside, under the spinning beams of the island's 117-foot-tall, whitewashed lighthouse. These thick shafts of light can be seen by ships more than 40 miles away and by you from your breezy hilltop table where you'll enjoy a 360-degree view and dine on Italian specialties like lasagna, gnocchi gorgonzola and chicken parmigiana. *Tip:* If you've climbed the lighthouse's 185 stairs on a Friday, Saturday, or Sunday in summer, this is also a good spot for lunch (you will, however, be sitting in its indoor dining room).

Gibbs Hill Lighthouse, 68 St. Anne's Rd. www.bermuda-dining.com. © **441/238-8679.** Lunch main courses $14–$25; dinner main courses $24–$36. Fri–Sun lunch 11am–3pm, Tues–Sun dinner 5:30–10pm. Closed Nov–Feb. Bus: 7 or 8.

Mediterra ★★ MEDITERRANEAN You'll "sail" from Greece to Italy to Spain and North Africa at this yachtlike eatery, with its porthole "windows" (actually inset sea paintings), its brass fixtures and burnished woods. And as you would on a ship, you'll be sharing the victuals—the menu is designed that way. From the tapas, meze, and antipasto appetizers to such large family-style dishes as paella or short rib lasagna, it's all meant to be doled out around the table. We've found that sharing evenly can be difficult, though: With food this terrific, hoarding instincts kick in. We must also sing the praises of the staff and chefs here for how well they accommodate children: The kid's menu isn't the usual sad chicken fingers. Instead children are offered "steaming fish," hummus and pita, and other healthy but simple dishes.

Fairmont Southampton, 101 S. Shore Rd. www.fairmont.com. © **441/238-8000.** Dinner main courses $22–$40. Daily 6–9pm. Closed Tues in winter. Bus: 7 or 8.

Jasmine Lounge ★★ INTERNATIONAL Attention hungry travelers: This is one of the few restaurants on Bermuda with continuous service from 11am in the morning until 11:30pm at night. (Most island restos shutter between lunch and dinner, and well before 11:30pm). It's also a very pleasant spot for a nibble, with swish living room–like decor (it is set in the lobby of the Fairmont). Come evening there's sometimes live music, and the bar part of the equation comes to the fore; this laid-back lounge has a very good craft cocktail menu. We'd suggest pairing their Bermuda Old Fashioned (with Maker's Mark, Gosling's Old Reserve rum, angostura bitters, and raw sugar) with the "Serious Burger," a big hunk of charred meat topped with Applewood smoked bacon, aged cheddar, roasted garlic aioli, and a fried egg).

Fairmont Southampton, 101 S. Shore Rd. www.fairmont.com. © **441/238-8000.** Main courses $16–$42. Daily 11am–midnight. Bus: 7 or 8.

Inexpensive

D&C Grill West ★★ CARIBBEAN/SOUL FOOD If you're staying near the west end or happen to be passing through Southampton parish en route to the Royal Naval Dockyard, this is a swell little spot to pick up an inexpensive take out meal (there are also no-frills tables beside the to-go counter). The menu is an ever-changing lineup of Jamaican and Caribbean specialties: jerk chicken, barbecue ribs, braised oxtail, peas and rice, macaroni and cheese, and savory Johnny bread. It's all delicious.

2 Middle Rd., Southampton Parish. © **441/292-5991.** Lunch and dinner main courses $11 per pound. Mon–Thurs 10am–8pm; Fri–Sat 10am–10pm. Bus: 7 or 8.

Rum Bum Beach Bar ★★ COMFORT FOOD Burgers in your bikini! This laid-back beach bar is located on the grounds of Horseshoe Bay Beach, making it the only restaurant in Bermuda where you can eat, drink and be merry without donning a coverup. That's right: Guys *don't* have to wear a shirt and shoes can be left off. Like the atmosphere, the menu is unapologetic in its simplicity, which means fried fish baskets, burgers, and barbecue chicken legs served alongside potent rum swizzles, buckets of beer and frozen drinks.

Horseshoe Bay Beach. www.fb.com/RumBumBeachBar. ☏ **441/238-0088.** Main courses $5–$17. May–Oct Mon–Fri 9am–8pm, Sat–Sun 10am–8pm. Bus: 7 or 8.

WARWICK PARISH

Expensive

Blû ★★★ INTERNATIONAL/SUSHI Blû has always been something of a miracle worker. Its menu is thicker than *War and Peace,* the largest on the island. When we say there is everything you could possibly want to order on it, we're not exaggerating. But incredibly, they do it all very, very well. Want sushi? Blû offers inventive, NY-style rolls. In the mood for Asian-fusion fare or a classic bowl of ziti primavera? Both will be top drawer, as will the thick cuts of meat they sear, and the many seafood dishes served here. The setting is pleasing too, serene and sleekly minimal with floor-to-ceiling windows overlooking Hamilton Harbour to the east and Granaway Deep to the west. The summer sunset views are scintillating (ask for a corner table). Prices are high, but as the only truly upscale restaurant in this corner of Bermuda, they don't have any problem finding customers (so get reservations).

In the Clubhouse of the Belmont Hills Golf Course, 25 Belmont Hills Dr. www.blu.bm. ☏ **441/232-2323.** Main courses $17–$47. Daily 6–10pm, Sun brunch 11:30am–2pm. Bus: 8.

Moderate

The Swizzle South Shore ★ PUB GRUB This is the sister restaurant of the original Swizzle Inn (p. 147), which first opened in Bailey's Bay in 1932 and is credited with inventing the Bermuda Rum Swizzle. It's not quite as vibrant as that beloved dive bar, but it is a solid choice for a casual lunch, dinner or yes, pitchers of its namesake cocktail—a potent punch made with Gosling's Black Seal and Gold rums, pineapple and orange juices, a dash of angostura bitters and a local sweetener called falernum—strained into small, stemmed cocktail glasses. Here you can nosh on burgers, sandwiches and other bar food while sitting on its outdoor roadside patio or grab a seat inside its dining room that looks much like a traditional English pub.

87 South Rd. www.swizzleinn.com. ☏ **441/236-7459.** Main courses $15–$32. Daily 11am–1am. Bus: 7 or 8.

Divots ★ PUB GRUB This unfussy sports bar is where to go after you've played 18 holes at Belmont Hills Golf Course or if you'd like a low-key place to unwind with a beer and a great view of Granaway Deep. Expect a basic

Dinner music in Bermuda is not hard to come by—you just know where to find it. One of the most prolific local musicians is guitarist Tony Brannon, who fronts a laid-back lounge act known as **The Big Chill** (www.the-big-chill.com). Playing mellow grooves similar to what you'd hear on an Ibiza beach, this trio makes the rounds at popular island restaurants like **Sea Breeze** at the Elbow Beach Hotel, the **Hamilton Princess Beach Club** in Southampton and **The Pink Beach Club** at The Loren from May through October (and at

select venues in winter). Another popular spot to catch live music is at **The Dock,** an open-air tapas lounge adjacent to the Waterlot Inn where you can hear ukulele impresario Mike Hind strum classic cover tunes in front of a quiet bay. And for lively reggae and soul favorites, check out who's playing at **Marcus'** located at the Hamilton Princess Hotel. The lineup and schedule often changes, but this popular restaurant often hosts live bands during dinner hours on Thursday, Friday and Saturday nights.

menu of burgers, sandwiches and salads, plus predictable starters like wings and chili. One nice perk here: Children who eat from the kiddie menu eat free on Wednesday nights.

In the Clubhouse of the Belmont Hills Golf Course, 25 Belmont Hills Dr. www.divots. bm. (*) **441/434-8687.** Main courses $15–$27. Tues–Fri 11am–10pm; Sat 9am–10pm; Sun 9am–9pm. Bus: 8.

PAGET PARISH

Expensive

Fourways Inn ★★★ STEAK & SEAFOOD   Housed in a restored 17th-century cottage with handsome stone archways, antique paintings and white-clothed tables set with silver and crystal, this upscale restaurant oozes old-school Bermuda. For that reason, and because it's also the main restaurant of the attached cottage colony that bears the same name, it attracts an older crowd of repeat guests who love it because it simply hasn't changed very much over the years. That goes for the menu, too, which features classic preparations of French and Continental cuisine like escargots in garlic cream, hazelnut crusted foie gras and hearty mains like chateaubriand for two and veal tenderloin (it's also famous for its steakhouse classics, like prime cuts of beef and decadent sides of creamed spinach and truffle fries). Whatever you do, don't pass up dessert, since Fourways serves the island's best soufflés.

1 Middle Rd., Paget Parish. www.fourways.bm. (*) **441/236-6517.** Reservations required. Main courses $36–$54. Mon–Sat 6:30–9pm, Sun brunch 11:30am–2pm. Bus: 8.

Mickey's Beach Bistro ★★★ SEAFOOD   Almost as iconic as the beach it sits on, Mickey's is a Bermuda classic. Located just twenty yards from the surf, right on Elbow Beach, every table has a view of the turquoise coastline, making this a perfect spot for breezy long lunches or romantic moonlit dinners. Astonishingly, the food is as stellar as the views, especially if you concentrate on treats from the ocean, like grilled line-caught fish (usually tuna, wahoo, or mahi-mahi); mussels and manilla clams in a garlic white wine broth; or its grilled seafood platter with octopus, shrimp, mahi-mahi and scallops.

Elbow Beach Hotel, 60 South Rd. © **441/236-9884.** Reservations recommended. Lunch main courses $20–$39; dinner main courses $28–$55. Daily noon–3pm and 6–9pm. Bus: 1, 2, or 7.

Beau Rivage ★★★ CONTINENTAL   Spearheaded by critically acclaimed chef Jean Claude Garzia—he was awarded the "Meilleur Ouvrier de France" in 1998 (France's highest honor for a chef)—Beau Rivage features an ever-changing menu of classic Continental dishes. Favorites include fois gras with a sauternes sauce, niçoise salad with grilled Bermuda tuna, Provençal-style lamb chops, and beef wellington with truffle sauce and tiger shrimp. Desserts are gloriously Gallic: crème brûlée, apple tarte tatin, and a soufflé of the day. For a special night, reserve the chef's table, an 8- to 12-seat table inside the kitchen where patrons are treated to a five-, seven-, or nine-course meal of the chef's choosing. The dining room is quite handsome and features panoramic views.

Newstead Belmont Hills Golf Resort & Spa, 27 Harbour Rd. www.newsteadbelmont hills.com. © **441/232-8686.** Lunch main courses $14–$40; dinner main courses $32–$52. Daily breakfast 7–10:30am, lunch 11:30am–2:30pm, dinner 6:30–11pm. Bus: 8.

Café Lido ★★ SEAFOOD   Think of this as a slightly more upmarket Mickey's Beach Bistro. It's in the same resort complex, with the same superb views, but from indoors. So you'll see that gorgeous swatch of blush-colored sand through the windows; at night they shine floodlights on the surf, an alluring sight. We like the Lido for an adult night out (families are firmly "encouraged" to eat at the resort's more casual sister restaurants, which include Seabreeze; see below). Here you'll find expensive but expertly prepared plates of Mediterranean-inspired seafood, hearty cuts of meat and one of the few dessert menus in Bermuda with an international cheese plate.

Elbow Beach Hotel, 60 South Rd. www.lido.bm. © **441/236-9884.** Dinner main courses $28–$42. Daily 6:30–9pm. Bus: 1, 2, or 7.

Moderate

Sea Breeze ★ SUSHI/TAPAS   If Mickey's and the Lido are full, this is your third choice for dining—and yes, it is a definite *third* choice—at the Elbow Beach Resort. An outdoor cocktail lounge with low-slung wicker couches and chairs, food seems to be a bit of an afterthought here, though you can get decent sushi and tapas. That being said, it is a fun place to hang, especially on the nights it has live music.

Elbow Beach Hotel, 60 South Rd. www.lido.bm. © **441/232-3999.** Dinner main courses $10–$16. Breakfast 7–11am, dinner 5–9:30pm. Bar 5pm–midnight. Bus: 1, 2, or 7.

Inexpensive

Paraquet Restaurant ★ DINER   You're more likely spot local cab drivers on their break than tourists eating at this no-frills roadside diner. Serving simple homecooked food, the Paraquet is where Bermudians go to get a cheap but tasty meal served reasonably fast (at $5.75, its hamburger is probably the least expensive in Bermuda).

68 South Rd. www.paraquetrestaurant.com. © **441/232-2253.** Main courses $5–$27. Daily 8am–midnight. Bus: 7 or 8.

Homer's Café ★★★ CAFE   Named for the 19th-century artist Winslow Homer, who famously painted many Bermuda landscapes, this cozy cafe is set inside the **Masterworks Museum of Bermuda Art**—a fitting location since many of the dishes it serves are artfully created. Order an avocado toast and you'll be treated to a fan of bright green avocado, drizzled with balsamic reduction and topped with dainty pickled onions and crumbled queso fresca; try a fruit or vegetable smoothie and you'll be eating your garnish, typically fresh mint picked from the garden; or dig into one of its Mexican specialties like *mollete,* a flat bread with guacamole, refried beans and salsa fresca. Whatever you choose, have your food brought to you in the pleasant outdoor courtyard where you'll sit within eyeshot of a large steel sculpture commemorating John Lennon's time spent writing songs on the island.

Masterworks Museum of Bermuda Art, Botanical Gardens, 183 South Rd. www.bermuda masterworks.org. © **441/299-4001.** Lunch main courses $5–$10. Mon–Sat 9am–4pm. Bus: 1 or 9.

Ice Queen ★ FAST FOOD   The closest thing Bermuda has to McDonald's is this hole-in-the-wall takeaway place. It's open all day long, but you'll find mostly Bermudians queued up at night, long after the Hamilton bars have closed, to scarf down greasy burgers and fried fish sandwiches. As its name suggests, the place is also a go-to for soft serve ice cream and milkshakes. Bring cash; credit cards are not accepted.

Rural Hill Plaza. www.fb.com/IceQueenBermuda. © **441/236-3136.** Sandwiches and sides $6–$10. Daily 10am–5am. Bus: 7 or 8

CITY OF HAMILTON (PEMBROKE PARISH)

Bermuda's capital is also the island's biggest transportation hub, which means getting to the City of Hamilton for breakfast, lunch or dinner is as easy as hopping on any bus heading east from points west or vice versa. The public ferry is another good option, however for both modes of transportation, check schedules since times and routes sometimes change.

Expensive

Barracuda Grill ★★★ SEAFOOD   When Hollywood super-couple Michael Douglas and Catherine Zeta-Jones used to live in Bermuda, this was the restaurant they patronized most frequently. Maybe it was the expertly prepared seafood or perhaps, the dimly lit dining room and nicely spaced tables, both of which provide unusual privacy and the ability to have a eavesdrop-proof conversation. Whatever the reason, this City of Hamilton favorite remains one of Bermuda's best, even if today's VIPs are power-lunching

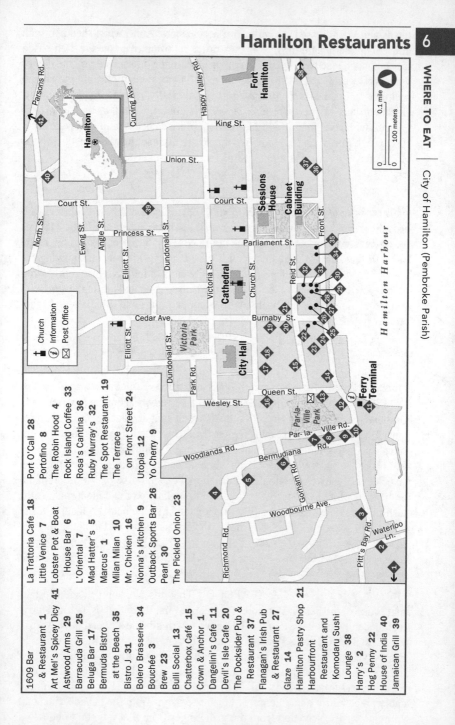

1609 Bar
& Restaurant **1**
Art Mel's Spicey Dicy **41**
Astwood Arms **29**
Barracuda Grill **25**
Beluga Bar **17**
Bermuda Bistro
at the Beach **35**
Bistro J **31**
Bolero Brasserie **34**
Bouchée **3**
Brew **23**
Bulli Social **13**
Chatterbox Café **15**
Crown & Anchor **1**
Dangelini's Cafe **11**
Devil's Isle Cafe **20**
The Docksider Pub &
Restaurant **37**
Flanagan's Irish Pub
& Restaurant **27**
Glaze **14**
Hamilton Pastry Shop **21**
Harbourfront
Restaurant and
Komodaru Sushi
Lounge **38**
Harry's **2**
Hog Penny **22**
House of India **40**
Jamaican Grill **39**

La Trattoria Cafe **18**
Little Venice **7**
Lobster Pot & Boat
House Bar **6**
L'Oriental **7**
Mad Hatter's **5**
Marcus' **1**
Milan Milan **10**
Mr. Chicken **16**
Nonna's Kitchen **9**
Outback Sports Bar **26**
Pearl **30**
The Pickled Onion **23**

Port O'Call **28**
Portofino **8**
The Robin Hood **4**
Rock Island Coffee **33**
Rosa's Cantina **36**
Ruby Murray's **32**
The Spot Restaurant **19**
The Terrace
on Front Street **24**
Utopia **12**
Yo Cherry **9**

129

locals and well-dressed socialites not movie stars. Amid walls sheathed with unusual modern paintings, you can order a roster of exquisite fish-based dishes that change with whatever comes in from local fishermen on the day of your arrival (imported fish is also served). The best examples are the seared rockfish with a Dark n' Stormy glaze and locally foraged loquat chutney. Decadent cuts of meat are also *de rigueur*, like the beef tasting, a meata-palooza with boursin-stuffed filet mignon, braised cheeks, and sous vide short ribs. *Tip:* If you're up for some live music after dinner, head downstairs to the Hog Penny pub, which often features local acoustic acts.

5 Burnaby Hill. www.barracuda-grill.com. ☎ **441/292-1609.** Lunch main courses $20–$36; dinner main courses $27–$71. Mon–Fri noon–2:30pm, daily 5:30–10pm.

Bolero Brasserie ★★★ CONTINENTAL   Helmed by Chef Johnny Roberts, this Front Street favorite offers a seasonal menu of French bistro classics like steak tartare, escargot and duck confit. But don't expect it all to be on the menu during a return visit since Chef Roberts prides himself on changing the menu daily, depending on what's fresh (or what's biting). No matter what you order, you can expect to do it in an artfully decorated dining room with vaulted ceilings, exposed beans, whimsical paintings and a harbor view second-story balcony.

95 Front St. www.bolerobrasserie.com. ☎ **441/292-4507.** Lunch main courses $18–$50; dinner main courses $25–$50. Mon and Sat 6–10pm; Tues–Fri noon–2:30pm and 6–10pm.

Harbourfront Restaurant & Komodaru Sushi Lounge ★★★ INTERNATIONAL/SEAFOOD/SUSHI   Located adjacent to the Bermuda Underwater Exploration Institute, this is an elegant and accomplished restaurant. It has quiet dockside tables where you can sit outside next to the water and a chic indoor dining room that looks out upon Hamilton Harbour. Wherever you choose to sit, you'll watch boats bobbing on their moorings as you dine on an eclectic, creative selection of international cuisine (like pan-fried branzino on truffled white bean puree) in addition to its lineup of excellent maki rolls, sashimi, and other Asian fare (like the togarachi roll, a beloved local favorite made with spicy tuna, Japanese mayo, tobiko, scallions, and tempura bits).

40 Crow Lane, E. Broadway. www.harbourfront.bm. ☎ **441/295-4207.** Lunch main courses $16–$44; dinner main courses $19–$44. Daily lunch 11:45am–2:30pm, dinner 6–9:30pm, sushi 5–9:30pm.

Harry's ★★★ STEAK & SEAFOOD   This upscale, sophisticated restaurant is one of the best in Bermuda for steak lovers. In the 1950s, before Harry, its founder, boarded the Pan Am Clipper to Bermuda, he stopped in New York to dine at a then-famous steakhouse named Peter's Backyard. His meal was so exceptional he returned to Bermuda with a suitcase full of sirloin, the first unfrozen prime beef that island had ever seen. Decades later, based on that experience, Harry's beef is still full of flavor, aged for 21 days, and impeccably prepared for an audience of businesspersons from the island's financial community. The selection from the grill ranges from filet mignon to boneless rib-eye to double thick Welsh lamb chops. It's also an excellent spot for sea-food, and for small bites: Head to the bar, where you can sit on high top tables and choose from a menu of small plates while sipping a proprietary batch of Gosling's rum especially blended for the restaurant (it's served from a mini barrel behind the bar). The waterfront patio, where you can watch sailboats pull in and out of Hamilton Harbour, is perfect for a breezy lunch.

96 Pitts Bay Rd. www.harrys.bm. © **441/292-5533.** Lunch main courses $12–$42; dinner main courses $32–$65. Mon–Sat noon–10pm.

Little Venice ★★ ITALIAN This is one of the most prominent Italian restaurants in Bermuda, a staple that has been here as long as anyone can remember. An enduring specialty is its veal saltimbocca—thin cut veal chops with prosciutto, marsala wine and fresh Bermuda sage. Other popular dishes include sous vide octopus with tomatoes, olives, capers and basil and an array of fresh pastas (including an excellent seafood gnocchi with shrimp, mussels, scallops, clams, and fresh local catch in a saffron cream). Its wine bar features one of the largest selections of wine in Bermuda, including several large format bottles, which is one of the reasons why you'll see this restaurant brimming with well-dressed locals at the stroke of 5pm.

32 Bermudiana Rd. (btw. Par-la-Ville Rd. and Woodbourne Ave.). www.littlevenice.bm. © **441/295-3503.** Lunch main courses $25–$42; dinner main courses $27–$46. Mon–Fri lunch noon–2pm, Mon–Sat dinner 6pm–closing.

Mad Hatter's ★★★ CONTINENTAL It might take some doing to find this well-hidden restaurant in northwestern Hamilton—it's located at the northern most end of Bermudiana Road, across from the Robin Hood pub and the Esso Gas Station. But once you get there, you'll be rewarded with some of the most inventive European cuisine in Hamilton. Named after the beloved Alice in Wonderland character, the restaurant is no less whimsical: Here you'll be asked to don one of its in-house collection of hats (pirate, court jester, Rasta dreads, or the like) before being sat at one of its cozy tables. Then you'll dive down the rabbit hole into an exquisite culinary world created by head chef Ben Jewett. Appetizers include jumbo lump blue crab cakes with sweet chili and ginger aioli, mussels in Thai coconut curry and a cognac and wild game pate served with sweet wine jelly and forest fruit compote. Entrees are equally as inventive—don't miss the Hoof & Feather, a venison chop with breast of duck and calvados flamed pears—but make sure you listen to the specials before you order, since this restaurant has an ever-changing rotation of in-season dishes, which sometimes outshine the regular menu.

22 Richmond Rd. www.madhatters.bm. © **441/297-6231.** Lunch main courses $26–$30; dinner main courses $39–$46. Mon–Fri lunch noon–2pm, Mon–Sat dinner 6–9pm. Closed Sun and public holidays.

Marcus' ★★★ CARIBBEAN/SOUL FOOD When celebrity chef Marcus Samuelsson, a winner of Top Chef: Masters, opened this chic harbor front restaurant in 2017, he ushered in a new standard of fine dining in Bermuda. Not only did he raise the bar, he effortlessly leaped over it.

Start your experience at the bar, behind which large floor-to-ceiling windows allow natural light and harbor views to pour in through airy shelves filled with craft rums and other high-end spirits. Cocktails here are over-the-top fabulous, mixed by skillful bartenders using fresh, house made ingredients (like their very own cilantro syrup in the Collie Buddz Collins, a vodka highball named for Bermuda's biggest reggae star, with lemon juice, muddled cucumber, and elderflower tonic).

When you're ready to sit down, grab a table inside so you can watch the chefs in the open kitchen work their magic. (There's also outdoor seating with views of megayachts in the Princess Marina, but we prefer dinner and a show). And now starts the parade of smartly dressed waiters, a crew who are attentive, knowledgeable and well-trained in the art of hospitality—a hallmark of Samuelsson's restaurants worldwide. They'll talk you through the seasonally changing lineup of locally sourced foods. Marcus' brings bold flavors to Caribbean-style southern cuisine, like such appetizers as cornbread madeleines with honey butter and tomato jam; crispy buttermilk cauliflower with sesame mayo; and fish chowder bites with Gosling's black rum aioli, every bit the essence of the traditional Bermuda stew. Main courses dazzle, too, with favorites like the Sinky Bay snapper—local catch cooked in a whole banana leaf with cucumber and coconut curry sauce—and the Seafood Bermuda Triangle, a playful spin on paella with a small local lobster called guinea chick. You may want to return to the bar after the meal: Marcus' features live reggae well into the night on Thursday, Friday and Saturday. *Tip:* The Sunday champagne brunch is one of the best on Bermuda and requires reservations well in advance.

Hamilton Princess Hotel, 76 Pitts Bay Rd. www.thehamiltonprincess.com ℂ **441/295-3000.** Lunch main courses $18–$49; dinner main courses $26–$49. Mon–Sat noon–3pm and 6–10pm. Bar 5pm–midnight. Sun champagne brunch 11am–3pm ($95 with champagne, $54 without).

Port O' Call ★★★ SEAFOOD   Since its inception, Port O' Call has been one of the island's most reliably excellent restaurants. It's hugely popular among locals for its killer power lunch (you'll see brokers wheeling and dealing at each table); those same island bigwigs return after work to crowd the black granite bar at happy hour, and smoke cigars on the shady sidewalk patio. The menu features the usual suspects—steaks, seafood and pasta dishes. But several times a night, the day's fresh catch is paraded through the dining room, and after oohing and aahing at how fresh and beautiful the seafood is, most order that and are quite happy they did. From September through March, try a spiny lobster—with no claws and a bigger tail, it's a sweeter version of New England's finest. *Tip:* Portions here are HUGE, so don't be shy about sharing.

87 Front St. www.portocall.bm ℂ **441/295-5373.** Lunch main courses $16–$38; dinner main courses $21–$45. Mon–Fri noon–2:30pm, Mon–Sat 6–10:30pm.

Moderate

1609 Bar & Restaurant ★★ INTERNATIONAL   Named for the fateful year in which Bermuda's first settlers crashed upon St. George's shores, this seasonally open restaurant at the Hamilton Princess Hotel couldn't possibly be closer to the water. In fact, the handsome dining room, with its modern glass walls and giant retractable windows, is perched over Hamilton Harbour, giving its diners the distinct feeling that they're eating aboard a ship. 1609 offers an all-day-and-night menu of light bites, including fresh salads and flatbread pizza, plus a handful of specialties from sea and land (like a classic lobster roll—the only one of its kind served in Bermuda). Come just for drinks? Order up a pitcher of red or white wine sangria or even better, the 1609 mojo on tap, made with Goslings light rum, mint, fresh lime and passionfruit juice.

Hamilton Princess Hotel, 76 Pitts Bay Rd. www.thehamiltonprincess.com. © **441/295-3000.** Lunch and dinner main courses $17–$49. Daily 9am–9pm. Closed winter.

Astwood Arms ★ PUB GRUB

With an imposing mirrored and hardwood bar that dominates its cavernous dining room, this Victorian-styled pub serves everything you'd expect from a restaurant that exudes old-school Britain. Pick on tasty bar snacks like Scotch eggs, cheesy chips with Cumberland sausage and fried fish fingers or choose from an extensive lineup of pub grub favorites like steak & ale pie, Cornish pasty, or liver & onions, pan fried with bacon and mashed potatoes. Grab a table inside or enjoy a pint on its pleasant sidewalk patio for some of the best people-watching on Front Street.

85 Front St. www.astwoodarms.bm. © **441/292-5818.** Lunch main courses $13–$25; dinner main courses $18–$33. Mon–Sat 11am–midnight; Sun noon–5pm.

Beluga Bar ★★ SUSHI

The basement of a shopping mall may be the last place you'd think about going to indulge in fine sushi rolls and freshly prepared sashimi, but don't count out this excellent sushi bar located within the bowels of Washington Mall. At Beluga Bar you'll be served by an affable team of Italian waiters and bartenders, who'll serve up colorful creations by beloved sushi chef, Sammy Wong. Don't leave without trying the Diamond Dragon, a maki roll with spicy tuna and mango topped with torch-fired Cajun shrimp or the Sammy Roll, with soft shell crab, avocado, mango, tuna and salmon.

Washington Mall, 18 Church St. (lower level). www.belugabar.bm. © **441/542-2859.** Maki rolls $11–$19. Mon–Sat 11:30am–2:45pm and 6–10pm; Sun 5–9:30pm.

Bermuda Bistro at the Beach ★ INTERNATIONAL

Despite the promise of a beachfront within this restaurant's name, it occupies the ground floor of a commercial building in the center of downtown Hamilton with nary a grain of sand in sight. Still there's a sense of vacation fun from the cheerful staff here, and an ambience that's one of the closest things to spring break in town. We're talking big-screen presentations of sporting events; stiff, party-colored drinks; a boisterous crowd; and uncomplicated bar food that never pretends to even approach fine cuisine. As the menu promises, its food will "fill your belly" with items that include burgers, pizzas, pastas, steaks, and simple preparations of fresh fish. A patio in front offers a great spot for people-watching, and although the full menu stops at 10pm, bar snacks are offered until midnight every night. In sync with this place's role as a jumping late-night singles bar, a DJ spins tunes nightly from 10pm till closing.

103 Front St. (at Parliament St.). www.thebeachbermuda.com. © **441/292-0219.** Full breakfasts $17; burgers, sandwiches, and pizzas $13–$23; main courses $19–$35. Daily 9am–10pm. Bar menu until midnight. Bar 9am–3am.

Bistro J ★ INTERNATIONAL Busy with the Hamilton workforce who tuck in for a quiet meal since its located down a hidden cobblestone lane between Reid and Front Streets, this small bistro eschews a traditional a la carte menu for a fixed-price two- or three-course lunch and dinner menu (offerings are identical from menu to menu; you just choose more or less). The menu changes daily, so visit the restaurant's Facebook page for a glimpse of its blackboard specials. But you can expect an international lineup of dishes, with daily entrees that always include pasta, meat, fish and vegetarian options

7 Queen St. www.bistroj.bm. © **441/296-8546.** Lunch and dinner 2-course meal $34; 3 courses $40. Mon–Fri noon–2:30pm, Mon–Sat 6–10pm.

Brew ★★ CAFE Featuring Bermuda's only wine-on-tap bar, draft beers from the Dockyard Brewing Company, and a wide selection of handcrafted coffees—including its very own nitro brew that's served cold and black—this brand-new Front Street cafe is like Starbucks on steroids. In the morning dig into egg wraps, oatmeal bowls and fresh pastries and at lunch, try its hearty bowls and pre-made sandwiches. The cafe transforms into a bustling wine and beer bar at night, adding flatbread pizzas and guacamole for two come nightfall.

53 Front St. www.irg.bm. © **441/542-2739.** Breakfast $7.95–$11; lunch $12–$15; evening bites (flatbreads $11.95, guacamole for 2 $25). Mon–Wed 7am–9pm; Thurs–Fri 7am–11pm; Sat 8am–10pm; Sun 9am–6pm.

Bulli Social ★★ BURGERS Fashioned as a gourmet burger bar, Bulli Social's tables are spread under a canopy of trees in a cordoned off section of Par-la-Ville Park. Its high-end burgers are all made with grass fed beef. Also on the bill are creatively topped "dawgs" (like the chihuahua, a hot dog with smoked jalapenos, habanero cheddar, green onions, and cilantro). Our faves are among the most inventive: the Threesome, a trio of sliders that includes a classic burger, the Jammy Dodger (with blue cheese and bacon jam), and the I.E.D. (with smoked jalapenos and candied bacon). As a side dish, you can't do better than classic poutine: French fries with gravy and your choice of toppings.

7 Queen St. www.bullisocial.com © **441/232-2885.** Lunch and dinner main courses $13–$20. Mon 11am–6pm; Tues–Sat 11am–closing.

Crown & Anchor ★ INTERNATIONAL Named for a popular Bermudian dice game that's played during the annual Cup Match cricket tournament, this chic, all-white restaurant is adjacent to the lobby of the Hamilton Princess Hotel. Even if you don't end up eating here, head in to see the museum-quality contemporary artwork on the walls of the hotel. And if you do dine here, it will be on sandwiches, pizza and hearty main courses. Grab a table on the outdoor terrace for views of the Princess Marina. In addition to breakfast, lunch and dinner, the restaurant also serves an elegant afternoon tea with petit fours and dainty finger sandwiches (weekends only; reservations required).

Hamilton Princess Hotel, 76 Pitts Bay Rd. www.thehamiltonprincess.com. (*) **441/295-3000.** Full breakfast $15; lunch and dinner main courses $17–$36. Buffet breakfast Mon–Fri 7–10:30am, Sat–Sun 7–11am. Daily all-day breakfast 7am–11pm, lunch 11am–5pm, dinner 5–11pm. Afternoon tea Sat–Sun 3–5pm (reservations required). Order food up to 10pm; bar closes at 1am.

Devil's Isle Café ★★★ INTERNATIONAL Winning our vote for best new restaurant on Bermuda, Devil's Isle is an angel when it comes to healthy eating. It has tons of options for both vegetarians and vegans (including an outrageously good sandwich with cashew cream, garlic spread, spinach, avocado, roasted tomato, and sprouts). And when it does do meat dishes, they are hormone free, and sourced from small farms. Its Harvest Bowls are a favorite, featuring fresh picked greens from local farms, as are its do-it-yourself Ramen Bowls which customers customize, picking their own noodles, broth, condiments and protein. If you want to get a little devilish, order one of their classic cocktails, some of which feature house-made liqueurs. Whatever you choose, you'll be enjoying it inside its industrially styled dining room that feels straight out of Williamsburg, Brooklyn (think hanging Edison bulbs and exposed metal ducts), or on its covered sidewalk patio, where you'll watch Hamilton's workforce scurry by during daylight hours. *A few tips:* If you've only got time for a smoothie, vegetable juice, or a really good cup of coffee (they roast their own beans), pop into its adjacent **Kaffe House,** which also sells small bites and to-go items. And if you're planning on sitting down for a meal, get a reservation. This place is tiny and hugely popular, even at lunchtime.

19 Burnaby St. www.devilsislecoffee.bm. (*) **441/292-3284.** Lunch and dinner main courses $10–$37. Cafe Mon–Thurs 8am–10pm; Fri 8am–11pm; Sat 9am–11pm; Sun 9am–10pm. Kaffe House Mon–Fri 7:30am–5pm; Sat 9am–5pm; Sun 9am–4pm. Reservations recommended.

The Docksider Pub & Restaurant ★ PUB GRUB Don't come to "Dockies" expecting gourmet cuisine, because that simply isn't part of the mentality of this sometimes rowdy drinking den where food is an afterthought to foaming mugs of beer, stiff drinks, and a crowd that roars its approval or disapproval of whatever's happening in the world of international sports. *Note:* Dockies has often opened its doors as early as 8am for TV broadcasts of major soccer, football, or rugby games from as far away as Australia.

121 Front St. www.docksider.bm. (*) **441/296-3333.** Main courses $11–$24. Daily 11:30am–9:30pm. Bar closes at 2am.

Flanagan's Irish Pub & Restaurant ★★ PUB GRUB Bermuda has many British pubs, but this is the only Irish one, and it's a lark. There's Guinness, Harp and Kilkenny on tap; shepherd's pie, fish & chips and bangers & mash on the menu; and Gaelic signs welcoming you inside, where of course, you'll be greeted by friendly bartenders who'll be happy to put your favorite sports game on for you. The pub is immediately across from the cruise ship docks in Hamilton, in a historic Front Street building.

In the Emporium Bldg., 69 Front St. www.flanagans.bm. © **441/295-8299.** Lunch main courses $11–$29; dinner main courses $13–$39. Daily 11am–5pm and 5–11pm. Bar Mon–Fri 11am–1am; Sat–Sun 9am–1am.

Hog Penny ★★ PUB GRUB The Hog Penny remains Bermuda's most famous and enduring watering hole, open since 1957, serving draft beer and ale to each new generation of mainlanders who head here, probably on the advice of their grandparents. The dark paneled rooms are decorated in the British style, with old fishing and farm tools, bentwood chairs, and antique mirrors. At lunch you can order pub specials (including shepherd's pie) or tuna salad and the like. The kitchen prepares several passable curries, including chicken and beef. Fish and chips and steak-and-kidney pie are the perennial favorites, and they are comparable to what you'd find in a London pub. Dinner is more elaborate; the menu might include a whole lobster, a fresh fish of the day (perhaps Bermuda yellowfin tuna), and excellent Angus beef. Hog Penny is also one of the few restaurants in town that features live nightly entertainment, so stick around for some of the best guitarists, singers and local acts on the island. Even the staff comments from time to time on this establishment's long-standing appeal as everyone's tried-and-true local: "We'll probably never redecorate, and we'll retain the same decor until the place falls down."

5 Burnaby Hill. www.hogpennypub.com. © **441/292-2534.** Lunch main courses $15–$27; dinner main courses $20–$29. Daily 11:30am–3pm and 5:30–10pm. Pub hours daily 11:30am–1am.

La Trattoria ★★ ITALIAN/PIZZERIA This family-oriented restaurant is tucked away in a narrow alley 2 blocks north of the City of Hamilton's harborfront. There's not a single cutting-edge or glamorous thing about it, and that's just what the loyal regulars like. The decor is straight out of old Naples, with a wood-burning pizza oven (the only one in Hamilton) and clear lacquered tabletops with hundreds of dried pasta noodles below. The attentive waitstaff serves generous portions of well-flavored Italian food. You'll find more than a dozen kinds of pizza, and the kitchen is happy to create variations for you. Pastas include lasagna and a delicious spaghetti *con ceci,* with chickpea sauce, shaved parmesan, and truffle oil. There are also heartier main courses (like the traditional veal marsala, pounded thin with mushrooms).

23 Washington Lane (in the middle of the block between Reid and Church sts.). www.latrattoria.bm. © **441/295-1877.** Pizzas $17–$19; lunch main courses $12–$29; dinner main courses $20–$35. Mon–Sat 11:30am–3:30pm, daily 5:30–10pm (to 10:30pm in summer).

The Lobster Pot & Boathouse Bar ★★ SEAFOOD A fixture on the Bermuda dining scene since 1973, the Lobster Pot is a perennial favorite for its campy nautical decor, fresh seafood specialties and award-winning Bermuda fish chowder—a spicy seafood stew traditionally served with a dash of Gosling's Black Seal rum and Outerbridge's Sherry Peppers sauce. And although the restaurant added an outdoor deck where meals can be enjoyed in

BERMUDA'S BEST fish sandwich

It's hard to find a restaurant in Bermuda that doesn't have fish sandwich on the menu. Next to the island's codfish and potatoes breakfast (typically served on Sat and Sun mornings) and bowls of hearty fish chowder, the fish sandwich is king—but not all are created equal. If you want a true taste of the island stick with a sandwich that's prepared Bermuda-style. That is, a deep-fried filet with cole slaw, lettuce, hot sauce and cheese served on raisin bread. Our picks:

o **Art Mel's Spicy Dicy** (9 St. Monica's Rd.; ℭ 441/295-3965): In Pembroke Parish, this hole-in-the-wall takeout place is commonly credited for creating the recipe. You'll lineup with locals for its shareable brick-sized sandwich.

o **The New Woody's Sports Bar & Restaurant** (1 Woody's Dr.;

ℭ 441/234-2082): This west end dive bar near Dockyard is where Bermudians gather to watch soccer and eat sandwiches with fried snapper or wahoo.

o **Mama Angie's** (48 York St.; ℭ 441/297-0959): The place to go in St. George's. After you get your order, have a picnic in nearby Somer's Garden.

o **The Swizzle Inn** (both outlets; see p. 147 and 125): Here you'll pair your sammys with pitchers of authentic Bermuda Rum Swizzle.

o **Rosa's Cantina** (121 Front St.; www.rosas.bm; ℭ 441/295-1912): Skip the tacos in favor of the winner of the Bermuda's Tourism Authority's Best Fish Sandwich Competition in 2015 (none have been held since). In the City of Hamilton.

the shade, not much else has changed in over 40 years. Its Bermuda stone walls are still trimmed with cedar planks; fishing nets, wooden oars and heavy brass bells still decorate most surfaces; and the feeling that you're dining in the bowels of an old sailing vessel permeates. Best of all, the food remains a consistently solid lineup of seafood dishes, including Bermuda cod fish cakes, conch fritters, Creole shrimp pasta and local catch of the day cooked Bermuda style, that is, pan fried with bananas and almonds.

6 Bermudiana Rd. www.lobsterpot.bm. ℭ **441/292-6898.** Lunch main courses $9–$36; dinner main courses $24–$40. Mon–Sat 11:30am–3pm, daily 5:30–11pm.

L'Oriental ★★ ASIAN/SUSHI Located just above Little Venice, this Pan-Asian restaurant gracefully mixes the cuisines of China, Malaysia, Thailand, and Japan. Within a mahogany-and-stone-lined room with bridges, a pagoda, and lots of Asian art, you'll find dimly lit tables, a sushi bar, and a *teppanyaki* table where a team of Japan-trained chefs prepares food on a super-hot grill in front of customers. That grilled fare is highly praised, as is the sushi here.

32 Bermudiana Rd. (above Little Venice restaurant). www.loriental.bm. ℭ **441/296-4477.** Lunch main courses $16–$30; dinner main courses $19–$60. Mon–Fri noon–2:15pm, Mon–Sat 6–10pm.

Outback Sports Bar ★ PUB GRUB This cavernous and windowless Front Street bar boasts 22 high-def televisions, the most in any Bermuda establishment. They're tuned to international sports matches: soccer, rugby, and cricket, plus baseball, football, basketball and hockey, if enough fans of the big four American sports are present. Because it's the sister bar to Flannagan's Irish Pub (located just next store), you'll find a similar menu of wings, burgers, sandwiches and hearty pot pies.

Emporium Building, 69 Front St. www.flanagans.bm. © **441/295-8299.** Lunch main courses $11–$29; dinner main courses $13–$39. Mon–Sat noon–1am; Sun 10am–6pm.

Pearl ★★★ SUSHI   Inventive preparations of fresh, locally caught fish, are the lure at this swank sushi bar just upstairs from Port O' Call on Front Street. In fact, we'd say Pearl has the very best sushi in Bermuda. Many of the dishes on the menu were invented here, like the rockfish *usuzukuri,* made with thin slices of local rockfish dressed in rice wine vinegar, toasted sesame oil, pickled onion and ginger or the hamachi carpaccio, local fish drizzled with jalapeno chili, garlic oil, cilantro and ponzu sauce. There's plenty to choose from, but often the best strategy is to allow the chefs to prepare you something special from whatever's been biting today. For seating, guests have a choice of the second-story outdoor balcony (nice views of the harbor) or the bustling dining room (nice views of the expert sushi chefs working their magic).

87 Front St. www.pearl.bm. © **441/295-9150.** Lunch and dinner main courses $12–$21. Mon–Fri noon–2:30pm and 5–10pm; Sat 6–10pm.

The Pickled Onion ★★ INTERNATIONAL   Think of this as much nicer version of T.G.I. Friday's: well-suited for families, with a something-for-everyone menu of sandwiches, salads, burgers, flatbread pizza, and entrees, all of which are consistently high quality. This place gets pretty busy with the lunch work crowd so if you're headed here midday, skip the ho hum dining room and make a reservation for its outdoor balcony, which overlooks Hamilton Harbour. The "P.O." (as it's called locally) is also a hopping after-dark venue—when the dinner hour is done, the tables and chairs are pushed to the side and live bands and/or DJs take over from Tuesday through Saturday.

53 Front St. www.thepickledonion.com. © **441/295-2263.** Lunch main courses $13–$30; dinner main courses $15–$40. Daily lunch 11:30am–5pm, dinner 5:30–10pm. Bar 11am–1am.

Portofino ★ ITALIAN   The warm and inviting decor of this trattoria, complete with hanging lamps and brick accent walls, evokes northern Italy. This place has its devotees, and some locals insist that it's the most romantic-looking Italian restaurant in Bermuda. Reliably tasty traditional fare, including 9-inch personal pizzas, is part of the appeal. If you'd prefer to eat outside, head to the pleasant sidewalk patio that's draped in colored lights at night.

20 Bermudiana Rd. www.portofino.bm. © **441/292-2375.** Pizzas $20; lunch main courses $13–$30; dinner main courses $15–$40. Mon–Fri 11:45am–2pm, daily 5:30pm–closing.

The Robin Hood ★ PUB GRUB   Woodsy-looking and percolating in a sense of nostalgia for Merrie Olde England, this comfortably rustic tavern has evolved into the local watering hole for many of Pembroke Parish's nearby residents. No one will mind if you drop in just for a drink or two, and many of your fellow elbow-benders traditionally do that many nights until the closing bell.

But if you're in the mood for food as well, you'll find the kind of fare that goes well with liquor and suds (that is, pizzas, burgers, steaks, and curries). In addition to airing live sporting events, the Robin Hood also hosts a popular Quiz Night on Tuesdays, when locals pack the place to flex their trivia muscles.

25 Richmond Rd. www.robinhood.bm. 𝒞 **441/295-3314.** Lunch salads and sandwiches $8–$13; pizzas $12–$29; main courses $11–$28. Daily 11am–10pm. Bar until 1am.

Rosa's Cantina ★★ MEXICAN Are we sending you here for spicy south-of-the-border cuisine? Yes and no. Most people go to Rosa's for the fish sandwich—the restaurant took first prize in the Bermuda Tourism Authority's Best Fish Sandwich Competition in 2015 (none have been held since). And we think its Mexican specialties, of which there are many, are also topnotch: burritos, chimichangas, quesadillas, tacos, and more.

121 Front St. www.rosas.bm. 𝒞 **441/295-1912.** Sandwiches, tacos, burritos, and fajitas $15–$23; main courses $20–$42. Sun and Tues–Thurs 11:30am–10pm; Fri–Sat 11:30am–11pm.

Ruby Murray's ★★ INDIAN Tucked away in a quiet, cobblestone alley off Front Street—take a selfie on the colorful stairs are illuminated by dozens of hanging lights—this sparsely decorated restaurant serves classic Indian cuisine with aplomb. Its menu covers traditional North Indian favorites, such as chicken tikka masala and lamb vindaloo, and adds in less well-known dishes from other parts of the subcontinent, like Goan coconut fish curry and *nalli goscht,* slow braised lamb shank with green chili, ginger, onion, and tomato.

Chancery Lane (off Front St.). www.rubymurrays.bm. 𝒞 **441/295-5058.** Lunch and dinner main courses $15–$29. Mon–Fri noon–2:30pm, Mon–Sun 5–10pm.

The Terrace on Front Street ★★ INTERNATIONAL Spiny lobster, a sweet, clawless cousin of the New England variety, is one of Bermuda's priciest specialties. Usually. But at the Terrace whole lobsters go for the good-for-Bermuda price of $59 (other restaurants typically charge $75). You can get yours curried, thermidor style or broiled with shrimp stuffing and each comes with a choice of two sides (for the same price, you can also get surf and turf: half a lobster with a 6-oz. filet mignon). Ask for a table on the outdoor veranda overlooking Hamilton Harbour; the patchwork decor of its main dining room is unimpressive at best. *Note:* The season for spiny lobster is September through March.

55 Front St. www.thetterracebermuda.com. 𝒞 **441/292-7331.** Lunch main courses $15–$26; dinner main courses $17–$59. Mon–Sat 11am–closing.

Utopia ★ ASIAN Wedged between a row of Front Street retailers and directly across from the public ferry dock, this eclectic restaurant has one of the very best views of Hamilton and its open-air roof deck has a lively cocktail bar that packs with locals on Friday nights. Because of its prime downtown location, Utopia tends to fill up for lunch with the Hamilton workforce who enjoy its urban Asian cuisine (like Korean chicken wings, Vietnamese pho, or Thai curry bowls), but don't overlook this three-story restaurant for dinner, specifically on Saturday night when it serves a traditional Ethiopian spread, with lamb,

Boundary (p. 123)   If the dozens of high-def TV's, which cover its walls and air popular international sports, aren't enough to keep your kids' attention, then certainly the billiards table, shuffleboard and Jenga will. Combine that with a family-friendly menu of down-home southern favorites and your kids might never want to leave.

The Frog & Onion (p. 119)   Beyond its approachable pub grub menu, this is where your family can dine inside a huge stone fireplace that was used to forge iron hoops for wooden barrels in the 1800s. There's also a boisterous video arcade located in the very back of the restaurant.

The Swizzle Inn (p. 147)   What kid wouldn't want to draw on the walls after a meal? That's right: Patrons of this beloved Bailey's Bay dive bar are encouraged to scribble graffiti on the walls or pin up their business card.

La Trattoria (p. 136)   This Italian restaurant serves Bermuda's best brick oven, wood-fired pizza. And the staff seem to genuinely enjoy serving kids, a big plus.

The Village Pantry (p. 145)   Make your own pizzas (you get the uncooked dough and lots of topping choices) and an open-air play area make the Village Pantry nirvana for families.

chicken and lentil dishes plus hearty sides like spinach and potatoes, cabbage and carrots, served along traditional *enerja* (Ethiopian bread made of teff flour). 17 Front St. www.utopia.bm. ⓒ **441/296-8788.** Lunch and dinner main courses $10–$26. Mon–Sat 11am–3pm, Tues–Sat 6–10pm.

Inexpensive

Art Mel's Spicy Dicy ★★ BERMUDIAN   A take-out spot for classic Bermuda fish sandwiches. Made with battered swai (a thin, flaky white fish similar to tilapia), its sandwiches are brick-sized behemoths that can easily be shared (most locals order one for lunch and save the other half for dinner). 9 St. Monica's Rd. ⓒ **441/295-3965.** Fish sandwich $13. Tues–Fri noon–10pm; Sat noon–8pm. **Note:** There is no bus service to Art Mel's.

Bouchée ★★ FRENCH   Arguably Bermuda's best breakfast spot, Bouchée features a lengthy eggs Benedict menu (including Norwegian style with smoked salmon; Portuguese style with chorizo, onions, and potatoes; and the *Homard,* with lumps of Maine lobster) plus pancakes, Belgian waffles, and whatever else you could possibly want before you set out on a day's adventure. The restaurant is on the western edge of Front Street, not far from the Hamilton Princess Hotel and near a row of office buildings, meaning it also gets crowded for lunch, when local workers come for French classics like chicken cordon bleu, croque-monsieurs, and quiches of all kinds. In the Outerbridge Bldg., 75 Pitts Bay Rd. www.bouchee.bm. ⓒ **441/295-5759.** Full breakfasts $10–$14; lunch main courses $14–$21; dinner main courses $18–$30. Daily 7:30am–2:30pm, Tues–Sat 6–9pm.

Chatterbox Cafe ★ CAFE   Another one of Hamilton's most consistently crowded lunch spots (it serves hundreds of office workers daily), Chatterbox boasts big voyeuristic front windows that allow peek-a-boo views of the passersby outside. Its most popular choices are pastries, sandwiches, and salads made to order; heartier dishes may include lasagna, grilled chicken or cod fish cakes—the menu changes daily.

In the Washington Mall, Reid St. © **441/295-3263.** Sandwiches $7–$12; daily specials $9–$11. Mon–Sat 6:30am–5pm; Sun 6:30am–3pm.

Mr. Chicken ★★★ FAST FOOD

Don't even think about walking into KFC (the only American restaurant chain in Bermuda). Why would you when located just two doors down from the Colonel is this beloved family-owned fried chicken shack? With crispy fried chicken sandwiches, tender chicken nuggets and fried chicken combo boxes with wings, thighs, and breasts served with cole slaw and cornbread muffins, this no-frills fast food joint has been serving droves of islanders inexpensive meals since it opened in 1985. *Tip:* For a real Bermuda breakfast, stop by on Sunday mornings when it serves traditional codfish and potatoes with all the trimmings.

27 Queen St. www.fb.com/mrchicken. © **441/292-6109.** Chicken sandwich $7.50; 6-piece chicken nuggets $5; 3-piece chicken dinner $13; codfish breakfast $16. Mon–Thurs 11am–10pm; Fri–Sat 11am–4am; Sun 8am–7pm.

D'angelini's Cafe ★★ BAKERY/CAFE

Located next to the public ferry dock in downtown Hamilton and a stone's throw from the gleaming new Visitor Services Center, this Italian-owned cafe serves fresh baked scones, croissants and muffins, plus a wide selection of hot pressed panini sandwiches (the menu changes daily, and they often sell out fast). Grab a seat inside or enjoy your espresso or cappuccino at one if its outdoor harbor front tables.

8 Front St. www.dangeliniscafe.com. © **441/295-5272.** Baked goods $2–$6; sandwiches $6–$8. Mon–Fri 7:30am–5pm; Sat 7:30am–4pm.

House of India ★★★ INDIAN

It may take some doing to find this hole-in-the-wall curry house on the northern edge of Hamilton—known locally as "backatown," which is Bermudian slang for "back of town"—but once you arrive, you'll be rewarded with some of the island's finest Indian cuisine. Because the setting is no frills, we'd suggest you head to the takeout counter (among the busiest in Bermuda), where locals line up nightly for the northern Indian-style vegetarian, beef, lamb, and chicken dishes, spice level moderated upon request. We particularly like the chicken tikka masala with its sweet and spicy cream sauce and the beef rogan josh, a hearty curry with yogurt and tomatoes. In addition to its a la carte dinner menu, the restaurant also features a daily lunch buffet.

Park View Plaza, 58A North St. www.houseofindia.biz. © **441/295-6450.** Lunch buffet $15; main courses $16–$23. Mon–Wed dinner 5:30–9pm, Thurs–Sun dinner 5–9:30pm, Mon–Fri lunch buffet 11:30am–2:30pm.

Jamaican Grill ★ CARIBBEAN/SOUL FOOD

Also in the "back of town," an area which, frankly, should only be visited during daylight hours, this super casual restaurant specializes in Jamaican and other West Indian dishes. Geared mostly to the takeout crowd who place their orders downstairs,

SATISFY YOUR sweet tooth

Thanks to a trio of sweet shops located on the western edge of Hamilton, it's easy to find a treat when candied cravings call. **Yo Cherry** (8 Bermudiana Rd.; www.yocherry.com; ✆ 441/292-2020) is known for ultra-creamy frozen custard, fruity sorbet or cups and cones of frozen yogurt in dozens of flavors. Guests self-sprinkle it all with more than 50 toppings (like chocolate "rocks," Sour Patch Kids, and marshmallows). Just next door is **Glaze** (10 Bermudiana Rd.; www.glaze.bm; ✆ 441/292-1122), a bakery and cafe with a sister location near City Hall on Church Street and a wide selection of fresh doughnuts, crullers and bite-sized holes (the glazed maple bacon doughnut is outrageous). Around the corner, is **Milan Milan** (3 Front St.; ✆ 441/293-3663), a cafe and gourmet food shop that sells traditional Italian treats like pistachio ricotta cheesecake, tiramisu, cannoli, and cookies of all kinds.

If you're closer to central Hamilton **The Hamilton Pastry Shop** (31 Reid St.; ✆ 441/295-2253), an outpost of the Dockyard original, sells delicate French pastries, apple turnovers and chocolate croissants. And if candy is your calling, make a beeline for **Treats** (The Washington Mall, 7 Reid St.; ✆ 441/296-1123). Located inside the Washington Mall nearest the Reid Street entrance, this tiny toy store sells traditional wrapped favorites (like Air Heads and Nerds) plus jelly beans and candy-by-the-piece. Fill a paper bag which will be weighed before you leave.

the restaurant has upstairs tables where you can dine on traditional dishes like jerk chicken, curried goat, and oxtail stew. Daily specials abound, but typical rotating dishes include ackee and saltfish, which is the national dish of Jamaica.

32 Court St. ✆ **441/296-6577.** Main courses $13–$29. Mon–Thurs 7am–9pm; Fri–Sun 7am–3pm.

Nonna's Kitchen ★ CAFE   If you're looking for an easy grab-and-go meal, head to this small cafe on Bermudiana Road. In addition to typical breakfast items in the morning and a full salad bar at lunch, Nonna's also features a revolving menu of hearty hot foods, like beef chili, pot pies and chicken curry.

4 Bermudiana Rd. www.nonnaskitchenbermuda.com. ✆ **441/295-7687.** Baked goods $2–$6; sandwiches $6–$8. Mon–Fri 7am–3pm.

Rock Island Coffee ★ BAKERY/CAFE   The java here (espresso, cappuccino, and more) is crafted from an international selection of beans roasted in-house. It can be sided by a fresh baked muffin, scone or pastry. There's limited seating inside, but if you can find one and you need to get online, Rock Island offers free Wi-Fi for all of its customers.

48 Reid St. www.rockisland.bm. ✆ **441/296-5241.** Coffee $3–$7; baked goods $2–$6. Mon–Fri 7am–6pm; Sat 8am–1pm.

The Spot Restaurant ★ DINER   Set on a street running downhill into downtown Hamilton's harbor, this local diner offers a welcome alternative to the high prices you're likely to find in many nearby restaurants. Originally established in the 1930s, and no-frills in looks, it attracts a clientele of off-duty police officers, cab drivers, and all kinds of local residents who appreciate the plentiful portions and lack of sticker shock. You'll find breakfast platters, West Indian specialties, and a full lineup of burgers, salads and sandwiches. No alcohol is served.

6 Burnaby St. ⊘ **441/292-6293.** Breakfast platters $7–$12; burgers, sandwiches, and salads $6–$13; main-course platters $8–$19. Mon–Sat 6:30am–10pm.

SMITH'S PARISH

Expensive

Island Brasserie ★★★ INTERNATIONAL   You'll be in good hands here, thanks to a team of well-trained waiters who serve meals with aplomb (a real treat, since service at many of the island's restaurants can be slow or inattentive). We'd suggest reserving a seat on open-air patio (lovely views of Castle Harbour) but the dining room, with its vaulted ceilings with exposed cedar beams and handsome blue banquettes, ain't too shabby, either (in fact, it defines elegance). On offer is a well-executed lineup of international fare, but consider ordering one of the chef's island-inspired favorites like honey rum glazed pork belly or the pan seared rockfish with banana and toasted almonds. *Fun fact:* The Pan Am Sky Club murals, which depict the world's great 19th-century seaports and hang on the walls as you enter, were commissioned for New York's Pan Am Building in 1965 by Pan Am Airways owner Juan Trippe. They were purchased at auction by his son Ed Trippe in 2006 and later installed in the restaurant, since the Trippe family owns part of the land that Rosewood Bermuda was built upon.

Rosewood Bermuda, 60 Tucker's Point Club Dr. www.rosewoodhotels.com. ⊘ **441/298-4000.** Lunch main courses $19–$38; dinner main courses $22–$38. Breakfast 7–11am, lunch 11am–5:30pm, dinner 5:30–10:30pm. Bus: 1 or 3.

Marée ★★★ INTERNATIONAL   Housed in a chicly minimalist glassed-in dining room at The Loren—an ultra-modern boutique hotel that opened in 2017 (p. 200)—this swanky restaurant serves price-fixed three- and four-course dinners only. Get here a little early so you can start your evening in the swellegent bar area (with its comfy banquettes and turned-out crowd). Then it's off to the dining room—crisp white linens, flickering candlelight and views of the sea—for a meal crafted from artisanal ingredients (sourced locally and from New England and New York). The menu changes often, but recent winners on it have ranged from charred octopus with chorizo to an arugula and bloomed basil salad to miso-glazed rockfish with charred bok choy, zucchini and saffron cream. For dessert, diners can select a traditional cheese plate, but that would mean missing the stupendous profiteroles with chocolate Grenache and pistachio ice cream. A top choice for special occasion dining.

The Loren, 116 South Rd., Tucker's Town. www.thelorenhotel.com. ⊘ **441/293-1666.** Reservations recommended. 3-course dinner $98. For an additional $27, add hor d'oeuvres and a cocktail. Tues–Sat 6–10pm. Bar Tues–Sat 5pm–midnight. Bar menu 5–11pm. Bus 1.

Sul Verde ★★★ ITALIAN Bermuda's best Italian restaurant, its name means "on the green," fitting since its outdoor balcony offers stunning views of Tucker's Point Golf Course (and Castle Harbour in the distance). That being said, the handsome indoor dining room is pretty swell, too, decked out in hardwoods and leather banquettes. The food is traditional southern Italian and expertly prepared whether you choose classic antipasto, house made pastas, or thin crust Neapolitan style pizza. Sul Verde also has a large selection of hearty entrees like eggplant parmigiana and sausage with spicy broccoli rabe. Here with a large group? Have the chef prepare a three-course, prix fixe, family-style dinner ($60 per person).

Rosewood Bermuda, 60 Tucker's Point Club Dr. www.rosewoodhotels.com. *(* **441/298-4000.** Lunch main courses $17–$30; dinner main courses $17–$42. Daily 11:30am–9:30pm. Bus: 1 or 3.

Moderate

Beach Club Restaurant ★★ INTERNATIONAL If you're searching for a breezy, oceanfront restaurant on the east end, don't miss this alfresco bistro located on the sands of Rosewood Bermuda's private beach club. At lunch you can sit alongside swimwear-clad hotel guests who've come from the beach or nearby pool to eat salads, sandwiches and a handful of signature dishes (like the cold seafood platter with lobster, crab claws, and blue point oysters, among others). And at dinner, don your best Bermuda shorts for a well-executed seafood selection, served under the stars.

Rosewood Bermuda, 60 Tucker's Point Club Dr. www.rosewoodhotel.com. *(* **441/298-4000.** Lunch main courses $18–$48; dinner main courses $18–$52. Daily 11:30am–3pm and 5:30–9:30pm. Bus: 1 or 3.

North Rock Brewing Company ★ PUB GRUB Despite what its name suggests, beer is not brewed at this traditional English pub near Collector's Hill. It does, however, serve locally brewed ales by On de Rock, a craft brewery that distributes kegs to a select group of bars and restaurants. What's on tap will depend on when you visit, but North Rock typically features at least three On de Rock beers at time including its IPA, Honey Ale and Belgian Blonde. When you're ready to eat, pick from a predictable menu of British pub grub (fish and chips and so forth) plus burgers, steaks, and heartier mains.

10 South Rd. *(* **441/236-6633.** Lunch main courses $15–$27; dinner main courses $19–$37. Daily noon–3pm and 6–9pm. Bar noon–9pm. Bus: 1.

The Pink Beach Club ★★★ INTERNATIONAL Situated on a wooden deck that seems to hover over the ocean, this airy seaside restaurant is the main dining room of The Loren (p. 200), meaning it's open for breakfast, lunch and dinner. It peaks at Sunday brunch, thanks to a three-course, priced-fix menu of truly imaginative breakfast dishes, like an eggs Benedict that comes with baby kale and braised short ribs and the curry tofu scramble with chick peas, braised greens and toasted naan. Meals later in the day also go international, but more broadly so than at other Bermuda venues; a lunch might include Vietnamese-style pork buns and a dinner chimichurri rubbed hanger steak. All will be delish.

The Loren, 116 South Rd., Tucker's Town. www.thelorenhotel.com. © **441/293-1666.** Lunch main courses $15–$26; dinner main courses $18–$48; brunch $50. Daily breakfast 7–11am, lunch 11am–5pm, dinner 5–10pm, Sun brunch 11am–3pm. Bus: 1.

Rustico ★★ ITALIAN/PIZZERIA You have three solidly good options for lunch after a visit to the Bermuda, Aquarium, Museum & Zoo: this place, AZU Beastro, and The Village Pantry (both below). You can see from the star ratings which one to pick, but if the Pantry is full, you won't be disappointed by the thin-crust pizzas or the tasty, homemade pastas here. Rustico is also casual enough to be kid friendly. Grab a table on its outdoor patio for views of Flatts Inlet.

36 N. Shore Rd. (in Flatts Village). www.bermuda-dining.com/rustico. © **441/295-5212.** Lunch main courses $14–$28; dinner main courses $14–$48. Mon–Thurs 11:30am–2:30pm and 5–10pm; Fri–Sat 11:30am–10pm. Bus: 10 or 11.

The Village Pantry ★★★ INTERNATIONAL This is an ideal spot to bring the kids for two potent reasons. It features an outdoor play with toys and a picnic table where tykes can blow off steam while the meal is being prepared. And what kid *doesn't* love a make-your-own pizza menu? Order one and your kids will get a dollop of uncooked dough and a selection of toppings that they can sprinkle on. For adults there are wholesome, often locally sourced dishes, like Korean poke bowls, French open-faced sandwiches, and Alsatian style flatbreads. Vegetarians and vegans are well taken care of, with lots of veggie offerings on the menu, and many items can be easily adapted to accommodate dietary requests. *Tip:* This small restaurant is often fully booked at lunch and dinner, so if you're stopping by before or after the Bermuda, Aquarium, Museum & Zoo be sure to make a reservation.

8 N. Shore Rd. (in Flatts Village). www.villagepantry.bm. © **441/478-2300.** Reservations recommended. Lunch and dinner main courses $17–$37. Daily 8am–10pm. Bus: 10 or 11.

Inexpensive

AZU Beastro ★ CAFE Located inside the Bermuda, Aquarium, Museum & Zoo (BAMZ), this small waterside cafe is fine for a quick, no-frills lunch. It serves a kid-friendly lineup of burgers, chicken nuggets, hotdogs and fries plus soups, salads and sandwiches. *Bonus:* It's directly beside the BAMZ's pirate-themed playground, so your kids can easily get their wiggles out on the slides, sandbox and climbing frames when snack time is over.

Bermuda Aquarium, Museum & Zoo, 40 N. Shore Rd., Flatts Village. http://bamz.org/azu. © **441/293-2727.** Lunch main courses $5–$15. Daily 9am–4pm. Bus: 10 or 11.

D&C Grill ★★ CARIBBEAN/SOUL FOOD Like its sister location in Southampton, D&C features a flavorful, ever-changing lineup of Jamaican and Caribbean specialties, like jerk chicken, barbecue ribs, braised oxtail,

| That Tastes *WELL*! |

If a dish tastes particularly delicious in Bermuda, and it's currently being enjoyed by a local islander who's licking his or her lips in blissful satisfaction, then perk your ears up for the ultimate compliment. No, you won't hear how "scrumptious" his fish sandwich was or how "delectable" her codfish cakes were. Other synonyms like "appetizing," "exquisite," or "heavenly" are barely in Bermuda's collective foodie lexicon. What you *will* hear however, is the boisterous phrase, "that tastes *well*!" which couldn't possibly be a higher accolade. If you want to make a Bermudian smile—and your meal was worthy of five stars—use it on your way out the door.

peas and rice, macaroni and cheese, and savory Johnny bread. Diners can eat in at a few small tables, but most grab the food and go.

69 Harrington Sound Rd., Devil's Hole. ⓒ **441/734-8717.** Lunch and dinner main courses $11 per pound. Mon–Thurs 7am–8pm; Fri 7am–10pm; Sat 8am–10pm. Bus: 1 or 3.

Rotisserie Grill ★ SOUL FOOD Slow-roasted rotisserie chicken served in quarter, half or whole portions along traditional side dishes like mac & cheese, peas and rice and collard greens—those are the offerings, and they're more than enough. Simply order at the walk-up counter, pay at the cashier and take your food to go, or grab a seat at one of the tables in its small dining room. It's located in a shopping center at the South Road end of Collector's Hill, so stop in if you're passing through this part of the island to points east or west.

8 South Rd. www.fb.com/therotisseriegrillbm. ⓒ **441/232-7444.** Lunch and dinner main courses $15–$38. Mon–Sat 11am–10pm; Sun 7:30am–8pm. Bus: 1.

Specialty Inn ★ DINER/SUSHI/BERMUDIAN Bermudian comfort food is what to get at this local's diner. It does really tasty versions of fish chowder, fried codfish cake sandwiches and on Saturday mornings from 6 to 11:30am, a traditional codfish and potato breakfast served Bermuda-style with boiled egg, avocado, banana, and tomato sauce. Its sushi bar is surprisingly good and does a heavy takeout business. No alcohol is served.

Collector's Hill, 4 South Rd. www.specialtyinn.bm. ⓒ **441/236-3133.** Lunch main courses $12–$20; dinner main courses $16–$28. Mon–Sat 6am–10pm. Bus: 1.

HAMILTON PARISH

Expensive

Tom Moore's Tavern ★ CONTINENTAL Originally built as a private home in 1652, this historic restaurant is where Irish poet Thomas Moore wrote some of his most well-known work while living there in the early 1800s (in fact, the calabash tree that he frequently refers to in some of his songs still stands near the restaurant to this day). The house still very much resembles its original self, which is why the inside of this somewhat dated restaurant has the feeling of your grandmother's dining room, with its carpeted floors and tufted floral chairs. But if you'd like a taste of old-school Bermuda charm, with a lineup of predictable international cuisine, this would be the place for you.

Walsingham Lane (in Bailey's Bay). www.tommoores.com. ℂ **441/293-8020.** Main courses $33–$51. Daily 6:30–10pm. Bus: 1 or 3.

Moderate

Swizzle Inn Bailey's Bay ★★ PUB GRUB   This landmark dive bar in Bailey's Bay is the original home of the Bermuda Rum Swizzle—a potent punch made with Gosling's Gold and Black Seal rums, pineapple and orange juices, a dash of angostura bitters and local sweetener called falernum. It's also Bermuda's oldest, since the casual restaurant opened in a 17th-century roadhouse in 1932. It's two fish sandwiches are among Bermuda's best (the Bailey's Bay, made with beer-battered fried snapper, and the Blue Hole, with island-spiced grilled wahoo), but don't skip the drinks—chiefly, its namesake rum swizzle, which is always served in iced-down pitchers and strained into small, stemmed cocktail glasses. Before you leave, pin your business card or scribble some graffiti on its walls and exposed wooden rafters. Yes, these activities are encouraged by management.

3 Blue Hole Hill (in Bailey's Bay). www.swizzleinn.com. ℂ **441/293-1854.** Lunch main courses $12–$20; dinner main courses $16–$32. Daily 11am–1am. Bus: 1, 3, 10, or 11.

Inexpensive

Bailey's Bay Ice Cream Parlour ★★ ICE CREAM   If you've got plans to visit the Crystal & Fantasy Caves in Bailey's Bay, then don't miss this family-friendly ice cream parlor, which is accessible via a shady tree-lined walkway. For all-natural, homemade ice cream, there's no comparable spot in Bermuda—the staff concocts at least 30 flavors in the shop's 40-quart ice-cream maker. You can enjoy Bermuda banana, coconut, cherries and white chocolate chips, or other exotic flavors at one of the outdoor tables.

2 Blue Hole Hill (in Bailey's Bay). www.fb.com/baileysbayicecream. ℂ **441/293-8605.** Ice cream $4.50 per scoop. No credit cards. Daily noon–7pm. Closed mid-Dec through Mar. Bus: 1, 3, 10, or 11.

ST. GEORGE'S PARISH

Except for a handful of restaurants located on the eastern tip of St. George's Parish, and one on St. David's Island, all of the below recommendations are in the Town of St. George's, which is accessible via buses 1, 3, 6, 10 or 11. For travelers searching for an affordable meal there's no better area, since the historic town features the highest concentration of moderate and inexpensive restaurants in Bermuda.

Expensive

Tempest Bistro ★★★ FUSION   Named for the Shakespearean play that was inspired by the real-life story of the *Sea Venture*—the ship that crashed upon Bermuda's shores in 1609—Tempest Bistro is housed in a handsome former military warehouse. With lanterns, exposed brick walls and wood-paneling, its setting is evocative of old school Bermuda. Its menu, however, is decidedly new school—the same chef/owners behind the City of Hamilton's whimsical Mad Hatter's (p. 131) are in charge here and they're an imaginative bunch. Recent dishes have included shrimp and scallop bourguignon, Mexican chile soup with corn fritters, and a splendid take on herb crab cakes. Service is warm and attentive. Because the restaurant gets a lot of repeat visitors, book well in advance.

22 Water St. www.fb.com/tempestbistro. ⓒ **441/297-0861.** Lunch main courses $17–$25; dinner main courses $33–$41. Wed–Sun noon–2pm, Mon and Wed–Sat 6–9pm.

Moderate

Blackbeard's ★★★ MEDITERRANEAN Snag an outdoor table and look out to sea: In 1609, the captain of the British ship *Sea Venture* purposefully sailed his vessel onto the very reefs you see in front of you. His ship, badly damaged by a hurricane, was foundering and only by wrecking it could he save the 150 souls aboard (they had been headed for the colony of Jamestown). You'll also see the jagged rocks that the survivors clambered onto, the first Westerners to set foot in Bermuda. Beyond them, Fort St. Catherine looms, one of the islands largest stone fortifications. If you were savvy enough to get a reservation for sunset, soon the sky will be streaked the pinks, purples, and oranges one usually sees only on orchids. This is, arguably, the best sunset view on the island, and inarguably, the most dramatic sea vista. And lucky you, you're seeing it all while dining on polished Mediterranean fare, and well-crafted cocktails. Sometimes life is good.

5 Coot Pond Rd., Fort St. Catherine's. www.stgeorgesclub.com. ⓒ **441/297-1200.** Main courses $22–$48. Daily 11:30am–10pm. Closed Nov–Mar.

The Wharf ★ INTERNATIONAL Situated on the St. George's waterfront, the Wharf has the largest outdoor dining area in the Town of St. George's. But don't let that stop you from a making a reservation since those coveted harbor view tables tend to go fast. The food isn't quite as scintillating as the views, but it's fine: pub grub, sandwiches and burgers at lunch, and a somewhat larger menu at dinner, which features much of the same plus a handful of international entrees (like chicken parmigiana, Wiener schnitzel, calves' liver, and surf and turf).

14 Water St. www.wharf.bm. ⓒ **441/297-3305.** Lunch main courses $10–$30; dinner main courses $20–$46. Daily 11:30am–10pm.

Wahoo's Bistro & Patio ★★★ SEAFOOD Wahoo's Bistro & Patio serves everything wahoo, a flaky white local fish that's as versatile as it is delicious. On the menu? Creamy wahoo chowder, smoked wahoo pâté, deep-fried wahoo nuggets, Baja-style wahoo tacos, ground wahoo burger or simply grilled wahoo with herbed butter, all served at tables on its waterfront patio. But even if you're not into wahoo you should still consider this narrow but brightly colored harbor front favorite for lunch or dinner while visiting historic St. George's. It's charming and urbane, focusing on such Continental mainstays (the chef is Austrian) as Wiener schnitzel and traditional pastas. Its

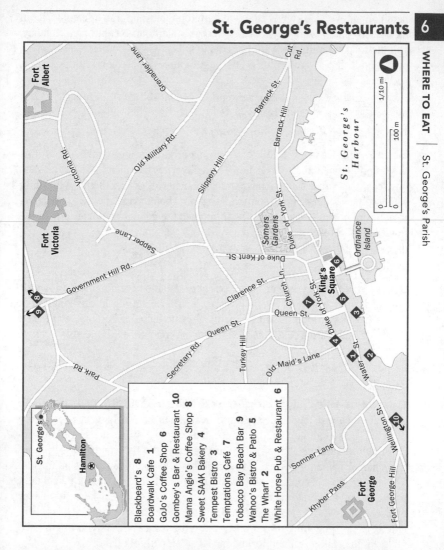

Blackbeard's **8**
Boardwalk Cafe **1**
GoJo's Coffee Shop **6**
Gombey's Bar & Restaurant **10**
Mama Angie's Coffee Shop **8**
Sweet SAAK Bakery **4**
Tempest Bistro **3**
Temptations Café **7**
Tobacco Bay Beach Bar **9**
Wahoo's Bistro & Patio **5**
The Wharf **2**
White Horse Pub & Restaurant **6**

Bermuda rockfish served with bananas and almonds also gets a big thumbs up. Grab a cup of gelato on your way out—the resto features an ice cream takeout counter near the front entrance.

36 Water St. www.wahoos.bm. ℂ **441/297-1307.** Lunch main courses $12–$18; dinner main courses $12–$42. Apr–Oct Mon 11:30am–5pm, Tues–Sat 11:30am–9:30pm.

White Horse Pub & Restaurant ★ PUB GRUB   The oldest tavern in St. George's is one of the most popular in Bermuda; it's always jammed. This white building with green shutters has a restaurant and cedar bar with a terrace jutting into St. George's Harbour. Sit in the main bar, where glasses hang from brass fixtures, TV's play soccer and other international sports and patrons perch on tall wooden swivel chairs at high top tables; or grab a seat outside in its outdoor patio, with views of St. George's Harbour. Neither area is fancy, and the food is straightforward bar eats (nachos, wings, burgers, sandwiches, pizza, English pub grub) plus a few larger entrees, including seafood, pasta, and steak.

8 King's Sq. www.whitehorsebermuda.com. ℂ **441/297-1838.** Lunch main courses $16–$22; dinner main courses $17–$35. Daily 11am–10pm. Bar until 1am (or later).

Inexpensive

Boardwalk Cafe ★ DINER   With decor straight out of the 1950s, this tiny family-owned diner serves homestyle favorites like meatloaf with mashed potatoes, egg salad sandwiches, and jumbo hot dogs smothered with chili. Many come just for a cup of soup or a bag of its homemade cookies—delicious varieties of both change daily. *Tip:* If you need to get online, this is one of the few spots in St. George's with free Wi-Fi.

Water St. ℂ **441/297-4819.** All plates $4–$15. Daily 10am–5pm.

Go Jo's Coffee Shop ★ CAFE   King's Square still has its wooden stocks, where prisoners were once publicly detained for common crimes. If you stick your head and hands in them, you'll be staring at this small cafe across the way, which is known for its gourmet cups of coffee, fresh baked goods (try the carrot cake), and light bites at lunchtime (like codfish cakes, tuna salad, or turkey and cheese).

7 King's Sq. ℂ **441/297-0614.** Coffee $3–$5; baked goods $2–$5; codfish cakes $9. Mon–Thurs and Sat–Sun 9am–5pm.

Gombey's Bar & Restaurant ★★ BURGERS/BERMUDIAN   Hang with the locals at the chill, al fresco beachfront bar, right next to a nature reserve. The soundtrack will be reggae and soca, the drinks are served in Solo cups, but boy are they strong, and the "Yummy"—a fish sandwich—lives up to its name. The only downside is something that could be seen as an upside: This is well off the beaten path, so you'll need to rent a scooter or take a taxi, as buses don't operate nearby. But that keeps the vibe real here (it's never overwhelmed with cruiseshippers). Bring the kids: Clearwater Beach is lovely and there's a sprawling playground next to the restaurant. As you might have guessed, the resto is named for the island's colorful folk dancers.

193 Cooper's Island Rd., Clearwater Beach, St. David's. www.facebook.com/gombeys 4955. ℂ **441/293-5092.** Lunch main and dinner main courses $10–$25. Daily 11:30am–7:30pm.

Mama Angie's Coffee Shop ★★ DINER/BERMUDIAN   A Traditional Bermuda fish sandwich in St. George's? There's no better place than this colorful hole-in-the-wall diner at the east of York Street. And you'll likely be the only tourist there. Either eat it at one of its small tables inside, or take it to go, and have a picnic at Somers Park just across the street.

48 York St. ℂ **441/297-0959.** Breakfast and lunch $5–$15. Mon–Thurs 8am–2:45pm; Fri 8am–2:30pm; Sat 8am–noon.

Sweet SAAK Bakery ★★★ BAKERY   What does SAAK mean? Good eats in this case, though in reality it is an acronym from the initials of the four siblings who run this bakery in St. George's. They use family recipes for their cinnamon buns, sliced cakes, sweet fruit breads, homemade granola and cookies. All is served alongside teas, coffee and hot cocoa with homemade marshmallows. SAAK also makes fudge once a week, but like all of its homemade goods, it sells out fast.

16 York St. www.sweetsaak.com. ⓒ **441/297-0663.** Baked goods $2–$8. Mon–Sat 9am–3pm.

Temptations Cafe ★ DINER   Popular with locals who've come for its affordably priced breakfast, quick-and-easy sandwiches at lunch or its large selection of ice cream by the scoop, this no-frills diner is the perfect pit stop.

31 York St. ⓒ **441/297-1368.** Breakfast and lunch $5–$15. Mon–Sat 8:30am–4pm.

Tobacco Bay Beach Bar ★ BURGERS   Located on a calm east end bay best known for snorkeling, this über-laid-back beach bar caters to the cruise passengers who rent its chaise lounges, kayaks and floating aqua bikes after being bussed there from their ship. Don't expect to be wined and dined—the place literally has six items on the menu: hamburgers, cheeseburgers, chicken wings, French fries, chicken tenders, and hotdogs, all served alongside frozen drinks, beers, and cocktails.

Tobacco Bay. www.tobaccobay.bm. ⓒ **441/705-2582.** Lunch options $5–$12. Mon–Thurs 10am–5pm; Fri 10am–sunset; Sat–Sun 10am–7pm. Closed winter.

RESTAURANTS BY CUISINE

ASIAN
Harbourfront Restaurant & Komodaru Sushi Lounge ★★★ ($$$, p. 130)
L'Oriental ★★ ($$, p. 137)
Utopia ★ ($$, p. 139)

BAKERY/CAFE
AZU Beastro ★ ($$, p. 145)
Chatterbox Cafe ★ ($, p. 140)
Boardwalk Cafe ★ ($, p. 150)
D'angelini's Cafe ★★ ($, p. 141)
Homer's Café ★★★ ($, p. 128)
Go Jo's Coffee Shop ★ ($, p. 150)
Glaze ★ ($, p. 142)
Nonna's Kitchen ★ ($, p. 142)
The Hamilton Pastry Shop ★★ ($, p. 142)
The Dockyard Pastry Shop & Bistro ★★★ ($, p. 120)
Milan Milan ★ ($, p. 142)

Rock Island Coffee ★ ($, p. 142)
Sweet SAAK Bakery ★★★ ($, p. 151)

BARBECUE
Boundary Sports Bar & Grille ★★ ($$, p. 123)

BERMUDIAN
Art Mel's Spicy Dicy ★★ ($$, p. 140)
Gombey's Bar & Restaurant ★★ ($, p. 150)
Mama Angie's Coffee Shop ★★ ($, p. 150)
Specialty Inn ★ ($, p. 146)

BURGERS
Bulli Social ★★ ($$, p. 134)
Gombey's Bar & Restaurant ★★ ($, p. 150)
Tobacco Bay Beach Bar ★ ($, p. 151)

KEY TO ABBREVIATIONS:
$$$** = Expensive   **$$** = Moderate   **$ = Inexpensive

CARIBBEAN/SOUL FOOD
D&C Grill East ★★ ($, p. 145)
D&C Grill West ★★ ($, p. 124)
Jamaican Grill ★ ($, p. 141)
Marcus' ★★★ ($$$, p. 131)
Rotisserie Grill ★ ($, p. 146)

CHINESE
L'Oriental ★★ ($$, p. 137)

CONTINENTAL
Beau Rivage ★★★ ($$$, p. 127)
Bolero Brasserie ★★★ ($$$, p. 130)
Mad Hatter's ★★★ ($$$, p. 131)
Tom Moore's Tavern ★ ($$$, p. 146)

DINER
Mama Angie's Coffee Shop ★★
   ($, p. 150)
Paraquet Restaurant ★ ($, p. 127)
Specialty Inn ★ ($, p. 146)
Temptations Cafe ★ ($, p. 151)
The Spot Restaurant ★ ($, p. 142)

FAST FOOD
Ice Queen ★ ($, p. 128)
Mr. Chicken ★★★ ($, p. 141)

FRENCH
Bouchée ★★ ($$, p. 140)
Tempest Bistro ★★ ($$$, p. 147)

ICE CREAM
Bailey's Bay Ice Cream Parlour ★
   ($, p. 147)
Yo Cherry ★ ($, p. 142)

INDIAN
House of India ★★★ ($$, p. 141)
Ruby Murray's ★★ ($$, p. 139)

INTERNATIONAL
1609 Bar & Restaurant ★★
   ($$, p. 132)
Aqua Terra ★★ ($$$, p. 121)
Devil's Isle Café ★★★ ($$, p. 135)
Beach Club Restaurant ★★
   ($$$, p. 144)
Bermuda Bistro at the Beach ★
   ($$, p. 133)
Bistro J ★ ($$, p. 134)
Blackbeard's ★★★ ($$, p. 148)
Blû ★★★ ($$$, p. 125)
Bone Fish Bar & Grill ★★ ($$, p. 118)

Breezes ★★★ ($$$, p. 118)
Coconuts ★ ($$$, p. 121)
Crown & Anchor ★★ ($$, p. 134)
Island Brasserie ★★★ ($$$, p. 143)
Jasmine Lounge ★★ ($$, p. 124)
Marée ★★★ ($$$$, p. 143)
The Pickled Onion ★★ ($$$, p. 138)
The Pink Beach Club ★★★
   ($$$, p. 144)
The Terrace on Front Street ★★
   ($$$, p. 139)
The Village Pantry ★★★ ($$, p. 145)
The Wharf ★ ($$, p. 148)

ITALIAN
Bella Vista ★ ($$, p. 123)
Café Amici ★ ($$, p. 119)
The Dining Room ★★ ($$, p. 123)
Little Venice ★★ ($$$, p. 131)
Portofino ★ ($$, p. 138)
Rustico ★★ ($$, p. 145)
Sul Verde ★★★ ($$$, p. 144)
La Trattoria ★★ ($$, p. 136)

MEDITERRANEAN
Mediterra ★★ ($$, p. 124)

MEXICAN
Rosa's Cantina ★★ ($$, p. 139)

PIZZERIA
Gulfstream ★★ ($$, p. 123)
La Trattoria ★★ ($$, p. 136)
Rustico ★★ ($$, p. 145)

PUB GRUB
Astwood Arms ★ ($$, p. 133)
Divots ★ ($, p. 125)
The Docksider Pub & Restaurant ★
   ($, p. 135)
Flanagan's Irish Pub & Restaurant ★★
   ($$, p. 135)
The Frog & Onion Pub ★★★
   ($$, p. 119)
Henry VIII ★★ ($$, p. 122)
Hog Penny ★★ ($$, p. 136)
North Rock Brewing Company ★
   ($$, p. 144)
Outback Sports Bar ★ ($$, p. 137)
Rum Bum Beach Bar ★★ ($, p. 125)
Somerset Country Squire Pub &
   Restaurant ★ ($, p. 119)

Swizzle Inn Bailey's Bay ★★
  ($$, p. 147)
The Swizzle South Shore ★★
  ($$, p. 125)
The Robin Hood ★ ($$, p. 138)
White Horse Pub & Restaurant ★
  ($$, p. 149)
Woody's Sports Bar & Restaurant ★
  ($, p. 120)

SEAFOOD
Barracuda Grill ★★★ ($$$, p. 128)
Blû ★★★ ($$$, p. 125)
Café Lido ★★ ($$$, p. 127)
Gulfstream ★★ ($$, p. 123)
Harbourfront Restaurant & Komodaru
  Sushi Lounge ★★★ ($$$, p. 130)
Lobster Pot & Boat House Bar ★★
  ($$, p. 136)
Mickey's Beach Bistro ★★★
  ($$$, p. 126)
Ocean Club ★★ ($$$, p. 121)
Port O' Call ★★★ ($$, p. 132)

Somerset Country Squire Pub &
  Restaurant ★ ($$, p. 119)
Wahoo's Bistro & Patio ★★★
  ($$, p. 148)

STEAK & SEAFOOD
Fourways Inn ★★★ ($$$$, p. 126)
Harry's ★★★ ($$$, p. 130)
Mickey's Beach Bistro & Bar ★★★
  ($$$, p. 126)
Waterlot Inn ★★★ ($$$$, p. 121)

SUSHI
Beluga Bar ★★ ($$, p. 133)
Blû ★★★ ($$$, p. 125)
Harbourfront Restaurant & Komodaru
  Sushi Lounge ★★★ ($$$, p. 130)
Henry VIII ★★ ($$, p. 122)
L'Oriental ★★ ($$, p. 137)
Pearl ★★★ ($$$, p. 138)
Seabreeze ★★ ($$, p. 127)
Specialty Inn ★ ($, p. 146)

TAPAS
Seabreeze ★★ ($$, p. 127)

WHERE TO SHOP

Bermuda, once widely hailed as a "showcase of the British Empire," is still that, at least in its variety of goods. The retail scene draws upon its British antecedents: Shopkeepers are generally both polite and discreet, and merchandise is unusual and well made. In addition, most retailers take full advantage of location. Shops usually occupy charming cottages or historically important buildings, making shopping even more fun. Even visitors who intend to do no more than window-shop are likely to break down and make a purchase or two.

These days, Bermuda's retail scene is vibrant—a development that can be directly attributed to the arrival of the 35th America's Cup in 2017. In preparation of the world's most prestigious regatta, a plethora of new shops and boutiques opened their doors in The City of Hamilton and beyond—and many of those stores are still thriving today.

In short, you'll find anything and everything to spend your U.S. or Bermuda dollars on, in stores that run the retail gamut: high-end boutiques selling leather shoes and designer clothes; large department stores with collections of perfumes, cosmetics and housewares; quaint, locally owned shops selling Bermuda-made jewelry and apparel; family-run souvenir stores where you can buy Bermuda-branded gear and trinkets; and a handful of specialty shops selling imported gifts and gourmet food items. Most of these will be found in the City of Hamilton, but some outer parishes are home to outposts of popular Hamilton favorites, so if you can't find your size or the color isn't quite right, it's worth asking if another branch has it.

Bermuda's Best Buys

In most cases, shopping on Bermuda isn't about bargains. Shops face huge import tariffs, plus employee-related taxes, leading to what some view as outrageously high prices. It also rarely pays to comparison shop since the price of a watch in a branch store in St. George's is likely to be exactly the same as it is in the main shop in the City of Hamilton. When discounts do happen, they tend to occur prior to restocking for busy shopping seasons. That means in the months leading up to December and in those just before June, you can sometimes find sales on designer goods. Considering there is also no sales tax in Bermuda, these periods are your best bet for finding a deal.

As is the case in most of its sister isles in the Caribbean, wine and spirits are a good buy since tourists are allowed 1 liter of wine and

1 liter of spirits duty-free upon departure—just be sure to buy yours at the departure lounge of L. F. Wade International versus a liquor store in town to save some cash. For example, a liter of Gosling's Black Seal rum costs $33.80 at **Gosling's Brother's** on Front Street; the same bottle if purchased at the departure lounge costs $16. Of all the bottles you might purchase, we'd recommend buying a bottle of Gosling's Old Rum. Housed in a handsome box, this high-end sipping rum is aged several years in charred oak barrels, giving it a rich, caramel complexity (it's also very hard to find outside Bermuda, which is why you should buy it here).

Authentic Bermudiana, products made on Bermuda or manufactured elsewhere exclusively for local stores, make great gifts. Top choices include jewelry boxes, sculptures and other gifts carved from local Bermuda cedar; handmade dolls made of palmetto leaves; coins commemorating the anniversary of the island's settlement; and works of art from local painters, all of which can be bought at the **Bermuda Arts Centre** (p. 92) and the **Bermuda Crafts Market** (p. 155) at the Royal Naval Dockyard. Philatelists will want to make a beeline for the **Perot Post Office** (p. 102) and its collection of limited-edition stamps. For other classy souvenirs, target a quartet of Bermuda's most acclaimed boutiques for island-inspired apparel, jewelry, ceramics and perfumes. These are **Alexandra Mosher Studio Jewellery** (p. 165); **The Island Shop** (craft goods, p. 164); **Lili Bermuda** (perfume, p. 164); and **TABS** (authentic Bermuda shorts, p. 162).

THE SHOPPING SCENE

Where to Go

THE CITY OF HAMILTON

By far the widest range of shopping choices in Bermuda is in the City of Hamilton (see "In the City of Hamilton," below). Most shops are located on Front Street, but some of the real shopping gems are found on Queen Street, which runs perpendicular to Front Street at its western end, and down Reid Street, which runs parallel. On these two thoroughfares you'll find a handful of apparel, jewelry and gift retailers—including the aforementioned TABS—plus one of the entrances to the Washington Mall, which is Bermuda's largest enclosed shopping area with shops and boutiques of all kinds (its main entrance is on Church St., just across from City Hall).

ROYAL NAVAL DOCKYARD

Because the Royal Naval Dockyard is Bermuda's main cruise port, this west end tourist hub is overflowing with retail options. In addition to a handful of popular Hamilton shops, which can be found in the Clocktower Mall—itself, a sprawling retail complex with shops galore—this is where you can buy a real piece of Bermudiana. Head to the **Bermuda Arts Centre** to peruse local artwork and hand-carved cedar sculptures or pop into the **Bermuda Crafts Market** for palmetto leaf dolls, sea glass jewelry, antique bottles and locally made foods. Nearby, you'll also find a handful of shops selling ceramics,

Bermuda rum cakes and blown glass vases, so if you're searching for a special island-inspired gift to bring back home, Dockyard is an excellent choice.

THE TOWN OF ST. GEORGE'S

If you're headed to St. George's to tour its historic sights and attractions, then by all means, walk down Water Street to peruse its shops and boutiques, of which there are many. But don't make a separate trip to the east end just to go shopping, since most St. George's boutiques are branches of existing stores that you'll find in the City of Hamilton. There are a few exceptions, like the not-to-be-missed Bermuda Perfumery, which is housed inside a historic 18th-century cottage, but even it has a smaller outpost in Hamilton.

What You Should Know

STORE HOURS

Stores in the City of Hamilton, the Town of St. George's, and the Royal Naval Dockyard are generally open Monday through Saturday from 9am to 5:30pm and most everything is closed on Sunday. When cruise ships are in port, businesses in Dockyard typically stay open later, and hours are typically extended throughout Bermuda during the busy December shopping period. But for the most part, don't expect any doors to be open past 6pm. The one exception is on Wednesday nights from May through September. Known as **Harbour Night,** it's when the City of Hamilton closes Front Street off to vehicular traffic and transforms itself into a large pedestrian street party, full of craft vendors and live music performances (and when popular brick-and-mortar shops are typically open late into the night).

FINDING AN ADDRESS

Some Front Street stores post numbers on their buildings, others don't. And even when they do, sometimes the number posted is the "historic" number of the building, which has nothing to do with where it's actually located (for example, the year that it was built rather than a physical address). Don't hesitate to ask for directions; most Bermudians are very friendly and willing to help.

SALES TAX & DUTY

There's no sales tax in Bermuda, but it's not a duty-free island. Depending on which country you're returning to, you may have to pay duty. See "Customs," in the "Fast Facts" section of chapter 10, for details.

IN THE CITY OF HAMILTON

By far one of the best evenings to open your wallet in the City of Hamilton is **Harbour Night,** when Front Street is transformed into a lively, pedestrian street party and shops stay open late into the night. Held every Wednesday between 7pm and 10pm from May through September, this festival boasts local vendors selling arts & crafts, food trucks with Bermudian specialties and live music performances throughout the night (if you're lucky, you'll catch a troupe of Gombey dancers, a wildly entertaining group of folk dancers who jump, bounce, and groove to the beat of thunderous drumming).

Department Stores

A. S. Cooper & Sons ★★   Traditionally, this store has been best known for its selection of crystal and bone china. It features Villeroy & Bosch, Wedgwood, Waterford and Portmeirion, many of which are sold at 15%-20% below U.S. prices, thanks to the special relationship Bermuda maintains with the U.K. But as Bermuda's largest department store it also has excellent coverage for cosmetics, perfumes, housewares, and women's and children's fashions. 59 Front St. www.ascooper.bm. ✆ **441/295-3961.**

Brown & Co. ★★   With a sprawling second-floor bookstore plus a Front Street retail space devoted to perfumes, colognes, designer sunglasses, and Body Shop products, Brown & Co. is a popular one-stop shop (it can get quite crowded with locals at lunchtime). Its Queen Street entrance is also a good place to go for Bermuda-branded clothes and souvenirs. 35 Front St. www.brown. bm. ✆ **441/279-5442.**

Gibbons Company ★   Sprawling and cost-efficient, Gibbons Company is a reliable, if not all that exciting, option for cosmetics, perfumes and such necessities as housewares and clothing. But if you're searching for Chanel, Dior, or Lancôme skincare, fragrance and beauty products this would be the place to go since it's Bermuda's exclusive seller of those brands. 21 Reid St. www.gibbons.bm. ✆ **441/295-0022.**

Marks & Spencer ★   This branch of the famous British chain carries the same merchandise as its sibling stores in the British Isles. You'll find men's, women's, and children's fashions in everything from resort wear to sleepwear, including lingerie. There are also well-tailored dresses and suits, dress shirts, blazers, and British-tailored trousers, as well as swimwear, toiletries, giftware, plus an entire section devoted to English foodstuffs. 18 Reid St. www.fb.com/ MarksandSpencerBermuda. ✆ **441/295-0031.**

Goods A to Z

ART

Bermuda Society of Arts (BSOA) ★★   The West Wing of Hamilton's City Hall (the island's Fine Arts Museum occupies the East Wing) is the permanent home of the oldest arts society on Bermuda. The site contains four separate gallery areas, where the artwork changes every 3 weeks. Styles range

157

Shopping in the City of Hamilton

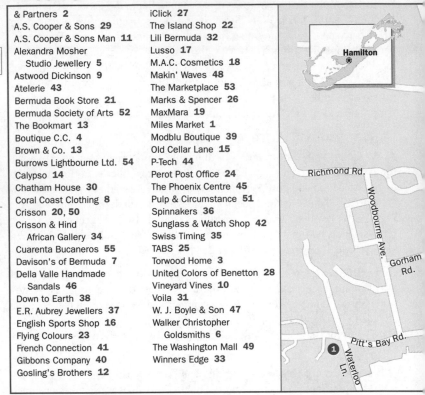

Hamilton

from the moderately avant-garde to straightforward representational, and every show includes dozens of examples of Bermudian landscapes, seascapes, or architectural renderings, any of which would make worthwhile home art. West Wing of City Hall, 17 Church St. www.bsoa.bm. © **441/292-3824.**

Crisson & Hind African Gallery ★★ Specializing in handcrafted creations from the Shona people of Zimbabwe, this handsome sculpture gallery features intricately carved busts, animals, wildlife scenes and more, all made from African stone (like verdite, butter jade, dolomite, and cobalt). Sculptures weighing up to 30 pounds can be packaged and taken onboard an aircraft as carry-ons; anything larger can easily be shipped internationally. In those instances, the gallery builds wooden crates for the sculpture then ships via DHL. 71 Front St. www.crissonandhind.com. © **441/295-1125.**

BEACHWEAR & SUNGLASSES
Makin' Waves ★ Bermuda's sole surf shop has laidback lifestyle apparel and accessories from brands like Billabong, O'Neill, Reef, Roxy and Quicksilver. With a huge selection of men's boards shorts and rash guards, plus an

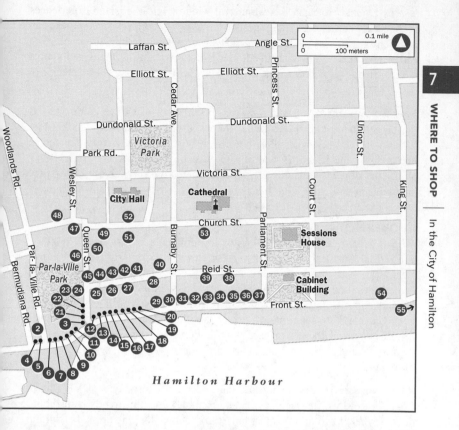

equally extensive lineup of bikinis, kids gear and sunglasses, Makin' Waves has everything one could ever need for a day at the beach. *One word of note:* In winter, this shop transitions its clothes to winter gear fit for the slopes, so if you've come from December through March, expect North Face jackets and Patagonia hoodies to replace most of what you'd typically see in summer. 11 Church St. www.makinwaves.bm. © **441/292-4609.**

Sunglass & Watch Shop ★ Bermuda's largest collection of designer shades carries Ray Bans, Oakley, Maui Jim, Prada, Versace, Michael Kors, Polaroid, Dolce & Gabbana, and Emilio Pucci. As its name suggests, in addition to sunglasses, this small shop also features a large selection of casual and designer watches including Hugo Boss, G Shock, Diesel, Lacoste and more. 13 Reid St. www.sunglassandwatchshop.bm. © **441/292-7933.**

BOOKS
Bermuda Book Store ★★ Head to this hole-in-the-wall bookshop for its large selection of specialty titles about Bermuda. For a humorous account

of expat life pick up Tracey Caswell's *Tea with Tracey; Mark Twain in Paradise* by Donald Hoffman is a wonderful window into the island experiences of the famed American writer; and *Tiny the Treefrog Tours Bermuda* makes an excellent gift for any child on your list since this beloved picture book from author and illustrator Elizabeth Mulderig features many of the island's most family-friendly attractions (like the Crystal Caves). 3 Queen St. www.bdabooks. bm. ℂ **441/295-3698.**

The Bookmart ★ Located on the second floor of Brown & Co., this is the biggest bookstore in Bermuda. It specializes in bestsellers, cookbooks, biographies and self-help titles, but also features a large section devoted to books about the island. In addition to an expansive selection of children's books, the store also features a small cafe where you can grab a coffee, pastry or sandwich and enjoy it on their open-air, second-story balcony. 35 Front St. www.bookmart.bm. ℂ **441/279-5441.**

CLOTHING

A. S. Cooper & Sons Man ★★ In Bermuda's largest menswear store, you'll find top designer brands—dress shirts, casual tops, slacks, shorts, swimwear, shoes and accessories—from Ralph Lauren, Brooks Brothers, Peter Milar, Lacoste, Perry Ellis, and other big names. Prices are generally "manufacturer's suggested retail," so in many cases, you'll pay what you would have at U.S. department stores, but with the benefit of paying no sales tax. Restocking sales, just prior to peak shopping seasons (so the months right before Dec and June), are particularly good here. 29 Front St. www.ascooper.bm. ℂ **441/295-3961.**

Atelerie ★★ Carrying designer labels from brands such as DVF, Rag & Bone, Vince, Joie, Rebecca Taylor, and Helmut Lang, this trendy ladies' boutique is where to go for that must-have top or show-stopping dress. In addition to its collection of high-end apparel, this chic boutique also carries a large selection of Bermuda-inspired jewelry, gourmet gifts and fashionable accessories, making it the go-to shop if you need something in a pinch for a special night out. 9 Reid St. www.atelerie.com. ℂ **441/296-0280.**

Boutique C.C. ★ Frequented by local ladies who come for its collection of effortless workwear from the likes of Catherine Malandrino, Gerry Weber, and Karen Kane, this fashion boutique is also known for its collection of evening gowns and moderately priced cocktail dresses. 1 Front St. www.fb.com/ BoutiqueCCBermuda. ℂ **441/295-3935.**

Calypso ★★   Calypso carries designer ladies wear from Eileen Fisher and Max Mara, casual beach-chic fashions and the most comprehensive selection of swimwear on Bermuda, including Vilbrequin. The shop also features Italian leather goods, espadrilles, hats, bags, Italian ceramics, beach wraps, and whimsical gift items (additional branches can be found at the Fairmont Southampton and the Royal Naval Dockyard). 45 Front St. www.calypso.bm. © **441/295-2112.**

Coral Coast Clothing ★★   Opened in 2017 by a pair of Bermuda businessmen who quit their day jobs to create a men's lifestyle brand, this shop sells its own lines of button down shirts, ties, polos, swim trunks, and Bermuda shorts, all of which epitomize the island life (evidenced by the playfully colored inside cuffs of its dress shirts and its blue angelfish logo, which appears on most garments). If you stop in, be sure to say hello to affable owners Sam Outerbridge and Adam Petty, who will likely be the ones helping you select your chicly tropical gear. 15 Front St. www.coralcoastclothing.com. © **441/707-7729.**

Davison's of Bermuda ★   Although this clothing shop, which sells Bermuda-branded shirts, hats, bags and gifts, has locations in the Royal Naval Dockyard and the Town of St. George's, this Front Street store is its main headquarters. Head there for brightly colored T-shirts, polos, hoodies, and Bermuda souvenirs of all kinds. 15 Front St. www.fb.com/Davisons-of-Bermuda-116367595082426. © **441/295-0088.**

English Sports Shop ★★   Established in 1918, this shop is one of the island's leading retailers of classic British woolen knitwear (i.e., hats, sweaters, ties, and the like) and until the arrival of TABS in 2016, it was one of the only places to buy traditional knee-length Bermuda shorts. They still sell shorts in a bouquet of colors—a linen/polyester blend that's $30 cheaper than the cotton/linen variety sold at TABS—but this beloved Bermuda shop also specializes in men's formalwear, its upstairs racks brimming with suits from Hugo Boss, Alexander of London, and Antonio Gardinni, plus an extensive collection of bow ties and cummerbunds. 49 Front St. www.fb.com/EnglishSportsShop. © **441/295-2672.**

Bermuda Shorts: A Quick History

It's hard to spend any time in Bermuda and *not* see a local strolling down Front Street in a pair of the eponymously named knee-length shorts. Regarded as formal business attire and traditionally worn with a blazer, collared shirt, tie and knee socks, these colorful shorts also transition well to casual gatherings, since their breezy, tropical hues can easily be paired with a simple polo shirt. But long before the shorts became a style icon, they were a utilitarian necessity. Originally worn by the British army to keep cool while stationed in India, the khaki shorts were eventually issued to soldiers based in Bermuda and by the 1930s, they had caught on with the rest of the population. For the best selection and the finest styles visit TABS, a Reid Street boutique in the City of Hamilton whose name stands for The Authentic Bermuda Shorts (p. 162).

French Connection ★   Head to this Reid Street branch of the popular British chain for chic urban-wear, trendy tops and casual clothes for both men and women. Because the FCUK brand is popular with expat locals, its apparel usually flies off the shelves, so expect hefty seasonal sales for anything leftover to make way for new inventory. 15 Reid St. www.calypso.bm. ✆ **441/295-2112.**

Lusso ★★   The high-end women's fashion boutiques on New York's Fifth Avenue are the model for this trendy shop. Here you'll find dresses, gowns and blouses from Lilly Pulitzer, Emilio Pucci and Moschino, plus a large selection of leather belts, handbags and shoes from Fendi, Prada, Ferragamo, and Jimmy Choo. Lusso also carries a small selection of men's ties and wallets, but in this chic store, you'll mostly find the men sitting on cozy leather couches. 51 Front St. www.fb.com/LussoBermuda. ✆ **441/295-6734.**

MaxMara ★   Ladies searching for casual beachwear or a fancy dress for a fun night out should pop into this tiny outpost of the celebrated Italian fashion house. In addition to its namesake brand, this store also sells clothes by SportsMax. 57 Front St. www.calypso.bm. ✆ **441/295-2112.**

ModBlu Boutique ★   Chic ladieswear from Raga, Blank NYC and Cooper & Ella, in addition to a large selection of accessories, jewelry and sunglasses are the lure here. Need a blowout or a quick styling? From Wednesday through Saturday, the shop offers hair services at its on-site Modbar salon (by appointment only). 46 Reid St. www.modblubermuda.com. ✆ **441/405-3250.**

Riihiluoma's Flying Colours ★★   This is everybody's favorite catchall emporium for inexpensive, impulse-buy souvenirs, Bermuda-branded stuff and T-shirts with perky slogans (such as "I Survived the Bermuda Triangle"). You'll also find paperweights, toys, beach coverups, sarongs, key chains, bracelets, necklaces, and more. The establishment's hard-to-spell name comes from the Finnish-born family that established it in 1937 and still manages it today. 5 Queen St. www.flyingcolours.bm. ✆ **441/295-0890.**

Spinnakers ★   The sister store of Flying Colours (see above), it has much of the same merchandise on its shelves. 99 Front St. ✆ **441/295-8228.**

TABS ★★★   Long before Bermudian designer Rebecca Singleton launched her flagship store in 2016, locals had been proudly wearing her island-inspired Bermuda shorts. This keen entrepreneur first sold her apparel online, hand-delivering the goods in pretty bags she stuffed herself. In no time her colorful shorts, whose acronym stands for The Authentic Bermuda Shorts, became the island's hottest, must-have item—a fact that was duly confirmed when TABS was chosen as the sole clothing sponsor of the 35th America's Cup in 2017. These days her breezy lifestyle brand has grown significantly, having added an extensive line of men's, women's and children's swimwear, cotton pique polos, knee-high socks and handsome pocket squares. But it's the classic Bermuda shorts that bring in the crowds. In colors reflecting the flora

WHERE TO SHOP | In the City of Hamilton

and fauna of the island (sea fan purple, hibiscus pink, kiskadee yellow) TABS shorts are lined with tropical patterns and feature Singleton's signature Bermuda triangle beltloop, a nod to the island's maritime lore. Shorts come in cotton twill, a cotton/linen blend or for women, comfortable stretch cotton. *Tip:* For another piece of only-in-Bermuda apparel, look for the shop's neon-colored Water Hazard trucker hats featuring popular Bermudian slang phrases (like Ace Girl or Full Hot). 12 Reid St. www.tabsbermuda.com. © **441/704-8227.**

United Colors of Benetton ★   This venerable Italian brand sells colorful shirts, blouses, pants, dresses, sweaters and accessories for the whole family. 24 Reid St. www.calypso.bm. © **441/295-2112,** ext. 105.

Vineyard Vines ★★   Preppy fashions are the hallmark of this New England outfitter which sells whimsically patterned ties, plaid and pastel-colored shirts, and Nantucket red shorts. Vineyard Vines is also home to a large selection of Bermuda-branded outerwear, perfect for those crisp fall days back home. *Tip:* For a fun photo, snap a picture at the sales desk, which resembles the transom of a large Bermuda boat. 27 Front St. www.ascooper.bm. © **441/295-3961.**

Voila ★   The exclusive seller of Longchamp Paris, this small Front Street boutique sells the esteemed brand's shoulder bags, purses and clutches plus a wide selection of accessories like belts, luggage and leather shoes. Butterfield Walkway. www.calypso.bm. © **441/295-2112,** ext. 120.

CONSUMER ELECTRONICS

iClick ★★   This authorized Apple reseller carries most of everything you'd expect to find at a typical Apple Store in the U.S. (laptops, iMacs, iPads, accessories, and the like), but at prices 30%-40% higher than U.S. advertised prices. Ouch! But if you need a cable, or some other piece of Apple equipment, this is where to find it. 20 Reid St. www.ptech.bm/iclick. © **441/542-5425.**

P-Tech ★★   Good for cameras, film, and accessories for Canon, Sony, Nikon, Pentax, Fuji, Olympus, and other big names. The store also carries electronics and top-of-the-line picture frames and camera bags. 37 Reid St. www.ptech.bm. © **441/295-5496.**

COSMETICS

M.A.C. Cosmetics ★   In addition to an extensive lineup of M.A.C.-branded beauty, makeup and skin-care products, this shop has a well-trained staff of makeup artists who offer walk-in makeovers and beauty tips. 53 Front St. www.gibbons.bm. © **441/295-8843.**

GIFTS

& Partners ★★   Opened in 2016 by husband and wife team, Peter Lapsley and Andrea Sundt, this modern design shop sells Scandinavian-inspired home decor, artwork, toys, jewelry and accessories, which are hand-picked during the couple's yearly scouting trips to Norway, Denmark and Sweden. In addition to high-design gifts, & Partners also supports local artisans stocking Beelovers Beekeeping candles made with Bermuda beeswax, jewelry by local designer

Shop The Lane

Before 1900, **The Old Cellar Lane**—a narrow, brick alleyway located next to The English Sports Shop—was one of the many stables along Front Street sheltering horses and carriages, Bermuda's main mode of transportation before cars were introduced to the island in 1946. These days it's home to a handful of small shops that you can stroll through with nary a horse in sight. Pop into **The Black Purl** for handknit gifts and its collection of wool, cashmere, and cotton yarn (www.blackpurlbda. com; (✆ 441/295-4544); **1609 Design,** selling tropical jewelry ((✆ 441/336-1326); **The Gem Celler,** a tiny shop specializing in semiprecious gemstones ((✆ 441/292-3042); **Mambo,** for casual men's and women's urban wear (✆ 441/295-3003); or **Meltdown,** a hole-in-the-wall ice cream shop with dozens of flavors (✆ 441/538-0065).

Rebecca Little and Fennel brand leather clutches from Bermuda's own Patrice Morgan. 46 Par-la-Ville Rd. www.andpartnersbermuda.com. (✆ **441/296-5250.**

Lili Bermuda ★★★   This outpost of the Bermuda Perfumery sells men's cologne and ladies perfume locally made with Bermuda botanicals (the original store is located in the Town of St. George's). Try Coral, a flowery perfume with hints of white roses and freesia or 64° west, a woodsy cologne named for the longitude of Bermuda with notes of citrus and cedar. 67 Front St. www.lili bermuda.com. (✆ **441/296-2885.**

Pulp & Circumstance ★   Tucked down a quiet pedestrian-only lane, this small-gifts emporium carries stationery, greeting cards, picture frames, candles, novelty items and more. It's also got a rotating inventory of seasonal items, so head here if you're searching for Christmas ornaments in winter or for festive gift ideas during typical Hallmark holidays. 4 Washington Lane (btw. Church and Reid sts.). www.fb.com/pulpbda. (✆ **441/542-9586.**

The Island Shop ★★★   No store better reflects the rich culture and natural beauty of Bermuda than this beloved ceramics, linen and glassware shop. Step inside this quaint shop and you'll immediately be greeted by shelves upon shelves of gorgeous, hand-painted (by owner Barbara Finsness) ceramic plates, platters, bowls, teapots, coasters and mugs. Designs feature local flora, fauna and architectural favorites (like the Bermuda buttery, which is a detached white-roofed building, once used to keep dairy items cool). The linens, pillows, napkins and glassware here also bear these designs. A uniquely Bermudian gift! 3 Queen St. www.islandexports.com. (✆ **441/292-5292.**

Torwood Home ★★   Formerly known as the Irish Linen Shop and recently renamed for the Somerset house where the business first began in 1948, this quaint corner boutique sells high-end gifts, private label home decor, and fine linens. The ground floor is filled with nautically inspired trays and platters, sterling silver picture frames and French candles from Cire Trudon (the world's oldest candlemaker). A second floor has the bed linens and tablecloths for which it was previously known. 31 Front St. (at Queen St.). (✆ **441/295-4089.**

GROCERS

Down to Earth ★   This small health store has the largest selection of organic foods and natural body products on the island. It also blends wholesome fruit and vegetable smoothies at its busy juice bar. 56 Reid St. www.fb.com/DownToEarthHealthBermuda. ℂ **441/295-3776.**

The Marketplace ★   The largest grocery store chain in Bermuda, it has branches scattered across the island. This outlet has an in-store bakery with organic items and precooked food to go. It's open until 10pm and keeps Sunday hours from 9am to 7pm. 42 Church St. www.marketplace.bm. ℂ **441/295-6006.**

Miles Market ★★   An upmarket collection of gourmet food items, Miles Market has everything you'd need for well-planned picnic (or a home-cooked meal), including Godiva chocolates, a fabulous selection of cheeses and prepared foods and aged beef, chicken skewers and fresh seafood at the butcher. 96 Pitts Bay Rd. (near Fairmont Hamilton Princess). www.miles.bm. ℂ **441/295-1234.**

JEWELRY

Alexandra Mosher Studio Jewellery ★★★   Take a teeny, tiny piece of Bermuda home with you. Local designer Alexandra Mosher creates handsome, hand-crafted, sterling silver jewelry, each of which incorporates tiny grains of pink sand. Her designs are so popular that her business has grown from a craft stand on the street to this swank shop. Here you'll find her "Reef Collection," which takes its inspiration from the island's south shore coral boilers; the "Fera Collection" with five-petaled flowers; and the "Critter Collection," featuring pink flamingos, sea turtles and jellyfish, among other beasties. For those who prefer gold to silver, there's her "One of a Kind" collection, it features white, yellow and rose gold rings set with precious gems like garnet, amethyst and milky peach diamonds. There's also a small selection of men's items, like silver and pink sand cufflinks, signet rings and tie bars. 5 Front St. www.alexandramosher.com. ℂ **441/236-9009.**

Astwood Dickinson ★★   This fine jewelry store, located across from the public ferry terminal, is an excellent resource for famous-name watches, including Breitling, Bremont, Cartier, Chanel, and Omega. Its other specialty is gemstone rings and gold necklaces. Their Bermuda collection of 18-karat gold mementos of the island, representing local flora, fauna, and landmarks, is handmade in the store's workshop. 25 Front St. www.ascooper.bm. ℂ **441/292-5805.**

Last-Minute Purchases: Good Old Duty-Free

Bermuda's airport is a darn good place to shop for gifts, especially considering they are duty-free. You'll find a large selection of spirits—like Gosling's Old Rum, an aged sipping rum, which is hard to find in the U.S.—plus Lili Bermuda perfumes, TABS Bermuda shorts, Bermuda Born handbags, Tiny the Treefrog children's books, and locally made gourmet food items like rum cakes and jams.

E. R. Aubrey, Jewellers ★   This small shop carries an extensive collection of gold chains and rings, but it specializes in jewelry made with precious and semiprecious gemstones, including diamonds, rubies, sapphires, emeralds, pearls, and the so-called Bermuda Lucky Stone, a four-colored lab-created stone representing friends, family, good health, and wealth. There are additional locations on Queen Street and at the Clocktower Mall in the Royal Naval Dockyard. 101 Front St. E. www.bermudaluckystone.com. 𝄞 **441/296-3171.**

Crisson Jewellers ★★   Family-owned and operated since 1922, Crisson is the exclusive Bermuda retailer for Rolex watches, which are sold at the lowest ticketed Swiss price, making its line of fine timepieces one of the best bargains in town (like everything else in Bermuda, you'll pay no additional sales tax). In addition to designer jewelry from John Hardy, David Yurman, Roberto Coin, Crisson is also the exclusive seller of Pandora charms and bracelets. It also has locations in the Royal Naval Dockyard and the Fairmont Southampton. 55 Front St. (main store); 16 Queen St. www.crisson.com. 𝄞 **441/295-2351.**

Swiss Timing ★   All the best names in Swiss and European watchmaking are found here, including Rodania, Certina, Oris, and Michel Herbelin along with a selection of semiprecious jewelry, gold chains, and bracelets. 95 Front St. www.swisstiming.bm. 𝄞 **441/295-1376.**

Walker Christopher Goldsmiths ★★   With one of the most unique collections of fine jewelry on the island, this shop is where to go if you're searching for heirloom jewelry that tells a story. In addition to its selection of South Sea pearls, fine gemstone rings and Bermuda-inspired gold jewelry, the shop also carries a large collection of rare coins—gold doubloons and silver "pieces of eight" salvaged from sunken galleons, as well as Greek and Roman coins that can be mounted and worn as pendants, earrings, and cuff links. Even Egyptian artifacts have been transformed into wearable art, and customers who have their own design in mind can work with a master jeweler to craft a one-of-a-kind piece. 9 Front St. www.walkerchristopher.com. 𝄞 **441/295-1466.**

LIQUOR

Burrows Lightbourn Ltd. ★   If Gosling Brother's doesn't have the exact bottle you're after, which could be the case since it stocks different brands than this competing wine and spirits importer, then head to this small Front Street shop on the east end of town to peruse its collection of gin, rum, scotch, tequila and more. 127 Front St. www.wineonline.bm. 𝄞 **441/295-1554.**

Gosling Brothers, Ltd. ★   This venerable store has been selling its world renowned rums since 1806. But that doesn't mean they're fully made here. Because Bermuda has no rivers or streams, it can't grow sugar cane, so the raw material (called rum distillate) comes from Barbados, Jamaica and Trinidad. It ships here in large stainless-steel tanks, before being aged and blended according to an old family recipe at the Gosling's Dundonald Street location (also in Hamilton). A portion that's destined for the local market stays behind and is bottled here, but the vast majority of the finished product gets put back

Make It the Mall

The Washington Mall, the island's largest indoor shopping center with dozens of retailers and restaurants, is where locals shop, and its outlets are worth a visit by tourists, too. Among the best of the bunch are **Atelerie** for designer ladies' apparel (p. 160); **Treats,** a tiny toy store that also sells candy by the piece (www. fb.com/TreatsBda; ℭ 441/296-1123); **The Harbourmaster,** with its collection of handbags, luggage, and leather goods (www.fb.com/theharbourmasterbermuda; ℭ 441/295-5333); **Sportseller** for athletic shoes, plus accessories and apparel for running and swimming (www.fb.com/sportseller.bermuda; ℭ 441/295-2692); **Gear and Gadget,** a phone and tablet accessory store that also replaces broken screens within 24 hours (www.irepair.bm; ℭ 441/824-2222); and **The Smoke Shop,** a local tobacconist that sells its own brand of cigarettes and electronic vaping devices (www.thesmokeshopbermuda. com; ℭ 441/296-2436). It has an extensive food court with some of the best sushi in Bermuda at **Beluga Bar** (www. belugabar.bm; ℭ 441/542-2859). The Washington Mall is closed on Sundays.

in those tanks and is transported to Bardstown, KY, where it's diluted, bottled and cased for international distribution. So what you'll get on Bermuda is the premium product. Your options: **Gosling's Black Seal rum** (used in cocktails, like the Dark n' Stormy and Bermuda rum swizzle, and in rum cakes and fish chowder), **Gosling's Gold Seal** (notes of caramel and vanilla), and **Gosling's Old Rum,** an aged sipping rum that comes in a handsome box. 33 Front St. www.goslingsrum.com. ℭ **441/298-7337.**

SHOES

Della Valle Handmade Sandals ★★   Owned by Vincenzo Della Valle—an Italian expat who's been living in Bermuda for nearly 20 years and who apprenticed with master sandal makers in Anacapri—this small boutique sells the bespoke sandals he creates based upon customer's requests. The strappy works-of-art feature leather soles and custom, bedazzled designs—so simply walk in the shop, choose your color, style and heel, and Vincenzo will whip up pair of sandals for you in about an hour (a final fitting when you pick up your sandals will take 15 min. more). 20 Reid St. www.dvsandals.com. ℭ **441/236-7263.**

W. J. Boyle & Son ★   In business since 1884, this shop has the best collection in town for men, women and children. It specializes in brand-name footwear from England, Spain and the United States including Clarks of England, Cole Haan, Enzo Angiolini, and Timberland. *Tip:* If your kids are in the need of a new pair of Crocs, this is the only place in Bermuda that sells them. 31 Queen St. ℭ **441/295-1887.**

STAMPS

Perot Post Office ★   Philatelists the world over visit this historic office to buy postage stamps from Bermuda. Highly prized by collectors, its stamps often feature historic figures and the island's flora and fauna. Stamps commemorating the 400th anniversary of Jamestown, Virginia, and the 19th-century sailing sloop *Spirit of Bermuda* are two of the most coveted. Open Monday through Friday from 9am to 5pm. Queen St. www.bpo.bm. © **441/297-7865.**

SPORTING GOODS

Winners Edge ★ Selling anything and everything for your cycling needs, this Front Street bike shop is the biggest and most reliable in Bermuda. In addition to a large selection of bicycles, the shop carries all the accessories and apparel you might need if you've forgotten a key piece of gear. The staff are accomplished cyclists and can help visitors map out worthwhile routes. 73 Front St. www.winnersedge.com. © **441/295-6012.**

TOBACCO

Chatham House Bermuda ★★ In 2016, the U.S. Treasury Department lifted the ban on bringing Cuban cigars to the United States, which means that you can now purchase unlimited quantities of cigars (and Cuban rum), as long as they're for personal use. This corner tobacconist on Front Street has one of the largest selections of Dominican, Jamaican, and, most notably, Cuban cigars like Cohiba, Monte Cristo, and Romeo y Julieta. The store also carries pipes, Swiss Army knives, postcards and Bermuda gifts. 63 Front St. www. bermuda.com/chatham-house. © **441/292-8422.**

Cuarenta Bucañeros Ltd. ★ Located above Hamma Galleries on the eastern edge of Hamilton, this organization sells boxes of the kinds of high-end cigars that go well with announcements of births, IPO stock buyouts, and corporate mergers. Montecristo, Romeo y Julieta, Trinidad, Cohiba, Partagas, and Hoyo de Monterrey are a few of the famous cigars for sale. 1 Lane Hill, East Broadway, 3rd Floor. www.cigarbox.bm. © **441/295-4523.**

ROYAL NAVAL DOCKYARD

For "only in Bermuda" products, the Royal Naval Dockyard excels. Beyond the **Bermuda Craft Market,** the **Bermuda Arts Centre,** the **Dockyard Glassworks,** and **Bermuda Rum Cake Factory** (all discussed below), it is home to the **Clocktower Mall,** which holds off-shoots of several Hamilton-based

---

Souvenir Spotlight: Bermuda's Underwater Treasure

In 2011, two intact bottles of perfume were found by divers in the bowels of a sunken 1860s Civil War blockade runner called the *Mary Celestia.* They brought them immediately to Isabelle Ramsay-Brackstone, owner of both **Bermuda Perfumery** (p. 171) and **Lili Bermuda** (p. 164). She had the perfume analyzed and then meticulously recreated the scent herself. Now sold under the name of the boat, in a handsome cedar box decorated with a silver coin depicting an image of the sunken ship at sea, this lovely eau de perfume is a piece of living Bermuda history—and one of the best souvenirs on Bermuda (it smells citrusy and tropical).

You may not have to leave your resort to get a gift or a new outfit. The **Hamilton Princess** (p. 197) has a modern retail corridor with two chic shops selling high-end men's and women's apparel: **FH For Him,** which sells Thomas Pink, Bugatchi, and Eton shirts among other menswear and shoes; and **For Her,** a ladies boutique with blouses, dresses and accessories from Elie Tahari, Chloe, and Pour les Femme by Robin Wright (www.luxury.bm; ℰ 441/298-6095). At **Rosewood Bermuda,** you'll find **Regali Boutique,** a handsome shop that sells casual menswear from The Love Brand plus dresses and blouses from Alice McCall, Alexis, and Keepsake (www.luxury.bm; ℰ 441/298-4035). And at the **Fairmont Southampton,** you'll find outposts of popular Front Street shops, including **Crisson Jewellers, The Island Shop** (pottery), **The English Sports Shop** (menswear and Bermuda shorts), **Calypso** (ladies resort wear), and **A. S. Cooper & Sons** (apparel).

stores. *Tip:* If you're passing through Paget Parish, another option for art buyers is **The Birdsey Studio** (5 Stowe Hill; ℰ **441/236-6658** or 441/236-5845), a commercial art gallery that's open by appointment only. Run by Jo Birdsey Lindberg—the daughter of Bermuda's best-known artist, Alfred Birdsey who died in 1996—this small gallery sells original artwork, watercolors and oils in compositions ranging from landscapes of Bermuda to architectural and nautical themes. You can also buy notecards reproduced from paintings by Alfred Birdsey.

Goods A to Z
ARTS & CRAFTS

Bermuda Arts Centre at Dockyard ★★★ Housed inside an old stone building across from the National Museum of Bermuda, this art gallery specializes in paintings and sculptures, mostly from Bermudian artisans (some of whom you can watch at work, since the Arts Centre also rents three studios to working artists). It features new exhibitions every 4 to 6 weeks from well-known local artists such as Christopher Grimes, Graham Foster and Jill Amos Raine. Goods will include inexpensive reproduction prints, mid-range originals and limited edition works of art, which can be shipped to your destination of choice if they're too big—or too precious—to be taken on a plane. 4 Maritime Dr. www.artbermuda.com. ℰ **441/234-2809.** Bus: 7 or 8.

Bermuda Craft Market ★★★ Boasting the largest collection of Bermuda-made crafts, products, jewelry and foods on the island, this bustling market is a perfect stop for a one-of-a-kind gift. In fact, most items are sold by the artists and craftsmen themselves, so do chat up your seller as they may have stories of how a particular piece was made. Peruse antique glass bottles, dolls made with palmetto leaves, sea glass jewelry, rum cakes, Bermuda books and maps, jams and jellies, cedar bowls and much, much more. The Cooperage Building. http://bermudacraftmarket.com. ℰ **441/234-3208.** Bus: 7 or 8.

Dockyard Glassworks and Bermuda Rum Cake Factory ★★
Around 1820, this soaring masonry workspace was a repair yard for high-masted ships. Today, every inch of the cavernous room is filled with glassware and baked goods that are created on-site and in most cases, in plain view. At the Glassworks pull up a chair and watch master blowers create colorful vases, paperweights and trinkets from hot molten glass. And at the Rum Cake Factory, sample a dozen different traditional Bermuda rum cakes in flavors like black rum, rum swizzle, chocolate, coconut, coffee, and banana. 1 Maritime Lane, Royal Naval Dockyard. www.dockglass.com. ✆ **441/234-4216.** Bus: 7 or 8.

Jon Faulkner Gallery ★★   With a large selection of colorful salt-fire pottery plus dozens of customizable house-number and name plaques (like "15 Chancery Lane" or "Welcome to the Smiths'") this eclectic shop also features a Paint-Your-Own-Pottery studio (no reservation necessary). 7 Camber Rd., Royal Naval Dockyard. www.jonfaulknergallery.com. ✆ **441/234-5116.** Bus: 7 or 8.

CLOTHING
Crown & Anchor ★   Housed in a former ship captain's home and named for the popular dice game that was originally brought to Bermuda in the 18th century by Royal Navy sailors, this men's and women's apparel retailer sells handsome, nautically inspired clothes. Find classically styled polos, gauzy beach dresses and accessories galore, plus a large selection of Bermuda-branded gifts. 4 Dockyard Terrace, Royal Naval Dockyard. ✆ **441/296-9552.** Bus: 7 or 8.

Makin' Waves ★   An outpost of the identically named surf shop in Hamilton, it carries a large selection of men's board shorts, rash guards, bikinis, kids' gear, and sunglasses. 5 Camber Lane, Royal Naval Dockyard. www.makinwaves. bm. ✆ **441/234-5319.** Bus: 7 or 8.

JEWELRY
In addition to the store below, there's an off-shoot of Crisson's in the Clocktower Mall (see below).

Diamonds International ★   The largest jewelry store in the Royal Naval Dockyard, it has vast selection of diamonds and gemstones, including several exclusive brands like Crown of Light Diamond, Safi Kilima Tanzanite,

Cool Off in the Clocktower Mall

The **Clocktower Mall** is a blissfully air-conditioned retail space where you can explore small branches of popular City of Hamilton boutiques, plus a handful of shops selling novelty items, gifts and apparel. Like all other stone buildings in the Royal Naval Dockyard, it was built for the British navy, originally constructed as a warehouse in 1856. These days it's where cruise ship passengers and west end residents head when they'd rather not drive to town to go shopping. The Mall has branches of **Crisson Jewellers, A. S. Cooper & Sons** (name-brand men's and women's apparel), and **Davison's of Bermuda** (Bermuda-branded T-shirts, hoodies, and hats). You'll also find a row of gift shops selling colorful souvenirs.

plus Marahlago, Forevermark diamonds, and Mont Blanc Watches. Storehouse Rd. and Camber Lane, Royal Naval Dockyard. www.shopdi.com. © **441/234-0500.** Bus: 7 or 8.

THE TOWN OF ST. GEORGE'S

Water Street, a pedestrian-only cobblestone lane holds most of St. George's shops and boutiques. The town is not a major shopping destination.

Goods A to Z

BOOKS

Long Story Short ★★ Housed in an 18th-century cellar underneath the historic Tucker House, this small but choice bookshop carries a large selection of books about Bermuda in addition to a quirky selection of gifts like local honey, spices, beeswax candles and custom-made hula hoops. The shop is also the starting point for a weekly haunted history tour, led by its affable owner Kristin White (tours are typically run on Thurs at 8:30pm; call for availability). Water St. www.kristindotcom.com. © **441/297-0448.** Bus: 1, 3, 6, 10, or 11.

CLOTHING

English Sports Shop ★★ At this branch of the beloved Hamilton men's and ladies apparel shop, you'll find classic British woolen knitwear, colorful Bermuda shorts and men's ties and belts with common island themes (think: longtails, maps, or sailboats). 30 Water St. www.fb.com/EnglishSportsShop. © **441/ 297-0142.** Bus: 1, 3, 6, 10, or 11.

Frangipani ★ Filled with colorful and casual fashion for women, this boutique has a large selection of comfortable cottons, bright silks, and soft rayons in addition to a fine collection of swimwear and unusual accessories. 13 Water St. www.fb.com/FrangipaniBermuda. © **441/297-1357.** Bus: 1, 3, 6, 10, or 11.

GIFTS

Bermuda Linens and Gifts ★ In addition to a selection of seasonal items—Christmas kitsch in December or orange-and-black everything around Halloween in October—this gift shop also stocks quirky novelty items, home decor, infant apparel, and hand-embroidered linens. 16 Somers Wharf. www. bermudalinens.com. © **441/296-0189.** Bus: 1, 3, 6, 10, or 11.

Bermuda Perfumery ★★★ Housed in a 1730s stone cottage called Stewart Hall, this historic perfumery creates perfumes and colognes inspired by Bermuda botanicals. Originally opened in 1928, the perfumery's signature perfume is Lily, which has a lush, floral bouquet modeled after the island's Easter lilies. Owner and master perfumer Isabelle Ramsay-Brackstone also frequently creates new scents, all of which evoke Bermuda. Men should try 64°W, a nod to Bermuda's longitude with notes of grapefruit and cedar. A popular unisex fragrance is Fresh Water, a bright. citrusy cologne with rosemary, neroli and clementine. The shop provides an informative tour on how its perfumes are made. Stewart Hall, 5 Queen St. www.lilibermuda.com. © **441/293-0627.** Bus: 1, 3, 6, 10, or 11.

BERMUDA'S BEST souvenirs

Bermuda-branded knick-knacks and trinkets clutter many shop's shelves. Our advice? Avoid those impulse buys and instead target a few pieces of authentic Bermudiana to take home with you. Here's our picks:

○ Landscape prints from Winslow Homer look for a painting called *Inland Water*, which features a pink Bermuda cottage in the foreground and still, flatwater in the distance). *Source:* **Masterworks Museum of Bermuda Art** (p. 96).

○ Sterling silver ladies' jewelry made with tiny grains of pink sand and handsome men's rings that mimic textures found in nature (like driftwood, sea urchins, or lichen) *Source:* **Alexandra Mosher Studio Jewellery** (p. 165).

○ Perfumes inspired by island botanicals, like Easter lily, jasmine, and Bermuda cedar. *Source:* **Bermuda Perfumery** and **Lili Bermuda** (p. 171 and p. 164).

○ Locally made arts and crafts, like dolls made from palmetto leaves or sea-glass jewelry. *Source:* **Bermuda Craft Market** (p. 92).

○ Hand-painted pottery, linens, and glassware featuring Bermuda plants, animals, and famous buildings. *Source:* **Island Shop** (p. 164 and 172).

○ Indigo Song sarongs featuring breezy Bermuda scenes (like its "Turtle Bay" print, of which 5% of the proceeds are donated to the Bermuda Turtle Project; also available at www.indigosong. com). *Source:* **Merch** (see below).

○ Bermuda shorts! *Source:* **TABS** (p. 162).

Gregory Nelmes Interior Design ★ Award-winning Bermudian designer Gregory Nelmes selects all the goods here. In addition to large array of home decor, rugs made from recycled materials, and fair-trade furniture, this boutique sells Bermuda-themed pillow covers, vintage bottles and artwork. 8 York St. www.fb.com/GregoryNelmesHome. ✆ **441/704-7740.** Bus: 1, 3, 6, 10, or 11.

The Island Shop ★★★ Another outlet for the hand-painted pottery, glassware and linens of local artisan Barbara Finsness. See more on p. 164. Somers Wharf. www.islandexports.com. ✆ **441/297-1514.** Bus: 1, 3, 6, 10, or 11.

Merch ★★ This small boutique has an excellent selection of tropical gifts, books, jewelry and apparel. Buy locally made candles from the Limestone + Cedar Co. with scents including Tank Rain, Dark Rum and Gombey Spice; cards and stationery with vintage Bermuda scenes from Nettleink Paper; or kicky cotton sarongs in flora and fauna patterns from Indigo Song. Stiles House, 1 King's Sq. http://themerch.space. ✆ **441/703-4500.** Bus: 1, 3, 6, 10, or 11.

Vera P. Card ★ This family-owned shop is known for its gifts from around the world, including one of the island's largest collections of Lladró, Hummel, and Swarovski figurines; Czech, Austrian, and Bohemian crystal; European cuckoo clocks; limited edition porcelain plates; and a large selection of fine and costume jewelry. 22 Water St. ✆ **441/295-1729.** Bus: 1, 3, 6, 10, or 11.

JEWELRY

Davidrose Jewelry ★★   Jewel encrusted Bermuda triangle jewelry are the show stoppers at this family-owned jeweler, but fans also covet Davidrose's 18-karat gold Nautical Collection featuring marlin, tuna, hooks and propellers. Davidrose has a sister location on Front Street in Hamilton. 20 Water St. www.davidrosestudio.com. ☎ **441/293-7673.** Bus: 1, 3, 6, 10, or 11.

La Garza ★★   Owner/designer Tara Cassidy uses items found in nature in most of her creations. Those include earrings and hairclips made with preserved lionfish fins, necklaces crafted from dark bits of shells and sea urchins, and pendants of crab molts and claws. Her Plastisea Collection is a stunner, featuring rings and other wearables made from colorful bits of plastic she finds washed upon the shore. Block House, 5 Bridge St. www.lagarzabermuda.com. ☎ **441/705-2787.** Bus: 1, 3, 6, 10, or 11.

Saltwater Jewellery ★★   Owned by mother-daughter team Kelli and Roseclair Thompson, this airy boutique features one-of-a-kind bracelets, necklaces, and earrings made with sea glass found on Bermuda's beaches, in addition to pieces incorporating Venetian glass, semiprecious stones and freshwater pearls. 29 Water St. www.saltwaterjewellery.com. ☎ **441/519-9906.** Bus: 1, 3, 6, 10, or 11.

TOBACCO

Churchill's Ltd. ★   Bermuda's only walk-in humidor is here and its crammed with premium Cuban cigars including Cohiba, Monte Cristo, and Romeo y Julieta. Churchill's also carries a wide selection of wine and spirits. 27 York St. ☎ **441/297-1650.** Bus: 1, 3, 6, 10, or 11.

BERMUDA AFTER DARK

I t's no secret that Bermudians like to party. In a country that claims not one but two national cocktails—the Dark n' Stormy and the rum swizzle—burning the midnight oil is a long-held tradition that's practiced at beachside bonfires, coastal parks and most notably, in the City of Hamilton where the majority of the island's bars and lounges are found. Sure, you might not find as much to keep you busy in the wee hours of the night as in some big city destinations, but with the right attitude and a little bit of rum, anything is possible in Bermuda.

In fact, there's a saying in Bermuda that's commonly uttered by witty bartenders and old-school islanders, all of whom wear their affinity for the bottle like a badge of honor. According to these old salts, the island is home to "65,000 alcoholics clinging to a rock," and while the adage is meant to be taken in jest, there *is* a hint of truth to it. Make no mistake: Bermudians like to drink and on any given night—but even more so on Fridays and Saturdays—you too can join the rum-fueled party.

Like most of its sister isles in the Caribbean, Bermuda's nightlife scene is governed by seasonality, which means from May through September you'll find the most happening, since this 5-month summer stretch is the island's busiest. After dark parties are also somewhat weather dependent, since popular events like Friday night happy hours in the City of Hamilton, and its festive Wednesday night street party known as Harbour Night, are typically held in outdoor venues. But no matter when you visit, you're bound to find a group of boisterous locals bellied up to the bar.

Bermuda is also a place where you can catch the occasional concert or comedy show from professionals who are flown in to perform—so you don't necessarily have to join the tippling masses to enjoy the evening. These events tend to happen to during the summer months and are centered around popular holidays like **Bermuda Heroes Weekend** in June, when international reggae and soca acts perform and at **Summer Splash** during the Cup Match cricket festivities in August when similar artists put on lively shows across the island. Another popular annual event is **Just for Laughs,** a comedy fest which features professional comedians from around the globe who perform at the Mid-Ocean Amphitheatre in January.

There's no one website that lists every event on a given night, so you'll have to do some surfing to find out exactly what's happening during your visit. A good place to start is **Nothing to Do in Bermuda** (**www.nothingtodoin bermuda.com**), which publishes events, performances, and movie listings and is updated regularly. Also check Bermuda's two main ticketing sites: **www.bdatix.com** and **www.ptix.bm**, both of which list dramatic, live music and comedy performances. Another useful resource is **www.bermuda.com**, an all-encompassing site that has a regularly updated events calendar (just click on "Things to Do" to navigate to the page).

From mid-January to early March the island is treated to a smattering of cultural performances at the **Bermuda Festival of the Performing Arts.** Be sure to buy tickets in advance since these performances sell out fast to a local population that's otherwise starved of big-name performances.

Finally, a word about transportation. Public buses and ferries are unreliable in the evening. If you've indulged, take a taxi wherever you might be headed for the night—and certainly back to your hotel. Road safety is a serious issue in Bermuda and riding two-wheeled scooters after a drink or two is a foolish risk. For a taxi, simply call Island Taxi at ℮ **441/295-4141** or download the app Hitch, which is similar to Uber, except for licensed taxi drivers.

BARS & LOUNGES
The City of Hamilton

Astwood Arms ★   This traditional English pub is among the newest in Bermuda, but you wouldn't know it by looking at its massive wooden bar, which hovers over a weathered-walled dining room. Predictably, it's popular with British expats who come for its pub grub menu and draft beers. 85 Front St. www.astwoodarms.bm. ℮ **441/292-5818.**

Bermuda Bistro at the Beach ★★   Despite its name, this thumping sports bar is located in the middle of Front Street, not far from where the cruise ships dock. Locals and tourists alike come here for cheap eats until midnight, to catch a game on one of the many TVs, and for DJs and live bands on some Friday and Saturday nights. 103 Front St. www.thebeachbermuda.com. ℮ **441/292-0219.**

Brew ★★   This is Bermuda's one and only wine-on-tap bar. It features eight seasonally rotating wines, all of which have been infused with nitrogen to prevent oxidation and loss of flavor, hand-pulled into a glass from a wall of silver taps. Beer lovers won't be disappointed either, since this after-work spot is one of the few bars in Hamilton where you can also get locally brewed draft beers from the Dockyard Brewing Company. Target this bar for a glass of vino before heading out to dinner in town. 53 Front St. www.irg.bm. ℮ **441/542-2739.**

Bulli Social ★   Imbibe in an open-air courtyard next to one of Bermuda's lushest parks. This gourmet burger bar's al fresco patio is covered by a canopy of trees making it a delightful place to spend a few hours, early in the evening

Feed the Late-Night Need

If you've stayed out past last call and you're in the need for a late-night "greeze"—Bermudian slang for a big, filling meal—line up with the locals at one of two fast food joints that stay open until the wee hours. There's **Mr. Chicken** (27 Queen St., City of Hamilton; ℂ **441/292-6109**) for fried chicken sandwiches, chicken nuggets, burgers, subs, and fried-fish dinners until 4am on Friday and Saturday nights. And at **Ice Queen** (Rural Hill Plaza; ℂ **441/236-3136**), just outside town in a small Paget Parish strip mall, many of the same flash-fried guilty pleasures are offered plus chicken wings, fish sandwiches and creamy milkshakes. This hole-in-the-wall takeout spot is open until 5am daily.

(it closes around 11pm most nights). 7 Queen St. (next to Par-la-Ville Park). www.bullisocial.com. ℂ **441/232-2855.**

Cosmopolitan Ultra Lounge & Night Club ★★ Simply called Cosmo by locals, this is Bermuda's only true nightclub. Open on Friday and Saturday nights from 10pm until 3am, it's where Bermuda's 20- and 30-something crowd goes to dance the night away to thumping house, soca, and electronic music played by live DJs. Grab a drink at one of its two bars and join the crowds on the dancefloor or grab a seat in its mood lit Ultra Lounge, where rainbow-colored lights illuminate the crowd. 95 Front St. ℂ **441/705-2582.**

Crown & Anchor ★ Located in the lobby of the Hamilton Princess Hotel & Beach Club, this casual bar and restaurant draws a mature crowd who come to hear live music on the weekends and who sit on its outdoor patio to enjoy a harbor front cigar—a large collection of Cuban varieties are sold behind the bar. It stays pretty mellow until close (typically around 11pm), so if you're staying at the hotel or even nearby, this is a good spot for a quiet martini. Hamilton Princess Hotel, 76 Pitts Bay Rd. www.thehamiltonprincess.com. ℂ **441/295-3000.**

The Docksider Pub & Restaurant ★★ Known as Dockies, this is the rowdiest sports bar in Bermuda, a no-frills, drink-till-you're-drunk pub where you can get cheap food until late and watch just about any sporting event on its many TVs. On Fridays and Saturdays expect live DJs and a young, boisterous crowd demanding drinks at its long cedar bar, tossing darts or playing Ping-Pong (or beer pong) at its in-house tables. This is also one of the few bars in Hamilton that stays open until 3am, so if you're searching for a late-night swizzle, this would be the place. 121 Front St. www.docksider.bm. ℂ **441/296-3333.**

The Dog House ★★★ Its tagline is "It's Where We All End Up"—a true statement if ever there was one. This industrial-looking hotspot is where Hamilton's hardcore partiers close out the night: It's the only place in the city open until 3am 7 days a week. The revelry extends to drink service: Along with 20 beers on tap, 100-ounce self-serve tubes are available for beer, Dark n' Stormies, or whatever else your drinking team desires. To keep the party going, dance music is pumped in by live DJs through a state-of-the-art sound system.

The Dog House often hosts bands too; check its website for the changing lineup. 93 Front St. www.doghouse.bm. ℂ **441/232-3644.**

Flanagan's Irish Pub & Restaurant ★★   On the second floor of a landmark building in the heart of Hamilton's business district, this restaurant and pub is one of Bermuda's most visible symbols of Irish nationalism and "the 100,000 welcomes" that often go with it. This traditional Irish pub has all the trappings including Guinness, Kilkenny, and a dozen other beers on tap and a handful of TVs behind its hardwood bar broadcasting sporting events. *Tip:* If your favorite game is not being shown, head downstairs to its sister location, the Outback Sports Bar (see below), which has the most TVs in Bermuda. Emporium Building, 69 Front St. www.flanagans.bm. ℂ **441/295-8299.**

Harry's Restaurant & Bar ★★   Located on the waterfront, this upscale restaurant is where the island's power brokers gather after work, since it's just far enough off the beaten path to avoid the crowds that typically descend upon Hamilton. The Friday happy hour on its torch-lit patio is a real scene. 96 Pitts Bay Rd. www.harrys.bm. ℂ **441/292-5533.**

Hog Penny ★★★   A common piece of Bermuda folk lore is that this traditional English pub was the inspiration for *Cheers,* the bar featured in the eponymously named 1980s sitcom. It's not true, but you will find a similar bunch of suds-soaked locals at the bar, all who have come for its cozy British stylings, tap beer, and the friendly bartenders. Open nightly until 1am, this tiny pub in the center of Hamilton gets especially busy on Thursday, Friday and Saturday nights, when it hosts live music from a handful of local musicians. Norm and the gang may not be bellied up to the bar, but after a few beers, it's likely that a few new Bermuda friends will know your name. 5 Burnaby St. www.hogpennypub.com. ℂ **441/292-2534.**

Little Venice Wine Bar ★★   This cozy trattoria has one of the largest collections of wines on the island. Pull up a stool at the granite-topped bar or grab a table at its open-air sidewalk patio, which will stay open until the last drops of fine chianti or full-bodied cabernet are sipped. 32 Bermudiana Rd. www.littevenice.bm. ℂ **441/295-3503.**

Outback Sports Bar ★★   Featuring 23 high-def TVs including a 63-inch flat screen from which the biggest sporting events are broadcast, there's not a bad seat in the house for sports fans. There with friends? Then reserve one of

---

Harbour Night in the City of Hamilton

On Wednesday nights from May through September, the City of Hamilton blocks off all vehicular traffic on Front Street to make way for a menagerie of crafts vendors, food trucks, and Gombey dancers (see p. 34). It all makes for a rousing summertime street party. Harbour Night is robustly attended by both locals and visitors, often with kids in tow as there are activities just for the wee ones in special family-friendly zones.

Marina Nights at the Hamilton Princess Hotel

The biggest night of the week in Bermuda is Friday, when the Hamilton workforce punches out of their day jobs and rum-punches in at the stroke of 5pm at a selection of bars and hotels that host boisterous happy hours. This one, hosted by the Hamilton Princess Hotel & Beach Club, is among the best since it draws well-dressed locals at a dockside venue adjacent to its luxurious Princess Marina, often crammed with gleaming white super yachts. Revelers sip cocktails harborside while listening to chilled-out lounge music played by a live DJ (May–Sept only). (76 Pitts Bay Rd.; www.thehamiltonprincess.com; ✆ **441/295-3000**.)

the booths, which feature personal screens that you can operate with a dedicated remote control for the table. The bar stays open until 1am, except on nights when it broadcasts major events like the Super Bowl when it stays open into the wee hours. Typical bar food like burgers, wings and chili is served until 10pm. Emporium Building, 69 Front St. www.flanagans.bm. ✆ **441/295-8299**.

The Pickled Onion ★★★   At night, after the dinner service, all the dining tables here make way for a dance floor. One of the few bars that features live music (Tues–Sat), it hosts open-mic nights, stripped-down acoustic ensembles, and raucous rock-'n'-roll bands. The bar usually stays open until 1am, but on Friday and Saturday nights, the band keeps rocking until 2am. 53 Front St. www.thepickledonion.com. ✆ **441/295-2263**.

The Robin Hood ★   More than most other pubs in Bermuda, this one attracts expatriates from the U.K. who join the soccer-crazed crowds to watch big-screen coverage of various British and European league competitions. Foaming pints of beer, hearty pub fare and some of Bermuda's best pizzas are also big lures. It's not the easiest place to find, as it is located at the western edge of Hamilton, about a 10-minute walk from Front Street. *Tip:* Tuesday nights, it hosts its über-popular Trivia Night starting at 9pm. 25 Richmond Rd. www.robinhood.bm. ✆ **441/295-3314**.

The Terrace on Front Street ★★   With soaring vaulted ceilings, a handsome black granite bar and a decidedly upscale vibe, this Front Street bar and restaurant draws a more mature crowd then most others along the block. Head there for martinis and light bites on its glassed-in balcony overlooking Hamilton Harbour. It closes around 11pm on most days (open later on Fri and Sat). 55 Front St. www.theterracebermuda.com. ✆ **441/292-7331**.

Yours Truly ★★★   You could walk past Yours Truly several times in a night without knowing it was there—which is exactly what this well-hidden speakeasy is going for. Tucked away down a narrow alley called Chancery Lane (it runs perpendicular to Reid and Front sts.), this exclusive lounge is accessible by pushing a single-button doorbell that's adjacent to an unmarked matte-black door with a golden knob. Simply tap it, then wait a few minutes.

When your table is ready, a leather-aproned server will escort you inside the dimly lit room where you'll be given an extensive menu of craft cocktails, most of which are created with homemade syrups and bitters. The selection changes often, but favorites include the Mezcal Maid with smoky mezcal, lime, agave, and Thai basil or a traditional pisco sour. Closed on Sunday and Monday, the cocktail bar typically stays open to midnight or 1am. 2 Chancery Lane. www.yourstruly.bm. © **441/295-0429.**

Southampton Parish

Boundary Sports Bar & Grille ★★   With one of the largest selections of high-def TVs in Bermuda, plus four 60-inch televisions stacked into a rectangle that can be turned into one giant screen, Boundary is a mecca for sports fans, broadcasting games of the NFL, NBA, MLB and NHL, plus a large selection of British and European soccer. Open until midnight 7 days a week, the bar has several beers on tap and serves a menu of pub grub (kitchen closes at 10pm). It's in the Fairmont Southampton, above the Turtle Hill Golf Course clubhouse. Middle Rd. www.waterlotinn.com. © **441/238-8000.**

The Dock ★★   If you've got dinner reservations at the Waterlot Inn (see "Where to Eat," on p. 121) then get there a little early to enjoy this outdoor lounge on Jew's Bay. With dozens of low-slung couches and lounge chairs, its darn nice even if you're not going to the Waterlot: You can sip cocktails and nibble on tapas while listening to local musicians play mellow favorites (like ukulele impresario Mike Hind, who usually performs Fri and Sat). Open during the summer season from 5 to 10pm, the Dock is one of the best places on the west end to watch the sunset. Middle Rd. www.waterlotinn.com. © **441/238-8000.**

Henry VIII ★   Easily walkable from the Fairmont Southampton and The Reefs Resort & Club, this traditional English pub (hardwood bar, brass railings throughout) has a large dance floor. Musicians and/or DJs keep it filled on Thursday, Friday and Saturday nights. 52 S. Shore Rd. www.henrys.bm. © **441/238-1977.**

Jasmine Cocktail Bar & Lounge ★★   Located in the lobby of the Fairmont Southampton, this elegant lounge is a popular spot for mixing and mingling with an upscale and often nubile collection of revelers—it's chiefly where dolled-up Bermudians go before catching a show at the on-site Mid-Ocean

---

The Best Sunset Cruise Deal on Bermuda

Party boat **Über Vida** (www.ubervida. net; © **441/236-2222**), a multi-deck power catamaran, departs the City of Hamilton for a 90-minute cruise through nearby Paradise Lakes daily from May through September (at 6pm and 8pm). Passage is free; the enterprise makes its money back by selling booze at the bar ($8–$15 per drink; bottle service available). Which means it is a superb bargain for teetotalers in the market for a sunset spin around the harbor. *Tip:* If you've taken the 6pm cruise and care to take another cruise, simply stay onboard for the 8pm departure.

Amphitheatre and where hotel guests grab pre-dinner cocktails before hitting the town. With an extensive cocktail list, live entertainment nightly, and cozy corners perfect for canoodling, Jasmine Lounge is a top spot to begin or end a special night out. Fairmont Southampton, 101 South Rd. ℂ **441/238-8000.**

Royal Naval Dockyard

Bonefish Bar & Grill ★   A good option for visitors staying on the west end in summer and searching for a night out, Bonefish hosts a DJ on Monday and Wednesday nights who spins lively Latin tunes. Popular among cruise shippers, it serves a light bar menu from 10:30pm until midnight from May through September. Royal Naval Dockyard. www.bonefishbermuda.bm. ℂ **441/234-5151.**

The Frog & Onion Pub ★★   Converted from an 18th-century cooperage where barrels were once made for the British Navy, this British-style pub is within the solid stone walls of the Royal Naval Dockyard. Sprawling and steeped in a sense of English military history, it serves stiff drinks in oversized glasses, draft beers brewed on-site by the Dockyard Brewing Company, and bar snacks throughout the evening. It's also one of the few places on the west end that hosts live music until midnight but call ahead to see who's playing since schedules often change, and they don't update their website regularly. The Cooperage, Royal Naval Dockyard. www.frogandonion.bm. ℂ **441/234-2900.**

Snorkel Park Beach ★   This is a made-for-tourists beach bar at the Royal Naval Dockyard (you won't find locals here). Still, if you want an island-fest vibe and nightly shows with fire dancers, limbo competitions and live DJs, this may be the spot for you. And the drinks are far more potent than you'll get aboard the cruise ships docked nearby (if you'd like to wake up without a headache, stay far away from its signature cocktail, the Shark Oil, made with loads of 151-proof rum). Seasonal hours are subject to cruise ship schedules. Maritime Lane, Dockyard. www.snorkelparkbeach.com. ℂ **441/234-6989.**

Warwick Parish

Swizzle Inn ★★   In a parish that boasts few late-night establishments, thank goodness then for this sole roadside bar and restaurant, where nearby residents watch British and European soccer matches at its small wooden bar, and devotees of the original Bermuda rum swizzle share iced-down pitchers of the stuff on its large, open-air patio. *Note:* This is an offshoot of the original Swizzle Inn. 87 South Rd. www.swizzleinn.com. ℂ **441/236-7459.**

8

Bars & Lounges

BERMUDA AFTER DARK

Hamilton Parish

Conservatory Bar and Lounge ★★ This upscale gin bar features 21 types of that clear liquor which are mixed into an exquisite selection of craft cocktails. Grab a seat at its handsome white granite bar or pull up an arm chair next to the fireplace where you'll have views of its exposed cedar ceiling beams and the waters of Castle Harbour through French doors that open up to small outdoor balconies. Rosewood Bermuda, 60 Tucker's Point Dr. www.rosewood hotels.com. ✆ **441/298-4013.**

The Swizzle ★★ This is the original, the creator of Bermuda's famous tipple, and a famously friendly dive where patrons scribble their names on the wall or tack business cards to the ceiling (activities that are encouraged). Like its sister location in Warwick (see above) you can order typical pub grub until 10pm, but most people come for the eponymously named drink, which is served in iced pitchers or by the glass. There's live entertainment most nights during the summer. 3 Blue Hole Hill, Bailey's Bay. www.swizzleinn.com. ✆ **441/293-1854.**

Smith's Parish

North Rock Brewing Company ★ You won't find a rollicking crowd at this pub in sleepy Smith's Parish. But if you're staying nearby and care to grab a pint, this traditional English pub near the south end of Collector's Hill will do just fine. Featuring a selection of beers brewed by local craft brewery On de Rock, North Rock screens British and European soccer matches many nights. 10 South Rd. ✆ **441/236-6633.**

St. George's Parish

The Wharf Restaurant & Bar ★ Whether this waterfront bar and restaurant stays open past 10pm is completely dependent upon the crowd, but such is life in the Town of St. George's, which is a bit player in Bermuda's nightlife scene. Here you can drink tap beer or grab a cocktail at its large indoor bar or pullup table at its sprawling outdoor patio, but don't expect much more to keep you entertained in the evening hours. 14 Water St., Somers Wharf. www.wharf.bm. ✆ **441/297-3305.**

White Horse Pub & Restaurant ★★ Located on King's Square in the heart of St. George's, this dive bar is most crowded during happy hour (Mon–Fri 5–7pm), when draft beer and cocktails cost $5. Open until 11pm nightly, it's all about the sports on TV, the dart throwing competitions, and the gossip of the regulars—nearby residents consider this place a second home. King's Sq. www.whitehorsebermuda.com. ✆ **441/297-1838.**

THE PERFORMING ARTS

Dance

The **National Dance Foundation of Bermuda** (✆ 441/236-3319) stages performances, both classical and modern, around the island, featuring both

Bermuda's Gombey Dancers

No one cultural institution is as iconic as Bermuda's own Gombey dancers—the island's single most important expression of African heritage. The tradition dates to the mid-1700s, when enslaved peoples from African and Caribbean nations shared customs from their native countries. What developed over time was this colorful dancing troupe, which spins and whirls to the thumping beat of snare drums and whistles played by costumed performers. These dancers perform during parades and during Harbour Night in the City of Hamilton—a weekly Wednesday night street party held on Front Street from May through September.

local dancers and major artists imported from venues in Europe and North America. Check local events listings for upcoming performances or simply calls its offices for more. And if you'd like to dance, check out the website of the **Sabor Dance School** (www.bermudasalsa.com), which regularly hosts salsa dance nights at venues around Bermuda.

Musical Theater

The **Bermuda Musical and Dramatic Society** (founded in 1944; www.bmds.bm) and the **Gilbert & Sullivan Society** (www.gands.bm) both use local talent to produce Broadway-style musicals and other family-friendly performances. As well, Harvard University's **Hasty Pudding Theatricals** visit Bermuda to perform student-written drag burlesque musicals—a tradition that's endured for more than 50 years. The latter is typically held in March or April at the Earl Cameron Theatre in City Hall.

WHERE TO STAY

B ermuda is home to a wide variety of lodging options from small family-owned inns to sprawling resorts with bells-and-whistles galore. Facilities vary greatly in size and amenities within each category. This chapter is organized by the type of available accommodations to help you find your ideal place to stay.

PRACTICAL MATTERS
Choosing the Place That's Right for You

Accommodations in Bermuda basically fall into six categories:

- **Resort Hotels:** These large properties are Bermuda's most lavish, offering many facilities, services, and amenities—but they also typically charge the highest prices. The lowest rates, usually discounted about 20%, are in effect from early November to mid-March. Large resorts usually have private beaches, swimming pools and a selection of on-site restaurants, while others boast their own golf courses.

- **Small Hotels:** Bermuda's small hotels offer the intimacy of upscale inns, but with more amenities. At a small hotel, you might feel more connected to the island and its people. Another plus? They're often cheaper than the big resorts.

- **Cottage Colonies:** This uniquely Bermudian option consists of a series of bungalows constructed around a clubhouse, which is the center of social life, drinking, and dining. The cottages, usually scenically arranged on landscaped grounds, are designed to provide maximum privacy and are typically equipped with kitchenettes for preparing light meals. In many of the cottage colonies, breakfast isn't available; you can go out, or buy supplies and prepare your own meal. Most colonies have beaches or swimming pools.

- **Housekeeping Units:** These cottage or apartment-style accommodations (often called efficiencies in the U.S.) occupy landscaped estates surrounding a main clubhouse. All of them offer kitchen facilities—perhaps not a full, well-equipped kitchen, but a kitchenette at least where you can whip up snacks and breakfast. Most offer minimal daily maid service. Generally, housekeeping units are simpler and less expensive than cottage colonies.

- **Guesthouses:** These are Bermuda's least corporate accommodations. Most are family-run, and many are old Bermuda homes in garden settings. Generally speaking, they've been modernized to include en suite bathrooms and other amenities. In these moderately priced accommodations, you'll likely mingle with other travelers in small common spaces and have a commute to the beach.

o **House Rentals:** Widely available on websites like **Airbnb, VRBO, Home-Away,** and **FlipKey,** these are the least expensive accommodations in Bermuda. On these sites, one can easily find studio or one-bedroom apartments for less than $100 a night (like Panatola Studio, with water views for $95 a night) and full cottages with multiple rooms for around $200 per night (like Watercolours, a two-bedroom waterfront cottage that's owned by acclaimed local artist Carole Holding, who's been known to gift renters signed artwork from her collection). Expect all the comforts of home and then some: Many feature cushy island amenities like pools, beach access and lush tropical gardens. With the introduction of the Twizy—Bermuda's first electric-powered rental vehicle (see p. 207)—some homeowners have even installed on-site charging stations, so consider homes with dedicated "Oasis Points" if you're planning on zipping around the island in a four-wheeler. Like other watery destinations, homes closest to the beach (or with ocean or harbor views) will likely be the most expensive, but deals abound for travelers who don't mind being landlocked.

Rates & Reservation Policies

The rates listed throughout this chapter are real-time prices culled mostly from popular third-party booking sites, including HotelsCombined.com and Booking.com. The exceptions are some of the small inns and guesthouses listed below, as they don't appear on the major booking engines. That's not a mark against their quality; these places do such good business that they don't have to rely on "third-party" sites to stay full (and they don't have to pay commissions, which means they can offer better prices to their guests).

The rates listed in this chapter do not include taxes and service charges, which can increase the nightly fee. All room rates are subject to an 11.75% government occupancy tax, plus a tourism fee and service charge, which will be automatically tacked onto your bill (some hotels charge 10% of the bill, while others charge a per-diem amount). Keep in mind that the service charge does not cover service at the on-site restaurants and bars; for those you'll be paying a 17% gratuity for food and beverage bills, so don't be sticker shocked when the final tally arrives.

Bermuda's peak season is in the summer months of June, July and August, when the weather is warmest and its hotels are their fullest. However, deals—and equally pleasant conditions—can often be found in the handful of months just before and just after these months. Called shoulder season, room rates can drop some 40% despite the fact that the weather will be quite temperate (about 60°–70°F) in April and May or September and October. Another way to save: Book a package deal that includes hotel and airfare. See airline sites, Expedia, Priceline and the like for these types of offers.

For the purposes of grouping hotels in this chapter, any hotel with rooms costing more than $400 a night in high season is listed as "expensive." "Moderate" hotels are those costing between $250 and $400 a night. And anything less than $250 per night is classified as inexpensive (alas, those are the parameters in pricy

Bermuda). Note that some hotels offer a wide range of room types, and with them a wide range of prices. So it may be possible to score a $300 a night room if you'll forego a water view, in a hotel where most rooms are $400 a night. Ask.

best FOR FAMILIES

- **Elbow Beach Hotel** (Paget Parish; www.elbowbeachbermuda.com; ☎ 855/463-5269 or 441/236-3535): Situated on one of the longest pink sand beaches in Bermuda with gentle waves perfect for the littlest of swimmers, this full-service resort also boasts a spate of amenities specifically geared towards children (like a kids' club with video games and toys galore and hosted daily games and craft-making sessions). See p. 194.
- **Fairmont Southampton** (Southampton Parish; www.fairmont.com; ☎ 888/495-4173 or 441/238-8000): This sprawling resort has a lot of amenities for families: the Explorers Camp Kids' Club where children ages 5 and up can try arts and crafts and play video games; a waterslide-equipped kiddie pool; and a private pink sand beach in a calm, protected cove. Kids 5 and under eat free, and children ages 5 to 12 get 50% off the adult menu. See p. 189.
- **Grotto Bay Beach Resort** (Hamilton Parish; www.grottobay.com; ☎ 855/447-6886 or 441/293-8333): Since this is one of the only all-inclusive resorts in Bermuda, it's a great place for a value-minded family vacation. It also features tons to keep the kids busy, like a floating inflatable playground anchored off its private beach, on-site scavenger hunts, pizza pool parties and even subterranean caves to explore. See p. 200.
- **Newstead Belmont Hills Golf Resort & Spa** (Paget Parish; www.newstead belmonthills.com; ☎ 441/236-6060): Spacious accommodations that are good for groups are the lure here, many of which contain full kitchens—a money- and sanity-saving perk for families who don't want to eat out every meal. There's no beach, but the kids will love the harborside infinity pool. See p. 195.
- **Rosemont Guest Suites** (City of Hamilton, Pembroke Parish; www. rosemont.bm; ☎ 800/367-0040 or 441/292-1055): This all-suite hotel in the City of Hamilton has rates that are among the lowest in the capital for roomy digs with kitchenettes. Rosemont is a top option for intergenera- tional families since up to four rooms can be connected. See p. 199.

best BANG FOR YOUR BUCK

- **The Oxford House** (City of Hamilton, Pembroke Parish; www.oxford house.bm; ☎ 800/548-7758 or 441/295-0503): Centrally located in the City of Hamilton, this elegant Bermuda-style townhouse is one of the most affordable accommodations in the capital. See p. 199.
- **Salt Kettle House** (Paget Parish; www.saltkettlehouse.com; ☎ 441/236-0407): This family-run inn is a stone's throw from Hamilton—the cozy cottage is located directly across the harbor from town (to get there just hop on the public ferry a few steps away). Expect water views, peaceful gardens and warm Bermudian hospitality. See p. 197.

Bermuda Hotels

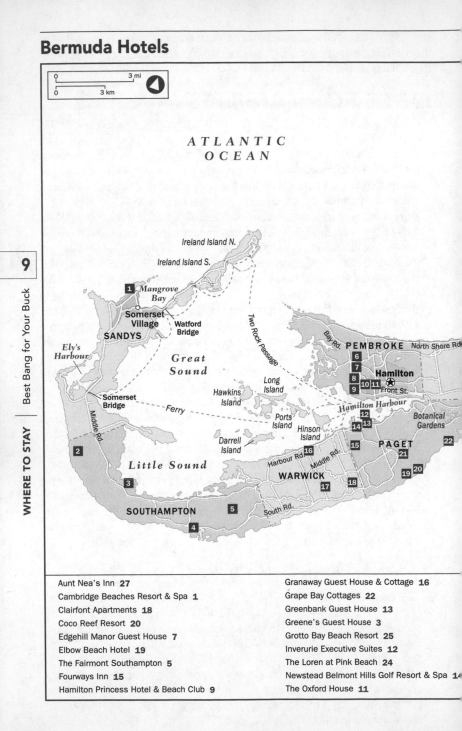

ATLANTIC
OCEAN

Ireland Island N.

Ireland Island S.

1 *Mangrove Bay*

Somerset Village

Watford Bridge

SANDYS

Ely's Harbour

Great Sound

Two Rock Passage

Bay Rd.

PEMBROKE North Shore Rd.

6
7
8 **Hamilton**
9 **10** **11** ★
Front St.

Somerset Bridge

— Ferry —

Hawkins Island

Long Island

Ports Island

Hinson Island

Hamilton Harbour

12
14 **13**

Botanical Gardens

2

Middle Rd.

Little Sound

Darrell Island

15 **PAGET**
21
22
19 **20**

Harbour Rd. **16**

Middle Rd.

3

WARWICK

17 **18**

SOUTHAMPTON **5**

South Rd.

4

Aunt Nea's Inn **27**
Cambridge Beaches Resort & Spa **1**
Clairfont Apartments **18**
Coco Reef Resort **20**
Edgehill Manor Guest House **7**
Elbow Beach Hotel **19**
The Fairmont Southampton **5**
Fourways Inn **15**
Hamilton Princess Hotel & Beach Club **9**

Granaway Guest House & Cottage **16**
Grape Bay Cottages **22**
Greenbank Guest House **13**
Greene's Guest House **3**
Grotto Bay Beach Resort **25**
Inverurie Executive Suites **12**
The Loren at Pink Beach **24**
Newstead Belmont Hills Golf Resort & Spa **14**
The Oxford House **11**

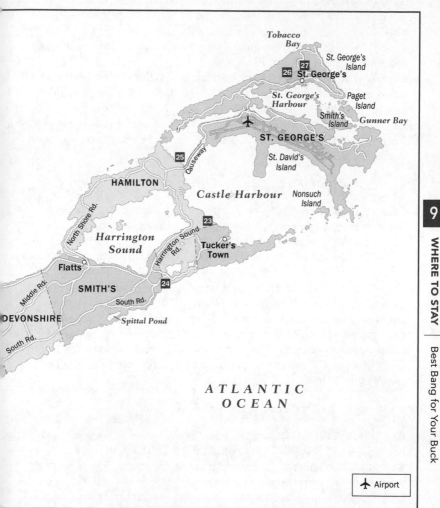

✈ Airport

See also the "Hamilton Hotels" map

- **Granaway Guest House & Cottage** (Warwick Parish; www.granaway. com; ☎ **441/236-3747**): This former private home from 1734 is a near picture-postcard cliché of Bermudian charm, with its light pink walls and whitewashed roof. Opening onto views of the Great Sound, it's been handsomely converted to receive guests with comfortable en suite rooms and lush private gardens. See p. 193.

- **Sandpiper Apartments** (Warwick Parish; ☎ **441/236-7093**): For visitors who'd prefer to cook their own meals and be within a 5-minute taxi ride to some of the island's finest slices of pink sand there's no better place. This recently renovated apartment complex in Warwick parish boasts spacious, inexpensive rooms with full kitchens just down the road from gorgeous Warwick Long Bay. See p. 193.

best SPLURGE

- **Rosewood Bermuda** (Hamilton Parish; www.rosewoodhotels.com; ☎ **441/298-4000**): Featuring a private beach, top class restaurants and spa, and some of the most luxurious rooms on the island—with oversized soaking tubs in large spalike bathrooms, handsome plantation-style hardwood furniture, and spacious outdoor balconies—this retreat is tailor made for special occasions. See p. 201.

- **The Hamilton Princess Hotel & Beach Club** (City of Hamilton; www. thehamiltonprincess.com; ☎ **441/295-3000**): Thanks to a recent infusion of more than $100 million by its owners, this landmark City of Hamilton hotel has regained its position as one of Bermuda's top resorts. It's added a host of new splurge-worthy amenities, like the island's best restaurant and a gorgeous new spa. The hotel boasts a multimillion-dollar collection of contemporary art in its public spaces. See p. 197.

most ROMANTIC

- **Cambridge Beaches Resort & Spa** (Sandys Parish; www.cambridge beaches.com; ☎ **800/468-7300** or 441/234-0331): This is the only resort in Bermuda where children 12 and under are not permitted, which is one of the reasons why honeymooners and couples have long made this adults-preferred retreat an island favorite. With four private beaches it's easy to find a secluded slice of sand to call your own. See p. 189.

- **The Loren at Pink Beach** (Smiths Parish; www.theloren.com; ☎ **844/384-3103** or 441/293-1666): Chic, modern, and stylish, Bermuda's newest resort upped the island's hip factor when it opened in 2017. All 45 rooms have views of the turquoise ocean. The hotel also has the two best restaurants on the east end. See p. 200.

- **The Reefs Resort & Club** (Southampton Parish; www.thereefs.com; ☎ **800/742-2008** or 441/238-0222): With pristine reef snorkeling just offshore, its pink sand beach is among Bermuda's best—as are its splurge-worthy club condos with spalike bathrooms and outdoor hot tubs for two. Ready for dinner? Then have the resort set up a table on the sand for an unforgettable meal under the stars. See p. 190.

SANDYS PARISH

Cottage Colony

EXPENSIVE

Cambridge Beaches Resort & Spa ★★★ If a hushed vacation is what you're after—one without raucous families, young children, and partying 20-somethings—you've found your Valhalla. Cambridge is the oldest and most celebrated cottage colony on the island, featuring four private beaches. That makes it possible to suntan without seeing another soul, which may be why celebrities and politicians have long made this adults-only retreat their pick (Bill and Hillary Clinton are among those bold-faced names). It's also entirely kid-free: Children 12 and under aren't accepted as guests.

On a peninsula overlooking Mangrove Bay in Somerset, the colony's 12 hectares (30 acres) of semitropical gardens and green lawns occupy the entire western tip of the island. The colony centers on an old sea captain's house that over the years grew into a compound of lounges, bars, dining rooms, and drawing rooms that give the feeling of a conservative country estate. Most notable restaurants here are **Breezes** (p. 118), the resort's open-air beachfront eatery, and **Tamarisk,** an elegant indoor dining room that features live entertainment nightly. The on-site **Ocean Spa** is newly renovated and quite swank; the property also has two tennis courts and a multilevel infinity pool.

As for rooms, they are capacious and decked out in a luxe version of island style, with exposed Bermuda cedar beams, fireplaces, and endless views of the water from private balconies or patios. Suites feature full living rooms with antiques, oversized bathrooms with whirlpool tubs, and a separate dressing area. The resort is approximately a 1-hour taxi ride from the airport, so plan your arrival and departure accordingly.

30 Kings Point Rd. www.cambridgebeaches.com. © **800/468-7300** in the U.S., or 441/234-0331. 94 units. Winter $332–$549 double; $359–$539 suite. Summer $529–$749 double; $799–$1,099 suite. Rates include breakfast. Bus: 7 or 8. **Amenities:** 3 restaurants, fitness center, spa, yoga classes, croquet, putting green, 2 pools, 2 tennis courts, watersports equipment/rentals, scooter rentals, free Wi-Fi.

SOUTHAMPTON PARISH

Resort Hotels

EXPENSIVE

The Fairmont Southampton ★★★ This sprawling 99-acre resort is Bermuda's biggest, some 593 rooms located inside one of the island's only high-rise buildings. It boasts one of Bermuda's finest locations, perched on a Southampton hill with 360-degree views of the Atlantic Ocean and the Great Sound harbor with its archipelago of islets and cays. The resort is directly adjacent to Horseshoe Bay Beach, easily the island's most iconic slice of sand.

But like others in this swank chain, it's a full-service resort, flush with on-site restaurants, amenities, and activities aplenty. In addition to three pools, tennis courts, PADI dive center, the 21,000-square-feet Willow Stream Spa, and its

BREAKING GROUND: bermuda's newest lodgings

A trio of properties will be opening soon after this book goes to press. Rising on the site of the former Surf Side Beach Club and perched on an ocean-hugging cliff in Warwick Parish, **Azura** (www.azura bermuda.com; ✆ **441/232-9000**) will feature fully equipped studio, one- and two-bedroom residences plus a handful of detached villas, all of which are privately owned and rented to visitors when not in use by their owners. Accepting guests in the fourth quarter of 2019, these units will have full kitchens and sweeping ocean views from their private balconies and patios.

In St. George's Parish the ground has broken on **The Residences at St. Regis** (www.theresidencesbermuda.com; ✆ **441/292-3921**), a 30-unit condominium-style hotel adjacent to Fort St. Catherine and directly overlooking it's sprawling pink sand beach. In addition to luxuriously appointment living areas, the hotel is also hoping to open the island's first casino when the property is unveiled in 2020.

And finally, for what will likely be unparalleled luxury on the west end, there's the **The Cove, a Ritz-Carlton Residence** (www.bermudaluxury residences.com; ✆ **441/707-7425**) taking shape on Morgan's Point in Southampton Parish. About a 5-minute walk from Port Royal Golf Course, these high-end homes will be surrounded by three private pink sand beaches and Caroline Bay Marina, a luxury boat slip where private vessels and mega yachts dock daily.

Turtle Hill Golf Course—an 18-hole executive par-three golf course loaded with ocean views—the resort has its own private pink sand beach, accessible via a quick trolley ride from the hotel lobby or a 10-minute walk. Its second floor is a bustling shopping area with outposts of some of Bermuda's most popular shops. The resort's nine restaurants will not disappoint either. In fact, they're so good, we've dedicated individual reviews to **Boundary** (p. 123), a family-friendly sports bar; **Mediterra** (p. 124), a tapas specialist; the **Waterlot Inn** (p. 121), an upscale steakhouse; **The Dock** (p. 126) and **Jasmine's Lounge** (p. 124) for cocktails and small bites; and the **Ocean Club** (p. 121), the resort's indoor/outdoor seafood restaurant.

Because this is the largest hotel in Bermuda, the resort typically hosts conventions and conferences, which can crowd its beach and lobby in the summer. But the Fairmont's swish contemporary rooms (all with private balcony), and the amenities mentioned above, keep most guests quite content. And when they need a break from their fellow guests, they can board a private ferry for rides to and from the City of Hamilton.

101 South Rd. www.fairmont.com/southampton. ✆ **888/495-4173** or 441/238-8000. 593 units. Winter $309–$539 double; $429–$1,005 suite. Summer $669–$939 double; $849–$1,389 suite. Children 5 and under eat free; kids ages 5–12 eat 50% off the adult menu. **Amenities:** Free ferry to Hamilton, 9 restaurants, 4 bars, beach club, children's programs, 18-hole golf course, fitness center, spa, 3 pools, watersports equipment rentals, PADI dive shop, scooter and Twizy rentals, free Wi-Fi.

The Reefs Resort & Club ★★★
This family-owned resort is one of Bermuda's most beloved. Most of its guests are repeat-visitors who come for its

Hamilton Hotels

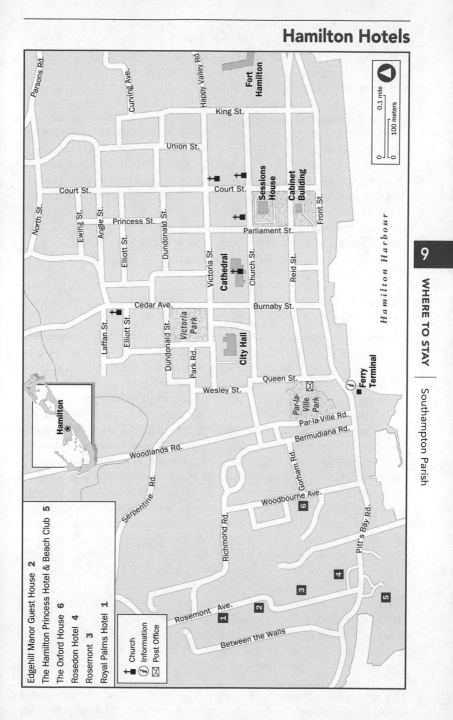

Edgehill Manor Guest House **2**

The Hamilton Princess Hotel & Beach Club **5**

The Oxford House **6**

Rosedon Hotel **4**

Rosemont **3**

Royal Palms Hotel **1**

Church

Ⓘ Information

✉ Post Office

Parsons Rd.

Curving Ave.

Happy Valley Rd.

Fort Hamilton

King St.

Union St.

Court St.

Court St.

North St.

Ewing St.

Angle St.

Princess St.

Elliott St.

Dundonald St.

Sessions House

Cabinet Building

Front St.

Parliament St.

Victoria St.

Cathedral

Church St.

Reid St.

Cedar Ave.

Burnaby St.

Laffan St.

Elliott St.

Dundonald St.

Victoria Park

Park Rd.

City Hall

Queen St.

Wesley St.

Par-la-Ville Park

Ⓘ Ferry Terminal

Par-la-Ville Rd.

Bermudiana Rd.

Woodlands Rd.

Hamilton ⊛

Hamilton Harbour

Serpentine Rd.

Gorham Rd.

6

Woodbourne Ave.

Richmond Rd.

Pitt's Bay Rd.

3

4

Rosemont Ave.

2

5

1

Between the Walls

0.1 mile

0

100 meters

0

9

WHERE TO STAY

Southampton Parish

191

oceanview rooms and sprawling Club Condos—two- and three-bedroom living spaces that are among the island's most luxurious. Lavishly appointed and thoughtfully designed, these units feature granite-topped kitchens with stainless steel appliances, oversized bathrooms with stand-alone soaking tubs and rain showers, oceanview balconies with outdoor whirlpools, and amazingly, sliding floor-to-ceiling glass walls that instantly convert the indoor living room into an open-air space. If the condos are beyond your budget, the newly renovated rooms and suites in the main hotel, are quite nice. All have private balconies or patios that face the ocean and a breezy island style (driftwood finish furniture and Bermudian artwork in living spaces, his-and-hers blue glass vanities, and glassed-in showers in bathrooms).

The hotel's secluded pink sand beach, with its craggy rock formations and ocean-penetrating coral boilers, is among the best in Bermuda (perfect for snorkeling). The resort also has one of the better spas on island. Called La Serena, its pre-and post-treatment relaxation room has floor-to-ceiling windows facing the ocean. Reviews for the on-site restos are on p. 121.

56 S. Shore Rd. www.thereefs.com. © **800/742-2008** or 441/238-0222. 60 units. Summer $675–$794 double; $1,098 suite; $1,925 2-bedroom condo. Winter $217–$699 double; $351 suite; $1,295 2-bedroom condo. Rates include breakfast. Bus: 7. **Amenities:** 2 restaurants, 2 bars, small fitness center, 2 pools, putting green, spa, game room, watersports equipment/rentals, free Wi-Fi.

Pompano Beach Club ★★   With 75 oceanview rooms perched on a Southampton cliff, this family-owned resort has the unique distinction of being located adjacent to an enormous sand bar, so guests can wade nearly two football fields in knee- to chest-deep water at low tide. It's just one of the reasons why the resort has so many repeat guests, including families who flock here for the dine-around ease (breakfast and dinner are included), and golfers who enjoy the proximity to Port Royal Golf Course, a neighboring 6,842-yard course that was once home to the PGA Grand Slam of Golf. Don't expect to be wowed by the rooms—they're drab and in need of a renovation—though with views like these most don't much mind. The resort has three very good on-site restaurants: Cedar Room, Coral Reef Café, and Ocean Grill, the latter with 30-foot-high, floor-to-ceiling windows that face the water.

36 Pompano Beach Rd. © **800/343-4155** or 441/234-0222. www.pompanobeachclub. com. 74 units. Winter $290–$330 double. Summer $540–$650 double. Rates include breakfast and dinner. Rockaway ferry to Hamilton. Bus: 7 or 8. **Amenities:** 3 restaurants, 3 bars, fitness center, day spa, tennis court, game room, pool, watersports equipment/ rentals, free Wi-Fi.

Guesthouses
INEXPENSIVE
Greene's Guest House ★   Budget travelers flock to this quaint Southampton inn not only for its low rates but for its peaceful environs—with just seven rooms in a tranquil residential neighborhood, this family-run guesthouse is the epitome of quiet. It also, at times, feels as if you could be vacationing in your Bermudian grandmother's house, what with its stately grandfather clock, Victorian hutch, and crystal chandelier all proudly displayed in the

dining room, where breakfast is served daily. Guests can lounge in the living room, where they'll find a television, board games, and a fireplace, or around the pool, which has a nice view of the Great Sound. Whale Bay Beach is a 10-minute walk away, Port Royal Golf Course is also nearby. Rooms are small and dated, but each has its own private bathroom, and some have water views.

71 Middle Rd. www.thegreenesguesthouse.com. © **441/238-0834.** 6 units. Year-round $180 double. Rates include full breakfast. Bus: 7 or 8. **Amenities:** Pool, free Wi-Fi.

WARWICK PARISH

Inexpensive

Sandpiper Apartments ★★   Built in 1979 and frequently upgraded, this apartment complex is a terrific bargain. Units feature handsome contemporary furniture, private balconies, full kitchens, and dining areas in addition to common outdoor amenities including a large pool, gas barbecue, and lounge chairs. Every apartment has a balcony, and there's daily maid service. Best of all is the fab location: just a 5-minute bus, scooter, or taxi from Warwick Long Bay and less than 10 minutes from Horseshoe Beach, plus the Swizzle Inn (p. 147) is just a few steps away. A real find.

1 Sandymount Lane. www.sandpiper.bm. © **441/236-7093.** 14 units. Winter from $125 studio, from $175 1-bedroom. Summer from $205 studio, from $260 1-bedroom. Extra adults in studio pay $25 each per night; in 1-bedroom pay $35 each per night. Bus: 7. **Amenities:** Pool, BBQ grill, free Wi-Fi.

Clairfont Apartments ★   If you don't mind being situated within a quiet residential neighborhood in Warwick Parish, this modest apartment complex is a more-than-decent choice for budget travelers. Units won't win any design awards, but they boast full kitchens with lots of living space (one-bedroom apartments have a king-size bed that can be split into twins, and two extra guests can sleep in the living area). Clairfont is just a 5-minute walk to Warwick Long Bay and Jobson's Cove, so getting to the beach—and to the nearby Warwick Long Bay playground with its swings, sandboxes and climbing frames—couldn't be easier. There's a pool, laundry facilities and a barbecue pit on-site, but little else on the property.

6 Warwickshire Rd. www.clairfontapartments.bm. © **441/238-3577.** 8 units. Year-round $160 studio; $185 1-bedroom. Bus: 7 or 8. **Amenities:** Pool, washer/dryer, barbecue pit, free Wi-Fi.

Guesthouses

INEXPENSIVE

Granaway Guest House & Cottage ★★   Originally built in 1734, this waterfront manor house embodies Bermudian charm, with its traditional stepped white roof, wooden window shutters, and daily continental breakfast served on fine Herend china. There are four en suite rooms on the property, and one private cottage that's perfect for anyone seeking additional seclusion—as if being tucked away among lush private gardens and well-manicured lawns, all of which overlook the Great Sound, isn't seclusion enough. Rooms are thoughtfully decorated, each with its own theme (flowered prints in The Rose Room, bone china decor with images of Queen Elizabeth in The Royals Room, and hand-painted Italian tile and a fireplace in the romantic cottage). You'll be well-served by public ferries to the City of Hamilton, which stop just down the street on Harbour Road.

Harbour Rd. www.granaway.com. ✆ **441/236-3747.** 5 units. Summer $175–$225 double; $250–$325 cottage. Winter $125–$175 double; $150–$225 cottage. Rates include continental breakfast (cottage excluded). Bus: 8. **Amenities:** Pool, free Wi-Fi.

PAGET PARISH

Resort Hotels

EXPENSIVE

Elbow Beach Hotel ★★★   This resort has long been a Bermuda legend, but it has been considerably downsized in recent years. When Elbow Beach rebranded as a "boutique" several years ago, it shed dozens of guest rooms from its inventory—units that were once housed in the hotel's butter-yellow main building. That building first opened its doors in 1908, and now stands largely empty (it's where you'll find the reception desk, concierge, gift shop, and guest lounge, but little else). The reason? Elbow Beach wanted to give its guests a more intimate experience, and they have, for the most part, succeeded. Rooms and suites are in low-slung detached cottages dotted throughout the 50-acre property and are still among Bermuda's most sought after. In rooms guests get soothing neutral decor and modern amenities, like iHome docking stations, personal espresso machines, rain showers and oversized soaking tubs. Each unit also features a private lanai-style patio, and some have stellar views of Elbow's iconic pink sand beach.

About that beach: It's the largest private slice of sand in all of Bermuda. Hotel guests get VIP treatment, relaxing on chaise lounges and flying a small flag attached to their beach umbrella when they want cold facial towels, or another frozen libation. There's a large heated pool where the littlest of swimmers can splash in the 1- to 3-feet wading area. There are three oceanview restaurants on-site, but don't miss a meal at **Mickey's** (p. 126), an alfresco bistro that we've named Bermuda's most romantic dinner spot.

60 South Rd. www.elbowbeachbermuda.com. ✆ **855/463-5269** or 441/236-3535. 98 units. Summer $375–$675 double. Winter $263–$375 double. Bus: 1, 2, or 7. **Amenities:** 3 restaurants, 2 bars, children's program, fitness center, spa, pool, games room, 5 all-weather tennis courts, free Wi-Fi.

Newstead Belmont Hills Golf Resort & Spa ★★★ Posh, post-modern, boutiquey, and stylish in an urban-hip way that's rather unusual in understated and conservative Bermuda, this hotel is unlike any on the island. It rises in a four-story avant-garde design that includes open-to-the-breeze-on-one-side corridors, lots of exposed limestone, a harborside infinity pool, and ample use of an exotic Brazilian hardwood *(jatoba)* for the interior louvers, doors, and trim. Rooms and studios are minimalist in design, each with a sleek full kitchen with granite countertops and stainless-steel appliances; sisal rugs on hardwood floors; spalike bathrooms with oversized soaking tubs; and private balconies, which look out upon the harbor.

This design, combined with the resort's amenities, and location, attracts the gamut of travelers. Business travelers appreciate its proximity to the City of Hamilton, golfers play its 6,100-yard oceanview course, and families enjoy the extra space that its one- and two-bedroom suites afford larger groups. Because Newstead is located directly on Hamilton Harbour, it has no beach, but popular slices of pink sand are merely a 10-minute taxi ride away. The hotel also runs a complimentary ferry to the City of Hamilton. *Tip:* If you book directly through the hotel's website, you'll receive complimentary round-trip airport transfers ($150 value). The hotel promises to match any lower rate found online (excluding auction sites, where the hotel brand is not known until booking is finalized, and those that sell package travel, such as airfare and hotel stays).

27 Harbour Rd. www.newsteadbelmonthills.com. 𝒞 **441/236-6060.** 60 units. Winter from $393 studio; from $508 1-bedroom; from $697 2-bedroom for 2. Summer from $515 studio; from $697 1-bedroom; from $980 2-bedroom. **Amenities:** 4 restaurants, 4 bars, fitness center, pool, spa, 2 tennis courts, complimentary ferry to Hamilton, complimentary round of golf, complimentary airport transfers, free Wi-Fi.

Small Hotels
MODERATE
Coco Reef Resort ★ In spite of its outdated decor and tired salmon-colored buildings (desperately in need of a paint job), this small resort does have one thing going for it: its splendid location, perched on a gorgeous expanse of Elbow Beach. Many of its rooms look right at it—a pink sand paradise flanked by the turquoise Atlantic—and that's clearly were you'll want to keep your gaze, as rooms feature tacky white wicker furniture and gaudy aqua and pink flowered curtains, pillows, and duvets. Still, they're clean with beds that are just fine. The on-site restaurant (also in need of a facelift) serves international cuisine but you'll do better taking quick walk down the beach to **Mickey's Bistro** (p. 126), **Lido** (p. 127), or **Sea Breeze** (p. 127). This hotel is a particularly good choice for golfers, since guests can play one round a day complimentary at **Belmont Hills Golf Course** (cart and clubs not included).

3 Stonington Circle. www.cocoreefbermuda.com. 𝒞 **800/648-0799** or 441/236-5416. 62 units. Jan to mid-Mar $179–$329 double; mid-Mar to mid-May $261–$332 double; mid-May to mid-Sept $297–$424 double. Bus: 7. **Amenities:** Restaurant, bar, pool, 2 tennis courts, complimentary golf, free Wi-Fi.

Housekeeping Units
MODERATE

Inverurie Executive Suites ★   One of Bermuda's most modern accommodations, this harbor-front condominium complex caters to business travelers and other extended-stay visitors who appreciate its proximity the City of Hamilton (the public ferry to town is just a stone's throw away, and a taxi takes 10 min.). In a cantaloupe-colored building on Harbour Road, offers studio suites equipped with kitchenettes and one-bedroom suites with full kitchens, all with executive work stations including a desk, ergonomic chair and G-link connectivity, smart TVs and spacious balconies facing Hamilton Harbour. You'll have daily maid service here but little else since most corporate guests use these suites only as a home base between meetings.

1 Harbour Rd. www.inverurie.bm. ℂ **441/232-5700.** 15 units. Winter from $185 studio; from $325 1-bedroom. Summer from $350 studio; from $549 1-bedroom. **Amenities:** Kitchenette in studio, full kitchen in 1-bedroom, free Wi-Fi.

INEXPENSIVE

Paraquet Guest Apartments ★   Pronounced "para-keet," these tastefully decorated tourist apartments are as close as Bermuda gets to a roadside motel offering simple, clean and inexpensive studio, one- and two-bedroom units, which to the delight of budget travelers are just a 5-minute walk to Elbow Beach and a 10-minute taxi to the City of Hamilton. For meals, there's the on-site Paraquet Restaurant—more of an American-style diner, actually. Guests can also grill their own food on the outdoor barbecue, which is located in a courtyard complete with shaded picnic tables.

72 South Rd. www.paraquetapartments.com. ℂ **441/236-5842.** 12 units. Summer from $205 double. Winter from $265 double. Bus: 1, 2, or 7. **Amenities:** Restaurant (guests get 10% off), free Wi-Fi.

Cottage Colonies
MODERATE

Fourways Inn ★   This posh little place feels like a secret hideaway. Pink-sided and airy, these Bermudian cottages occupy well-maintained gardens. The sands of Elbow Beach are within a 5-minute scooter or taxi ride. There's a freshwater pool on-site. The main building is a former private home dating from 1727. Each of the two-bedroom cottages is renovated and contain conservative, comfortable furniture. There's a medium-size grocery store across the road, but the kitchenettes are better suited for snack preparation than for making a feast. Or head for a meal to the well-regarded restaurant on-site (p. 126).

1 Middle Rd. www.fourways.bm.ℂ **800/962-7654** or 441/236-6517. 11 units. Apr–Oct from $266 double; from $356 suite. Nov–Mar from $158 double; from $189 suite. Extra person $40. Rates include continental breakfast. Bus: 8. **Amenities:** Restaurant, bar, pool, free Wi-Fi.

Guesthouses
INEXPENSIVE

Greenbank Guest House ★★   This charming guesthouse stands at the water's edge in Salt Kettle, just across the bay from the City of Hamilton.

Family owned for more than 60 years, with shady lawns and lush flower gardens, its atmosphere is relaxed and its service personal. Rooms vary in size, but many of them feature water views from the bedrooms; they're outfitted with simple wood furnishings, island-inspired artwork and in most cases, kitchens or kitchenettes (two units have a fridge only). There's no pool or beach, but guests can rent canoes for a paddle on the harbor or simply jump in for swim, since Greenbank is located directly on the water. Heading to Hamilton? Then hop aboard the public ferry, which docks just steps from the inn.

17 Salt Kettle Rd. www.greenbankbermuda.com. © **441/236-3615.** 11 units. Summer $190–$310 double. Winter $125–$255 double. **Amenities:** Canoe rentals, free Wi-Fi.

Salt Kettle House ★★★   As early as the 17th century, pirates and privateers would bring salt used to preserve meat and fish to Bermuda and store it in homes on an aptly named peninsula called Salt Kettle. This house was one of them, with parts of it dating back 200 years. These days, it's a quaint guesthouse that's been run by the same family for nearly a half century, with traditionally furnished rooms and cottages some of which are right on the water. Don't expect any bells and whistles here, but that's exactly the point. Salt Kettle House is a little slice of tranquility not far from the hustle and bustle of Hamilton (the public ferry dock to get to the city is steps from the inn).

10 Salt Kettle Rd. © **441/236-0407.** 6 units. Year-round $140–$160 double; $170 cottage for 2. **Amenities:** Public ferry nearby to the City of Hamilton, free Wi-Fi.

MODERATE
Grape Bay Cottages ★★   Small-scale and folksy, this "resort" consists of two cozy saltbox-style cottages, directly beside the sea, owned by Maria Frith. Each has comfortable, unpretentious furniture and lots of reminders of Bermuda's maritime traditions, as well as a fully equipped kitchen, a wide front veranda, and family-friendly ambience. The venue, which is often booked 6 months in advance, is about as laissez-faire as you'll find in Bermuda, but it's well suited to visitors who just want a little place of their own by the ocean.

Grape Bay Dr., off Middle Rd. www.gbcbermuda.com. © **441/236-2515.** 2 2-bedroom units. Apr–Oct $355 per night up to 4 people. Nov–Mar $270 per night up to 4 people. Bus: 7 or 8. **Amenities:** Twizy charging stations, free Wi-Fi.

CITY OF HAMILTON
Resort Hotels
EXPENSIVE
Hamilton Princess Hotel & Beach Club ★★★   This landmark luxury hotel launched Bermuda's tourist industry. Opened in 1884 and named for Princess Louise (Queen Victoria's daughter; she visited Bermuda in 1883), it was nicknamed the "Pink Palace" for its grand design and pastel paint job. More than 130 years later, the rose-colored hotel is one of Bermuda's most recognizable landmarks. It's also one of the island's most coveted reservations ever since a Bermuda-based billionaire bought the property in 2012 and infused more than $100 million into it in advance of the 35th America's Cup in 2017.

The number of new additions is staggering: a sleek harborfront infinity pool with hot tub and private cabanas; a 60-berth luxury marina that's home to gleaming white super-yachts; two new, and acclaimed, restaurants, **1609 Bar & Restaurant** (p. 132) and **Marcus'** (p. 131); an 8,200-square-feet **Exhale** spa and fitness center with adults-only pool; brand-new suites and completely refurbished rooms; plus a massive overhaul of its lobby and retail space, which now house the owner's multi-million-dollar collection of modern, pop, and contemporary art from the likes of Andy Warhol and Damien Hirst (see more about the artwork on p. 100).

As if all that weren't enough, its owners decided to make up for the hotel's lack of a private beach by buying one in Southampton (a free shuttle between the hotel takes about 20 min. and runs frequently). Called the **Hamilton Princess Beach Club,** this guests-and-members only beach club on Sinky Bay features has cheeky amenities, like in-water hammocks, a tiki bar and during the summer season, a casual alfresco restaurant.

76 Pitts Bay Rd. www.thehamiltonprincess.com. © **800/257-7544** or 441/295-3000. 458 units. Winter $399–$589 double; from $649 suite. Summer $649–$929 double; from $1,029 suite. **Amenities:** 4 restaurants, 4 bars, private beach club, spa, fitness center, luxury retail stores, watersports rentals, Twizy and scooter rentals, 2 pools, free Wi-Fi.

Rosedon Hotel ★★★   Originally built as a private home in 1906 and named after the original owner's son, this stately whitewashed mansion was converted into a boutique hotel in the 1930s. It's changed hands a few times since then, but much of the Rosedon's old-time charm remains, including its welcoming front porch and its cozy rooms with plantation style furnishings and crisp white linens. For visitors who'd prefer an upscale hotel in the City of Hamilton without the price tag of the Hamilton Princess (located across the street), there's no better option. In addition to a large heated pool and lush gardens with banana trees, birds of paradise and colorful hibiscus, the hotel has a very good on-site restaurant called Huckleberry, which specializes in sea-to-plate and farm-to-table cuisine (sit outside—the dining room is cramped and lacks character). It also offers guests a host of complimentary extras including a daily shuttle to Elbow Beach, daily afternoon tea with biscuits and cookies, a Tuesday night 1-hour rum swizzle party with hors d'oeuvres, plus two bicycles, which can be borrowed at any time.

57 Pitts Bay Rd. www.rosedon.com. © **441/295-1640.** 40 units. Winter from $299–$517 double. Summer $299–$689 double. **Amenities:** Restaurant, pool, complimentary afternoon tea, complimentary weekly rum swizzle party, complimentary bicycles, daily shuttle to Elbow Beach, free Wi-Fi. Closed Jan.

MODERATE

Royal Palms Hotel ★★   This boutique hotel on the outskirts of Hamilton is the epitome of Bermudian design and style. Comprising two 19th-century manor houses, the hotel is surrounded by lush orchards (guava, banana, avocado, and orange trees—and guests are allowed to pick fruit off them). Authentic details include an airy wraparound front porch with a swing and rocking chairs, a sunny glassed-in breakfast room with handsome Bermuda cedar tables, and a chandelier-clad sitting lounge with a brick fireplace and hardwood furniture. Rooms have all the touches of old-school Bermuda (like antique-styled lamps, hardwood furniture, and tufted armchairs) and most have kitchenettes with a microwave, refrigerator, toaster oven, and wet bar. continental breakfast is provided daily, as is complimentary red and white wine during evening happy hours. **Ascots,** its on-site restaurant, is a favorite off-the-grid hideaway among locals, but you'll find much better dining options if you simply take a short walk to town.

24 Rosemont Ave. www.royalpalms.bm. ℂ **800/678-0783** or 441/292-1854. 32 units. Summer $405–$435 double. Winter $299–$339 double. Rates include continental breakfast. **Amenities:** Restaurant, bar, pool, complimentary happy hour, free Wi-Fi.

Guesthouses
MODERATE
Edgehill Manor Guest House ★   If you're looking for a moderately priced room that's within a 10-minute walk to the hustle and bustle of Hamilton, this would be a good option—just don't expect to be wowed by the decor since most of its units are in desperate need of a facelift with tired white furniture and ghastly flower print duvets. Still, this no-frills guest house draws business travelers who crave a quick commute to town and families who enjoy the bigger rooms and suites, some of which have kitchens. There's a small pool on-site, and a free continental breakfast of fresh baked goods is served daily.

36 Rosemont Ave. www.edgehill.bm. ℂ **441/295-7124.** 14 units. Jan–Mar $184–$288 double. Apr–Dec from $339 double. Rates include continental breakfast. Bus: 7 or 8. **Amenities:** Pool, free Wi-Fi.

Housekeeping Units
MODERATE
Rosemont Guest Suites ★★   Not to be confused with the Rosedon Hotel around the corner, and located within walking distance of Hamilton's center, this collection of 47 studios and one-bedroom suites is often booked by large groups and families since as many as four units can be linked together (it's one of the few accommodations in Bermuda with multiple adjoining rooms). It's also a favorite among business travelers since it offers many amenities directly geared towards the corporate set (like free property-wide Wi-Fi, same-day laundry services, and complimentary continental breakfast with muffins, yogurt, and coffee). Rooms are nothing special—in fact, most feel as if they belong in a typical Holiday Inn Express—but they all feature balconies or patios that face the freshwater pool and full kitchens (if you'd like to stock the cupboards, simply walk 5 min. to nearby Miles Market).

41 Rosemont Ave. www.rosemont.bm. ℂ **800/367-0040** or 441/292-1055. 47 units. Summer $332–$383 suite. Winter $300–$320 suite. **Amenities:** Pool, complimentary continental breakfast, free Wi-Fi.

Guesthouses
MODERATE
The Oxford House ★★   With 12 rooms inside an elegant two-story townhouse, this small inn has all the personal touches of an elegant English

manor—one that reeks of a spiffy sense of Britishness thanks to its Welsh-born owner, Ann Smith. Built in 1938 by a doctor and his French wife, who requested that some of the architectural features follow French designs, the house boasts Doric columns, corner mullions, and urn-shaped balustrades, which flank the entrance portico. Inside, well-furnished, Victorian-style guest rooms have high ceilings and dressing areas and there's also a sunny upstairs sitting room. Here you won't be more than a 5-minute walk from all that the City of Hamilton has to offer, and you won't have to go very far for breakfast, since a complimentary spread is included each morning.

20 Woodbourne Ave. www.oxfordhouse.bm. ℂ **441/295-0503.** 12 units. Year-round $290–$310 double. **Amenities:** Continental breakfast, free Wi-Fi.

SMITH'S PARISH

Small Hotels

EXPENSIVE

The Loren at Pink Beach ★★★   When this hip hotel opened its doors on the site of the former Pink Beach Club in 2017, it ushered in a new era for Bermuda's hotels. This is, quite simply, the island's most contemporary property designwise, from its glass spiral staircase in the main building to its walls of windows, which allow natural light and Atlantic Ocean views to flood its lobby, restaurant and public areas. Rooms are no less stylish; in fact, they're downright gorgeous. Marble bathrooms feature walk-in rain showers, giant freestanding soaking tubs and Malin+Goetz beauty products; bedrooms boast handsome driftwood flooring, sleek minimalist furniture, and warm hues of white and gray; and spacious outdoor balconies have large sitting areas with airy steel wire railings, which allow for uninterrupted Atlantic Ocean views.

Its restaurants too, are among Bermuda's best: **Mareé** (p. 143), a tasting menu–only joint, and the **Pink Beach Club** (p. 144), an alfresco dining room that serves throughout the day. There's a full-service spa on-site and two world-class golf courses nearby—the **Mid Ocean Club** and **Tucker's Point**—but if you'd prefer to spend your time lazing at the hotel, opt for its über-private pink sand beach (unlike some hotel beaches, it's not attached to a larger public beach) or one of its two heated oceanfront pools (one for adults only).

116 S. Shore Rd., Tucker's Town. www.thelorenhotel.com. ℂ **844/384-3103** or 441/293-1666. 45 units. Summer $1,015–$1,100 suite. Winter $355–$455 suite. Bus: 1. **Amenities:** 2 restaurants, 2 bars, 2 pools, spa, fitness center, free Wi-Fi.

HAMILTON PARISH

Resort Hotels

EXPENSIVE

Grotto Bay Beach Resort ★★   It's the shoreline that makes Grotto Bay especially suitable for families. Alongside the calm waters of Castle Harbour, the resort's small beach barely gets a ripple of waves. The water is so still in fact, that it recently added a floating water park featuring a huge inflatable slide and trampoline about 30 yards from shore—a family-friendly romp within eyeshot of Grotto Bay's two other waterfront attractions. Both located on a pier adjacent to the resort, **Ana Luna Adventures** (p. 76) operates a 44-foot catamaran, which is available for half- and full-day sailing and snorkeling charters around the east end of the island; and **Dive Bermuda** (p. 74) takes guests on adventurous scuba adventures of all kinds, including dives to nearby sunken shipwrecks. The resort was named after the subterranean caves on property, and the nearby coastline is enchanting, with many natural caves and intimate coves.

Spread across 21 bougainvillea- and hibiscus-draped acres, the resort has 201 rooms housed in 11 cottages. Their styling is a bit too "old-style tropical" for our taste (think faux bamboo night tables, rattan headboards, and a color palette of brown and beige) but they're clean and comfortable. For those who choose the all-inclusive option, there are two bars and three on-site restaurants, which serve Continental cuisine. *Tip:* Truly memorable massages are offered at the Grotto Bay's **Nature Spa,** located deep inside one of the resort's stalactite-laden caves; treatment tables are nestled inside raised pergolas, which are housed on floating platforms above a freshwater lagoon.

11 Blue Hole Hill. www.grottobay.com. © **855/447-6886** or 441/293-8333. 201 units. Winter $249–$347 double. Summer $469–$499 double. Supplement for all-inclusive (3-day min. stay required) $114 per person per day; $84 per child ages 4–16 per day. Bus: 1, 3, 10, or 11. **Amenities:** 3 restaurants, 2 bars, children's programs, pool, 4 tennis courts, watersports equipment/rentals, dive shop, sailing excursions, spa, free Wi-Fi.

Rosewood Bermuda ★★★

When this east end retreat first opened in 2009, it was Bermuda's most luxurious resort. In 2011, Rosewood Hotels & Resorts took the reins and shined up an already glistening property—a years-long process that culminated with a $25-million renovation in 2018, which refurbished all of its guestrooms and suites, built the handsome new **Conservatory Bar & Lounge** (p. 181) in the lobby, reinvented its full-service **Sense** spa, and refreshed the look and menus of all of its restaurants including the **Island Brasserie** (p. 143), **Beach Club** (p. 144), and **Sul Verde** (p. 144). Thanks to the recent renovation, the resort's rooms are among Bermuda's finest featuring handsome hardwood furniture, spalike bathrooms with large soaking tubs, and spacious private balconies overlooking Castle Harbour.

What worked was kept untouched, like the clubby, British colonial atmosphere in the public areas and many amenities. The latter include a private beach club with a setting that's on par with Bermuda's best (just keep a keen eye on your littlest swimmers, as the tides here can be rough). The beach club, which is a 5-minute shuttle ride (free) from the hotel, features an alfresco restaurant, fountain-filled kiddie pool, and an oceanfront adults-only pool. Golfers will love the resort's Robert Rulewich–designed, championship-caliber course, with its 18 oceanview holes.

You'll be about a 20-minute taxi ride to the City of Hamilton and about 35 minutes from popular south shore beaches like Horseshoe Bay, but for unparalleled luxury on the east end of Bermuda (a mere 15 min. from L. F. Wade International airport), there's simply no place better.

60 Tucker's Point Club Dr. www.rosewoodhotels.com. © **441/298-9800.** 92 units. Summer $820–$1,355 double; $2,214–$4,230 suite. Winter $298–$664 double; $1,201–$2,167 suite. **Amenities:** 4 restaurants, 4 bars, 4 pools, 18-hole golf course, fitness center, spa, watersports equipment/rentals, free Wi-Fi.

ST. GEORGE'S PARISH

Cottage Colonies

EXPENSIVE

St. George's Club ★   Located in the Town of St. George's, this collection of one- and two-bedroom cottages also doubles as one of Bermuda's few timeshare accommodations. Don't worry! There are no hateful presentations to sit through here. Instead, guests get all the amenities one would need for a long-term stay. Newly renovated units face the ocean, pool or the now-defunct golf course and feature full kitchens, spacious living areas, and bathrooms with large sunken tubs and marble vanities. The sprawling 17-acre property is also flush with amenities, including three pools, two tennis courts, a clubhouse with laundry facilities, and a fitness center plus two restaurants (one on-site and another at nearby Achilles Bay, accessible via the hotel's shuttle bus). For those seeking a self-catered option on the east end, the St. George's Club is a fine choice, just don't expect much to hold your attention at night since the town is sleepy at best, even during peak season.

6 Rose Hill. www.stgeorgesclub.bm. © **441/297-1200.** 71 units. Summer $404–$449 1-bedroom cottage; $598–$664 2-bedroom cottage. Winter $292–$324 1-bedroom cottage; $440–$489 2-bedroom cottage. Bus: 1, 3, 6, 10, or 11. **Amenities:** 2 restaurants, 2 bars, 3 pools, 2 tennis courts, fitness center, watersports equipment/rentals, free Wi-Fi.

Guesthouses

INEXPENSIVE/MODERATE

Aunt Nea's Inn ★★   Named for the unrequited love of Irish poet Tom Moore who stayed here in 1804 and fell for the girl next store—literally, since Nea Tucker lived in the property adjacent to the inn—this historic guesthouse is within walking distance to all the Town of St. George's historic sites and attractions. Run by wife and wife couple Carolyn and Faith Bridges who bought the property in 2015 then totally refurbished it, the inn has 10 en suite rooms, all named and decorated for island flora and fauna (like Longtail, Angelfish, and Coral) and all of them include a complimentary continental breakfast. There's a large lawn and outdoor porch, but beyond these two public spaces, there's little else on-site.

1 Nea's Alley. www.auntneasinn.com. © **441/296-2868.** 10 units. Year-round $195–$350 double. **Amenities:** Complimentary breakfast, free Wi-Fi.

PLANNING YOUR TRIP TO BERMUDA

Settling into Bermuda is relatively easy. In this chapter, you'll find everything you need to plan your trip. That includes how to get around, make telephone calls, and get cash, plus what it takes to get married on island and much more. Let's get started.

GETTING THERE

By Plane

Flights from most East Coast gateways—including New York, Boston and Philadelphia—take less than 2 hours. Flights from Atlanta, Miami and Toronto take around 3 hours. And from London Gatwick (daily nonstop flights), the trip is just under 7 hours. Upon arrival you'll have to wait in line like everyone else to clear Bermuda customs, but American travelers returning home will have the added benefit of going through U.S. customs here in Bermuda, since the island is one of the few countries in the world offering "preclearance." This allows passengers to avoid the long lines of U.S. Immigrations and Customs back home.

Airfares fluctuate according to the season but for the most part, you'll pay the highest prices during peak summer season (July and Aug) and can often save up to 30% when traveling during the lowest of low season (Jan and Feb).

By Cruise Ship

Bermuda has long been a popular destination for the cruise ship crowd. Ever since 1905, when the steamship S.S. *Bermudian* first motored here from New York City, the island has lured ships big and small. Today, cruising to Bermuda is big business with more than 470,000 passengers arriving by boat in 2018 (a 13% uptick from the year before). **Most cruise ships tie up at King's Wharf** in the Royal Naval Dockyard—a bustling port of call with shops, restaurants and attractions galore—however **smaller ships** have been known to dock in the **City of Hamilton** and the **Town of St. George's.** While the cruise experience isn't for everyone it does provide a carefree, and in most cases, affordable vacation.

Rising behind the runways of L. F. Wade International is Bermuda's newest addition—a state-of-the-art airport terminal, which is expected to open by the end of 2020. When it's complete, the $250-million steel and glass structure will be home to a 182,000-square-feet ground floor, which will house extensive retail corridors and multiple restaurant options. Another added plus will be its six covered jetways where passengers can board airplanes without stepping foot outside—a considerable upgrade.

Itineraries range widely depending on the cruise line, but most include 4 days at sea with 3 days in port. The season typically lasts from mid-April through mid-November, however a few ships make occasional port calls in the off-season.

We recommend buying cruises through travel agents rather than directly through the cruise line. That's because agents who sell a lot are often rewarded by the cruise line with perks they can pass on to their customers, like free upgrades, a waiving of onboard gratuities, and more. Reputable agencies include **Cruises Only** (www.cruisesonly.com), **Cruise Brothers** (www.cruisebrothers.com), **Vacations to Go** (www.vacationstogo.com), and **Galax-Sea Cruises and Tours** (www.cruisestar.com).

GETTING AROUND

Arriving from the Airport

Planes arrive at Bermuda's **L. F. Wade International Airport** (**BDA;** www.bermudaairport.com; ✆ **441/293-2470**), about 9 miles east of the City of Hamilton (30-min. taxi), 13 miles from Southampton (40-min. taxi), and 17 miles from Somerset (50-min. taxi). The Town of St. George's is about a 10-minute taxi from the airport. Because you aren't allowed to rent a car in Bermuda, and buses don't allow passengers to board with luggage, you must rely on a taxi, minivan or private car to reach your hotel.

LEAVING THE AIRPORT BY TAXI

There are hundreds of taxis in Bermuda and cabbies typically meet all arriving flights. Hotels do offer transportation, but usually the prices they charge are a good $10 to $15 higher than the metered taxi rate.

Which is not to say taxis on Bermuda are cheap. They're not. They usually move slowly, meters rise alarmingly fast, and taxi fares will inevitably represent a significant percentage of your day-to-day spending money. Regrettably, this situation can't be avoided. Nonresidents are forbidden to drive cars and your only other option involves either walking (not practical on many of Bermuda's narrow roads), renting a bicycle (not recommended for similar reasons), two-wheeled scooters (more on that later), and Bermuda's latest rental vehicles, electric-powered Twizys, which can seat two passengers, but cannot fit even one piece of luggage.

Unless the taxi has been specifically called to pick you up, the meter should read $4.15 when you first get in a cab. After that, expect to pay $7.90 for the first 1.6km (1 mile) and $2.75 for each additional 1.6km (1 mile) for up to four passengers. The following is a sample of taxi fares, including a tip of 10% to 15%, from the airport: To any point within the City of Hamilton, expect a metered fare of around $40 to $50; to points in and around St. George's, around $20 to $30; to points near Tucker's Town, around $35; to such south-shore beach hotels as Elbow Beach, around $50 to $60; and to such far-distant points as the west end, around $70. Fares increase by 25% between midnight and 6am, as well as all day on Sundays and holidays (the rate jumps 50% for five to seven passengers at any time, and luggage carries a surcharge of $1 per piece). In almost every case, a meter determines the fare, unless you ask for a sightseeing tour of the island, which can be pre-arranged before you step inside the taxi. Tours are usually a minimum of 3 hours in length and cost $50 an hour for one to four passengers and $70 an hour for five to seven passengers (you can cover half the island in 3 hr. and the entire island in 6 hr.).

> ### "What Color Is Your House?"
>
> If you're one of the growing number of visitors who've rented a private cottage and need a taxi to pick you up, make sure that you have your home's single most important piece of information on hand before calling the dispatcher: its color. That will invariably be the first question you'll be asked after dialing for a cab since house numbers are usually hard to spot. Also make note of your rental's other features like window shutters (or lack thereof), flagpoles or other specifics since cabbies routinely use these details to identify Bermuda's candy-colored homes.

At the airport, cab drivers typically wait at the taxi stand just beyond the main exit. If a taxi is not there, you can call **Bermuda Island Taxi** (𝄢 441/295-4141) or **BTA Dispatching** (𝄢 441/296-2121). Another good option is to download an app called **Hitch** to your smart phone, which works like Uber but with licensed taxi drivers (www.hitch.bm). Note that taxi drivers who use the Hitch app are the only cabbies who accept credit cards, so make sure you have cash on hand before departing the airport.

Arriving by Cruise Ship

Depending on your ship, you'll likely arrive King's Wharf in the Royal Naval Dockyard where taxis and public transportation await. But a handful dock in the City of Hamilton where hailing a cab or hopping on a bus or ferry is also a breeze. If your ship is docking in the Town of St. George's, you might consider arranging a taxi in advance since the east end port is considerably sleepier than its Hamilton and Dockyard counterparts. *Tip:* To save money on sightseeing excursions, consider booking through such companies as **CruisingExcursions.com** and **ShoreTrips.com.** Both offer the same types of trips as the cruise lines do (they're often exactly the same), but for groups that are capped at 12 people (so a van rather than a bus) and often far less money than you'd pay for a cruise line tour (or even a tour by private taxi when you arrive).

(But Not) by Car

Bermuda is one of the few countries in the world where visitors are not permitted to rent a car. In fact, even residents are allowed only one car per household, two strict vehicular laws that help keep congestion on the island's narrow roads down and emissions low. If you want to get around in Bermuda, you'll have to reply on taxis, buses, ferries, bicycles, scooters and four-wheeled electric vehicles called Twizys.

By Scooter

Dependence on cabs and rented two-wheeled motor scooters—locally called bikes—is simply a fact of Bermudian life that newcomers quickly accept as part of the island's charm. Although not having a car at your disposal is inconvenient, Bermuda's tourism advertisements make it seem just wonderful: a happy couple zipping around the island on a sunny day, helmets on and smiles wide. What the adverts don't tell you is that the roads are narrow, driving on the left side of the road can be confusing and Bermudians—who own cars and pay dearly for the privilege—feel that the road is theirs (so just pull off to the side of the road if a car is tailgating or wants to pass). During inclement weather, scooter riders are likely to be edged close—sometimes disturbingly close—to the shoulder; after rainstorms, they'll almost certainly be splattered with water or mud. Many accidents occur on slippery roads after it's rained, especially involving those not accustomed to using a motor scooter.

Who should rent a scooter and who should avoid them altogether? Frankly, the answer depends on your experience, physical fitness and time of day. Although scooters can be a lot of fun during a sunny day, they can be wildly dangerous after dark—and of course, after you've had a few Dark n' Stormies, which is not at all advisable. Considering the hazards, visitors who are physically fit and confident on two wheels will have a blast renting a scooter. But if you're at all apprehensive, whether because of your physical ability or current road or light conditions, then consider taking a taxi to avoid a trip to the emergency room.

You must be 16 or older to rent a scooter, helmets are required by law and some vehicles are big enough to accommodate two adults. Among the rental companies listed below,

Rules of De Road

Bermuda is polite to a fault, but you wouldn't know it by listening to all that honking. What's all the ruckus? Bermudians commonly use their car horns to say hello while passing other motorists—typically friends or family—while on the road. Flashing one's headlights is another common way to say hi, a maneuver that can also mean you've got the right of way. And when you see a car gently nudging its front end into a main thoroughfare from a secondary road, it's best to let them go. Bermuda's narrow roads have lots of blind spots, so cars slowly roll into turns to avoid oncoming traffic.

fees tend to be roughly equivalent—so shopping around for a better deal is usually a waste of time. On average, scooters for one rider rent for $55 for the first day, $95 for 2 days, $135 for 3 days, $165 for 4 days, $188 for 5 days, $207 for 6 days and $225 for 7 days. Scooters for two riders cost about $75 for 1 day, $127 for 2 days, $170 for 3 days, $200 for 4 days, $227 for 5 days, $247 for 6 days, and $267 for 7 days. You'll also have to pay a one-time fee of $30 for insurance, which is valid for the length of the rental.

With several offices across the island, the two main operations that rent scooters are **Oleander Cycles** (www.oleandercycles.bm; © **441/236-5235**), with locations at Cambridge Beaches Resort & Spa, Grotto Bay Beach Resort, The Reefs Hotel & Club, the City of Hamilton, the Town of St. George's, and the Royal Naval Dockyard; and **Smatt's Cycle Livery** (www.smattscyclelivery.com; © **441/295-1180**), with rental locations at the Hamilton Princess Hotel & Beach Club, Fairmont Southampton, and Rosewood Bermuda. A third option is **Elbow Beach Cycles** (www.elbowbeachcycles.com; © **441/296-2300**), which rents scooters from its sole location at Elbow Beach Resort in Paget Parish.

By Twizy

Though you can't rent a car you can still get around on four wheels. Called a **Twizy,** this electric-powered vehicle is similar to a golf cart, but instead of riding side-by-side, its two passengers sit front-to-back in a low-to-the-ground cockpit that features a windshield but no windows. Simply hop in, turn the key, release the parking brake and press the accelerator. In no time you'll be safely zipping around Bermuda in an environmentally friendly, seatbelt-equipped vehicle with side impact protection and an airbag for the driver. A full charge will last up to 55 miles (plenty of power for a 21-sq.-mile island), but if you need to "refuel" along the way, there are charging stations at hotels and at popular attractions. Thanks to the clever folks at **Current Vehicles** (www.currentvehicles.com; © **441/296-8949;** $129 per day plus mandatory $30 insurance fee)—the company that rents these vehicles from the Hamilton Princess Hotel & Beach Club and the Fairmont Southampton—finding these "Oasis Points" is simple, since all you have to do is consult an app that you download to your smart phone, which also works offline.

Since these zippy vehicles are all the rage with locals and tourists alike, they tend to book up fast, so make a reservation long in advance of your arrival. No Twizys left? Then consider renting a similar electric-powered vehicle called an Anaig Quick from **Oleander Cycles** (www.oleandercycles.bm; © **441/295-0919**), which has 13 in its fleet ($115 per day plus mandatory $40 insurance fee), or a larger hatchback-style electric car called a Tazzari that you can also rent by the day ($150 per day plus $40 mandatory insurance fee).

By Bicycle

Pedaling a bicycle—or a push bike as it's called on the island—up Bermuda's steep hills can be challenging, but if you're looking for a more natural means of locomotion than a scooter or if you plan to explore Bermuda's many trails, you can rent mountain bikes at most cycle liveries (from $40; see above). Serious road riders should head to **Cycle Works,** in the City of Hamilton, which rents Specialized Roubaix carbon and Focus Cayo aluminum race bikes for $95 per day (www.bicycleworks.bm; © **441/297-8356**). As with scooters, exercise caution: Roads are narrow and sometimes slippery, and remember to stay on the left. See "Biking," in chapter 4, for more details.

By Bus

With 11 routes covering the island, most of which run every half hour throughout the day, Bermuda's bus network services nearly all hotels, guesthouses, restaurants and attractions. Regularly scheduled buses go to most of the destinations that interest visitors in Bermuda but be prepared to wait since they don't always run on time or on certain days of the week. For example, some buses don't operate on Sundays or holidays, so be sure you know the schedule before you wait on the roadside.

Bermuda is divided into 14 zones, each about 2 miles long. The rate is $3.50 within the first three zones and for longer distances the fare is no more than $5 (generally for rides from the City of Hamilton to Dockyard, St. George's, or Hamilton Parish). Just make sure you have a ticket or coins since bills are not accepted and drivers will not make change. For those planning to use the bus often—or the ferry for that matter since the below prices are the same for those traveling by water—consider buying a Transportation Pass available for 1 day ($19), 2 days ($32), 3 days ($44), 4 days ($49), 7 days ($62), 1 month ($69), or 3 months of unlimited use. These passes and individual tickets are sold at the ferry terminal on Front Street, post offices across the island or the **Central Bus Terminal** on Washington Street in the City of Hamilton, where all routes begin and end (at Church St.; © **441/292-3851;** Mon–Fri 7:15am–7pm, Sat 8am–6:30pm, Sun and holidays 8:30am–5:30pm).

It's sometimes confusing to identify where buses actually stop along the roadside since not all bus stops are equipped with covered shelters. When in doubt, look for a blue or pink pole on the side of the road. Blue poles indicate routes heading west and pink poles indicate those heading east.

By Ferry

One of the most scenic and efficient ways of getting around the island is the government-operated ferry service. In Bermuda there are two kinds: two-tiered, air-conditioned **fast ferries** that zoom from the City of Hamilton to Dockyard across the Great Sound and from Hamilton to St. George's via the North Shore; and older navy-and-white **commuter boats,** which operate between the hotel-filled parishes of Paget, Warwick and Southampton to the City of Hamilton. The easiest way to tell where a ferry is headed is by its colored route. Ferries to Paget and Warwick are on the Pink Route; Somerset and Dockyard are on the Blue Route (which also takes scooters aboard); Rockaway in Southampton is the Green Route; and on weekdays in summer only, Dockyard and St. George's are well-served by the Orange Route.

Getting Around

PLANNING YOUR TRIP TO BERMUDA

The cost of a single fare varies by route. One-way adult fares to Paget, Warwick, and Southampton cost $3.50 while one-way adult fares to Dockyard and St. George's cost $5. Cash or coins are not accepted so purchase tickets, tokens or transportation passes in advance at the ferry terminal on Front Street in the City of Hamilton. Like buses, you can buy money-saving Transportation Passes ranging from 1 day to 3 months (see "By Bus" for pricing). For more info about public ferries, contact the **Department of Marine and Ports** (www.marineandports.bm; ✆ **441/295-4506**).

PLANNING AN ISLAND WEDDING

Considering its proximity to the U.S. East Coast and the fact that no cases of the Zika virus have ever been reported in Bermuda—a plus for expectant or soon-to-be-expectant mothers—destination weddings are big business on the island. Couples who would like to get married in Bermuda must file a "Notice of Intended Marriage" with the Registry General—a form that can be downloaded on their website (www.gov.bm/getting-married-bermuda). Note that the form must be printed on white, legal-sized paper (8.5" x 14") to be accepted and completed and mailed to the Registry General along with a cashier's check or money order for $368. Copies of divorce decrees or death certificates, if applicable, must also be included.

Once the Registry General receives the "Notice of Intended Marriage," it will be published, including names and addresses, in the island's local newspaper. Assuming there is no formal objection, the registry will issue the license 15 days after receiving the notice, which will then be valid for 3 months.

Civil ceremonies can be performed weekdays or Saturday mornings in the Registry's Marriage Room for $245 or outdoors on government parks or beaches for $450. Churches can be contacted individually and booked for a fee. Many hotels can help make wedding arrangements—reserving the church and clergy, hiring a horse and buggy, ordering the wedding cake, and securing a photographer. There are also very good wedding planners on the island, including **Das Fete** (www.dasfete.com; ✆ 441/400-5048), **The Bridal Suite** (www.bridalsuitebermudaweddings.com; ✆ 441/292-2025), **Bermuda Bride** (www.bermudabride.com; ✆ 441/295-8697), **To Have and To Hold Wedding and Event Planning** (www.ththbda.com; ✆ 441/236-7473), and **Bermuda Event Solutions** (www.weddingsolutions.bm; ✆ 441/236-9469). Weddings in Bermuda range from simple ceremonies on the beach to large-scale extravaganzas at the Botanical Gardens. Other popular sites include yachts and the Unfinished Church (p. 110). If you're doing the planning on your own and need an excellent photographer, you won't go wrong with either **Gavin Howarth** (www.gavinhowarth.com; ✆ 441/532-3234) or **Amanda Temple** (www.amandatemple.com; ✆ 441/236-2339).

[FastFACTS] BERMUDA

Area Code The area code for all of Bermuda is **441.**

Banks The main offices of Bermuda's banks are in the City of Hamilton. Most banks and their branches are open Monday to Friday 9am to 4:30pm, however some close at 4pm. Banks are closed Saturdays, Sundays, and public holidays. Many big hotels will cash traveler's checks, and there are ATMs all around the island.

HSBC Bermuda has several locations across the island and its main branch is on 6 Front Street in the City of Hamilton (www.hsbc.bm; ℂ **441/299-5959**).

The **Bank of Butterfield** is on 65 Front St. in the City of Hamilton, with other locations in Sandys and St. George's parishes (www.butterfieldgroup.com; ℂ **441/295-1111**).

Clarien Bank is on 19 Reid St. in the City of Hamilton (www.clarienbank.com; ℂ **441/296-6969**).

With the exception of one ATM at the HSBC Front Street branch and another inside the departure lounge of L. F. Wade International Airport, ATMs dispense only Bermuda dollars.

Business Hours Most commercial businesses are open Monday through Friday from 9am to 5pm, while retail shops are generally open Monday through Saturday from 9am to 5pm (some stay open until 6pm). Shops in the Royal Naval Dockyard tend to stay open later when cruise ships are in port.

Customs Visitors may bring into Bermuda duty-free up to 50 cigars, 200 cigarettes and 1 pound of tobacco; 1 liter of wine and 1 liter of spirits; and other goods with a total maximum value of $50. All imports may be inspected on arrival. For additional information on temporary admission, export and customs regulations, and tariffs, contact **Bermuda Customs** at ℂ **441/295-4816** or visit the Bermuda Customs website at **www.customs. gov.bm**.

Dentists For dental emergencies, call **King Edward VII Memorial Hospital,** 7 Point Finger Rd., Paget Parish (www.bermudahospitals.bm; ℂ **441/236-2345**). The hospital maintains lists of dentists on emergency call.

Disabled Travelers Bermuda is not a great place for persons with disabilities since public buses are not geared for passengers in wheelchairs and many of its roads (especially in the Town of St. George's) are cobblestone. Getting around the island is a bit difficult even for the agile, who must rely on scooters, bicycles, buses and taxis. However, you can ask your hotel to check on the availability of mini buses operated by private individuals. The most accessible hotels in Bermuda are its resort hotels, including the Hamilton Princess Hotel & Beach Club, the Fairmont Southampton and Rosewood Bermuda (see chapter 9 for listings).

Doctors In an emergency, call **King Edward VII Hospital,** 7 Point Finger Rd., Paget Parish (ℂ **441/236-2345**), and ask for the emergency department. For less serious medical problems, ask someone at your hotel for a recommendation. In general, the quality of health care on the island is on par with most U.S. cities.

Dress Well-tailored Bermuda shorts are acceptable on almost any occasion, and many men wear them with jackets and ties. On formal occasions, they must be accompanied by navy blue or black knee socks. Aside from that, Bermudians are rather conservative in their attitude toward dress—bikinis, for example, should only be worn on the beach and shirtless walks anywhere there's not water nearby is verboten.

Drinking Laws Bermuda sternly regulates the sale of alcoholic beverages. The legal drinking age is 18, and most bars close at 1am (some close as early as 10pm and others as late as 3am). Some bars are closed on Sunday. You can bring beer or other alcohol to the beach legally, but the moment you walk on the streets with an open container of alcohol, you risk a fine.

Driving Rules Visitors cannot rent cars. To operate a motorized scooter, you must be age 16 or over. All scooter drivers and passengers must wear helmets. Driving is on the left side of the road, and the speed limit is 32kmph (20 mph) in the countryside, 24kmph (15 mph) in busy areas.

Drug Laws In Bermuda, there are heavy penalties for the importation of, possession of, or dealing of unlawful drugs (including marijuana). Customs officers, at their discretion, may conduct body searches for drugs or other contraband goods.

Electricity Electricity is 110 volts AC (60 cycles). North American appliances are compatible without converters or adapters. Visitors from the United Kingdom or other parts of Europe need to bring a converter.

Embassies & Consulates For Residents of the U.S.: The American Consulate General is located at Crown Hill, 16 Middle Rd., Devonshire (http://hamilton.usconsulate. gov; ℂ **441/295-1342;** Mon–Fri 8am–4:30pm).

For Residents of Canada The Canadian Consulate General (Commission to Bermuda) is at 73 Front St., Hamilton (ℂ **441/292-2917**).

For Residents of the U.K. As Bermuda is a British territory, Britain does not maintain a consulate in Bermuda. For emergency travel documents, contact the

Bermuda Department of Immigration, 30 Parliament St., Hamilton (www. immigration.gov.bm; ℂ **441/295-5151**).

For Residents of Australia The Australian High Commission in Ottawa, Canada (www.canada.embassy.gov. au; ℂ **613/236-0841**), provides consular assistance.

Emergencies To call the police, report a fire, or summon an ambulance, dial ℂ **911.** The nonemergency police number is ℂ **441/ 295-0011.** For air-sea rescue, contact the Rescue Coordination Center, ℂ **441/297-1010.**

Family Travel Bermuda is one of the best vacation destinations for the entire family. Toddlers can spend blissful hours in shallow seawater or pools geared just for them, and older kids enjoy boat rides, horseback riding, hiking, and snorkeling. Most resort hotels help in finding babysitters, and many have supervised kids' activities.

Outside the Town of St. George's and the City of Hamilton, walking with a baby stroller is difficult—most roads don't have sidewalks or adequate curbs. It is extremely dangerous to carry a baby on a scooter, as baby seats are not provided. Buses, taxis, and ferries are the safest ways to travel around Bermuda with a baby. For some recommendations on where to stay and eat, refer to "Best for Families," on p. 185, and "Family-Friendly Restaurants," on p. 140.

Gasoline All of the scooters available for rental by a nonresident of Bermuda have 50cc engines that require regular unleaded gasoline.

Health Pack **prescription medications** in your carry-on luggage, and carry them in their original containers, with pharmacy labels. Carry the generic name of prescription medicines in case a local pharmacist is unfamiliar with the brand name. Contact the **International Association for Medical Assistance to Travelers** (**IAMAT;** www.iamat.org) for tips on travel and health concerns in Bermuda, and for lists of local doctors. The **U.S. Centers for Disease Control and Prevention** (www.cdc.gov; ℂ **800/232-4636**) provides up-to-date information on health hazards by region or country and offers tips on food safety.

Cuts All cuts obtained in the marine environment must be taken seriously because the high level of bacteria present in the water can quickly cause a cut to become infected. The best way to prevent cuts is to wear a wet suit, gloves, and reef shoes. If you get a coral cut gently pull the edges of the skin open and removing any embedded coral or grains of sand with tweezers. Next, scrub the cut well with fresh water, and then press a clean cloth against the wound to stop the bleeding.

Sunburns & Exposure Limit your exposure to the sun, especially between the hours of 11am and 2pm and during the first few days of your trip. Use a sunscreen with a high protection factor and apply it liberally. Also, as you travel around Bermuda it's always wise to carry along some bottled water to prevent dehydration.

Seasickness A great deal of the population tends toward seasickness. If you've never been out on a boat, or if you've been seasick in the past, make sure you take any seasickness prevention measures that work for you **before** you board; once you set sail, it's generally too late. On the boat, stay as low and near the center of the boat as possible. Stay out in the fresh air and watch the horizon. If you start to feel queasy, drink clear fluids like water, and eat something bland, such as a soda cracker.

Hospitals **King Edward VII Memorial Hospital,** 7 Point Finger Rd., Paget Parish (www.bermudahospitals. bm; ☏ **441/236-2345**), has a highly qualified staff and Canadian accreditation.

Insurance Although close to the United States, a visit to Bermuda is, in essence, "going abroad." You can encounter all the same problems in Bermuda that you would in going to a more remote foreign destination. Therefore, it's wise to purchase travel insurance, especially policies covering medical care. Consider insurance marketplaces like InsureMyTrip. com and SquareMouth.com.

Internet Access In late 2018, the Bermuda Tourism Authority rolled a program that offers free Wi-Fi for 1 hour at such sites as the Visitor Services Centers in the Royal Naval Dockyard, the City of Hamilton, and St. George's; the Hamilton Ferry Terminal; the Hamilton Bus Terminal; and the St. George's Ferry Dock at Penno's Wharf. The network to connect to is called "BERMUDAWiFi." You'll be kicked off after 60 minutes but can get back on by simply going through the registration again. Additionally, the public library in the City of Hamilton, which is adjacent to the Bermuda Historical Society Museum, offers five computer stations where you can get free internet access for 30 minutes with a photo I.D. Washington Mall, L. F. Wade International Airport and most accommodations in Bermuda also have free Wi-Fi.

Legal Aid Your consulate will inform you of your limited rights and offer a list of attorneys. (See "Embassies & Consulates," above.) However, the consulate's office cannot interfere with Bermuda's law-enforcement officers.

LGBTQ Travelers Bermuda is tolerant of gay and lesbian travelers, but the island still lags far behind North American and European countries when it comes to laws and policies affecting the LGBTQ community. In 2013, Bermuda's Parliament voted in favor of the Human Rights

Amendment Act, which finally added sexual orientation to the list of prohibited grounds of discrimination—an act which was integral in a 2017 Supreme Court ruling on same sex marriage. During a landmark case that was brought by a gay couple, the Court ruled any ban on such a union was discriminatory and violated human rights, so the couple were legally married a month later by the Registry General. That same year a new, considerably more conservative government was voted into power and with it came roll backs on marriage equality. A new law was passed effectively making same sex marriage illegal and the fight for LGBTQ rights in Bermuda continues to this day. That said, it's unlikely gay travelers will encounter any overt discrimination, but public signs of affection will definitely turn heads in this über-conservative country.

Mail Deposit regular mail in the red pillar boxes on the streets. You'll recognize them by the monogram of Queen Elizabeth II. The postage rate for airmail letters up to 10 grams and for postcards is 70¢ to the United States and Canada, 85¢ to the United Kingdom. Airmail letters and postcards to the North American mainland can take 6 to 8 days, to Britain possibly a little longer.

Mobile Phones Most travelers can use their cell phones while in Bermuda, but you should check international rates with your

WHAT THINGS COST IN BERMUDA

	US$/BD$
Taxi from the airport to center of Hamilton	$40.00
Double room, moderate	$300.00
Double room, inexpensive	$200.00
Three-course dinner for one without wine, moderate	$50.00
Bottle of beer	$6.00
Cup of coffee	$4.00
Admission to most museums	$10.00
Average daily scooter rental	$55.00

carrier before switching your phone on, since roaming costs tend to be sky high while traveling overseas. To alleviate extra fees, consider buying a local SIM card from **Digicel** (10 Church St.; www.digicel.bm; © **441/500-5000**), which sells inexpensive plans and cards that you can use while you're on the island. You'll need to have a phone that you can unlock, and your phone number will change while here, but at least you won't pay exorbitant roaming rates during your stay.

Money & Costs Legal tender is the Bermuda dollar (BD$), which is divided into 100 cents and pegged to the U.S. dollar on an equal basis (BD$1 equals US$1). U.S. dollars are interchangeable with Bermuda dollars and are widely accepted in shops, restaurants, and hotels. Currency from the United Kingdom and other foreign countries is not accepted but can be easily exchanged for Bermuda dollars at banks. Bring enough petty cash to cover incidentals, tipping, and transportation to your hotel before you leave home, or withdraw money upon arrival at an airport ATM. For up-to-the-minute currency conversions, visit **www.xe.com**.

THE VALUE OF THE BERMUDIAN DOLLAR VS. OTHER POPULAR CURRENCIES

BD$	Aus$	Can$	Euro (€)	NZ$	UK£	US$
BD$1.00	A$.7	C$.7	€1.1	NZ$.66	£1.3	$1.00

ATMs These machines are plentiful in Bermuda. Do remember that many banks impose a fee every time you use a card at another bank's ATM, and that fee can be higher for international transactions (up to $5 or more) than for domestic ones (where they're rarely more than $2). In addition, the bank from which you withdraw cash may charge its own fee.

Credit Cards Visa, Mastercard and American Express cards are widely accepted across the island. Do know that all will carry some sort of foreign transaction fee. Still, credit cards are safer to use than cash, and have an excellent exchange rate.

Newspapers & Magazines Bermuda has one daily newspaper, the *Royal Gazette*, which publishes Monday to Saturday. Major U.S. newspapers, including the *New York Times* and *USA Today*, are scarce, but many resort hotels will provide guests with a copy of a Times Fax, which includes U.S. and international news.

Passports A passport is required of all travelers entering Bermuda, and that passport must be valid a minimum of 45 days from

213

the date of your arrival. Any traveler staying in Bermuda longer than 3 weeks must apply to the **Chief Immigration Officer** in person at the Government Administration Building, 30 Parliament St., Hamilton (www.immigration.gov.bm; ℰ **441-295-5151**). You will be asked to fill out an immigration application for an extended stay, which must be approved by authorities.

Pets   To take your pet with you to Bermuda, it must be a minimum of 10 months of age, and if it's a dog, it must not be a member of any of the approximately 20 breeds that local authorities define as dangerous. You'll need a special permit issued by the director of the **Department of Agriculture, Fisheries, and Parks** (www.animals.gov.bm; ℰ **441-236-4201**). The island has no quarantine facilities, so animals arriving without proper documents will be refused entry and will be returned to the point of origin. Some guesthouses and hotels allow small animals, but most will not; inquire in advance. Always check to see what the latest regulations are before attempting to bring a dog or another pet—including Seeing Eye dogs—to Bermuda.

Pharmacies   Bermuda has pharmacies located across the island, but none are open 24 hours, so if you need a prescription filled between the hours of 6pm and 9am, go straight to the hospital. The biggest chain

is **Phoenix Centre,** with a large pharmacy in Hamilton at 3 Reid St.

Post Offices   The **General Post Office,** 56 Church St., Hamilton (ℰ **441/297-7866**), is open Monday to Friday from 8am to 5pm, Saturday from 8am to noon. Post office branches and the Perot Post Office, Queen Street, Hamilton, are open Monday to Friday from 8am to 5pm. Some post offices close for lunch from 11:30am to 1pm. Daily airmail service for the United States and Canada closes at 9:30am in Hamilton. See also "Mail," above.

Safety   Bermuda has always been considered a safe destination, especially when compared to certain countries of the Caribbean. However, there is some petty crime and you should be alert in certain neighborhoods, especially at night. In the City of Hamilton, it's wise to stay clear of north Court Street, an area referred to as "backatown," which is Bermudian slang for "back of town." It's perfectly fine to wander these streets during the day, but at night it attracts gang members and nefarious types who won't think twice about grabbing your purse. About those handbags: It's common for thieves on scooters to snatch bags right out of the basket of rental scooters, while you're driving on the road. To protect yourself, use a bungee cord to keep it in place. Bermuda's beaches are safe,

but do take your belongings if you go for a long stroll.

Smoking   In the spring of 2006, the government of Bermuda passed a law banning smoking in enclosed public places. Tobacconists and other stores carry a wide array of tobacco products, generally from the United States, England and the Caribbean.

Taxes   Bermuda charges visitors a Passenger Tax before they depart from the island; it's hidden within the cost of an airline or cruise-ship ticket. Frankly, you might never know that a tax has actually been imposed, but if you're interested, $25 of the cost of your airline ticket, and $60 of the cost of your cruise-ship ticket, goes to the Bermudian government. Children age 2 and younger are exempt from paying this tax.

All room rates, regardless of the category of accommodations or the plan under which you stay, are subject to a government tax of 7.25%.

Telephones
To make international calls: To make international calls from Bermuda to North America, simply dial 1. For countries besides the U.S. and Canada, first dial 00 and then the country code (U.K. 44, Ireland 353, Australia 61, New Zealand 64). Next, dial the city or area code and local number.

To call Bermuda:
1. Dial the international access code: 00 from the U.K., Ireland, or New

Zealand; or 0011 from Australia. From North America, no international access code is necessary; just dial 1.

2. Dial country code 441.
3. Dial the local number.

For directory assistance: Dial 411 if you're looking for a number inside Bermuda, and dial 0 for numbers to all other countries.

For operator assistance: If you need operator assistance in making a call, dial 0.

Toll-free numbers: There are no toll-free numbers in Bermuda. Calling an 800 or 888 number in North America from Bermuda costs the same as an overseas call.

Time Bermuda is 1 hour ahead of Eastern Standard Time (EST). Daylight saving time is in effect from the second Sunday in March until November 1.

Tipping In most cases, a service charge is added to hotel and restaurant bills. In hotels, the charge is in lieu of tipping various individuals, such as bellhops, maids, and restaurant staffers (for meals included in a package or in the daily rate). Otherwise, a 15% tip for service is customary. Taxi drivers usually get 10% to 15%.

Toilets The City of Hamilton and St. George provide public facilities, but only during business hours. In the City of Hamilton, toilets are at City Hall, in Par-la-Ville Gardens, Albouy's Point, and inside the Washington Mall. In St. George's, facilities are available at Town Hall, Somers Garden, and Market Wharf. Outside of these towns, you'll find restrooms at the public beaches, at the Botanical Gardens, in several of the forts, and at service stations. Often, you'll have to use the facilities in hotels, restaurants, and wherever else you can find them.

Transit Information
For info about ferry service, visit www.marineandports.bm. For bus info, check www.gov.bm/bus or call ℂ **441/292-3854** or 441/292-3851.

Visitor Information
The website of the Bermuda Tourism Authority (BTA; www.gotobermuda.com) is an excellent one-stop shop for info. The BTA's Visitor Services Centres on Front Street in the City of Hamilton, in St. George's and at the Royal Naval Dockyard have a team of tourism ambassadors to answer questions and high-tech touch-screen kiosks where you can book excursions.

Water Tap water is generally safe to drink.

Weather Go to www.weather.bm. For average temperatures in Bermuda, see "When to Go," in chapter 2.

10

PLANNING YOUR TRIP TO BERMUDA | Weather

Index

See also Accommodations and Restaurant indexes, below.

Photo Credits

Map List

Frommer's Bermuda, 18th edition

Published by
FROMMER MEDIA LLC

ISBN 978-1-62887-438-9 (paper), 978-1-62887-439-6 (e-book)

Editorial Director: Pauline Frommer
Editor: Pauline Frommer
Production Editor: Heather Wilcox
Cartographer: Roberta Stockwell
Photo Editor: Meghan Lamb
Assistant Photo Editor: Phil Vinke
Cover Design: Dave Riedy

For information on our other products or services, see www.frommers.com.

Frommer Media LLC also publishes its books in a variety of electronic formats. Some content that appears in print may not be available in electronic formats.

Manufactured in the United States of America

5 4 3 2 1

ABOUT THE AUTHOR

David LaHuta is a Bermuda-based travel journalist who's been reporting on the island since he relocated to its pink sand shores in 2009. Originally from New York City, LaHuta has written about Bermuda for the *New York Times*, *Travel+Leisure*, and AFAR and has also covered the country extensively as the host of the Bermuda Channel, a television network broadcast exclusively across the mid-Atlantic archipelago. He has profiled Bermuda as a correspondent for Outside Television, has written in-depth online guides for Frommers.com, and contributes videos, stories, and social media dispatches from the English colony for Islands.com. A sought-after travel expert, LaHuta has visited more than 60 countries and reports on the people and places making news in the world today for publications including *Outside*, *Delta Sky*, and *Robb Report*, among others. He's been an on-camera contributor for *American Morning* (CNN), *Forbes's Luxe 11* (Travel Channel), and *Good Day New York* (FOX) and was also the adventure correspondent for *The Rachael Ray Show*. A graduate of the University of Maryland College of Journalism, LaHuta enjoys boating, surfing, and beachcombing with his wife and two sons near their home in Warwick. For more about his work, visit www.David LaHuta.com and follow him on Twitter and Instagram @davidlahuta.

ABOUT THE FROMMER TRAVEL GUIDES

For most of the past 50 years, Frommer's has been the leading series of travel guides in North America, accounting for as many as 24% of all guidebooks sold. I think I know why.

Though we hope our books are entertaining, we nevertheless deal with travel in a serious fashion. Our guidebooks have never looked on such journeys as a mere recreation, but as a far more important human function, a time of learning and introspection, an essential part of a civilized life. We stress the culture, lifestyle, history, and beliefs of the destinations we cover, and urge our readers to seek out people and new ideas as the chief rewards of travel.

We have never shied from controversy. We have, from the beginning, encouraged our authors to be intensely judgmental, critical—both pro and con—in their comments, and wholly independent. Our only clients are our readers, and we have triggered the ire of countless prominent sorts, from a tourist newspaper we called "practically worthless" (it unsuccessfully sued us) to the many rip-offs we've condemned.

And because we believe that travel should be available to everyone regardless of their incomes, we have always been cost-conscious at every level of expenditure. Though we have broadened our recommendations beyond the budget category, we insist that every lodging we include be sensibly priced. We use every form of media to assist our readers, and are particularly proud of our feisty daily website, the award-winning Frommers.com.

I have high hopes for the future of Frommer's. May these guidebooks, in all the years ahead, continue to reflect the joy of travel and the freedom that travel represents. May they always pursue a cost-conscious path, so that people of all incomes can enjoy the rewards of travel. And may they create, for both the traveler and the persons among whom we travel, a community of friends, where all human beings live in harmony and peace.

Arthur Frommer